ARISTOTLE AND LAW

In *Aristotle and Law* George Duke argues that Aristotle's seemingly dispersed statements on law and legislation are unified by a commitment to law's status as an achievement of practical reason. This book provides a systematic exposition of the significance and coherence of Aristotle's account of law and also indicates the relevance of this account to contemporary legal theory. It will be of great interest to scholars and students in jurisprudence, philosophy, political science and classics.

George Duke is Associate Professor at Deakin University, Melbourne. His main research areas are the philosophy of law, constitutional theory, and the history of political and legal thought. Duke has published in a wide-range of international journals on these topics, including *Classical Quarterly*, *Legal Theory*, *Ancient Philosophy*, *History of Political Thought*, *International Journal of Constitutional Law*, and *European Law Review*. He is also the co-editor of *The Cambridge Companion to Natural Law Jurisprudence* (2017).

Aristotle and Law

THE POLITICS OF *NOMOS*

GEORGE DUKE
Deakin University

CAMBRIDGE
UNIVERSITY PRESS

CAMBRIDGE
UNIVERSITY PRESS

University Printing House, Cambridge CB2 8BS, United Kingdom

One Liberty Plaza, 20th Floor, New York, NY 10006, USA

477 Williamstown Road, Port Melbourne, VIC 3207, Australia

314–321, 3rd Floor, Plot 3, Splendor Forum, Jasola District Centre, New Delhi – 110025, India

79 Anson Road, #06–04/06, Singapore 079906

Cambridge University Press is part of the University of Cambridge.

It furthers the University's mission by disseminating knowledge in the pursuit of education, learning, and research at the highest international levels of excellence.

www.cambridge.org
Information on this title: www.cambridge.org/9781107157033
DOI: 10.1017/9781316661741

First published 2020

A catalogue record for this publication is available from the British Library.

Library of Congress Cataloging-in-Publication Data
NAMES: Duke, George, 1974– author.
TITLE: Aristotle and law : the politics of nomos / George Duke, Deakin University.
DESCRIPTION: Cambridge, United Kingdom ; New York, NY, USA : Cambridge University Press, 2020. | Includes bibliographical references and index.
IDENTIFIERS: LCCN 2019032189 (print) | LCCN 2019032190 (ebook) | ISBN 9781107157033 (hardback) | ISBN 9781316661741 (epub)
SUBJECTS: LCSH: Aristotle. | Natural law – Philosophy. | Law – Political aspects – Philosophy. | Nomos (The Greek word)
CLASSIFICATION: LCC K434.A7 D85 2020 (print) | LCC K434.A7 (ebook) | DDC 340/.112–dc23
LC record available at https://lccn.loc.gov/2019032189
LC ebook record available at https://lccn.loc.gov/2019032190

ISBN 978-1-107-15703-3 Hardback

For my parents

ἐρωτηθεὶς τί ποτ᾽ αὐτῷ περιγέγονεν ἐκ φιλοσοφίας, ἔφη, τὸ ἀνεπιτάκτως ποιεῖν ἅ τινες διὰ τὸν ἀπὸ τῶν νόμων φόβον ποιοῦσιν.

When asked what advantage he [Aristotle] had ever gained from philosophy, he replied: that I do without being ordered what some are constrained to do by their fear of the law.

Diogenes Laertius, *Lives of the Philosophers* V.1.20.

Contents

Acknowledgements

Chapters 4 and 5 contain material that has been revised from articles published in *History of Political Thought*: 'Two Functions of Aristotle's Common Advantage' (2016) 37: pp. 195–215 and 'Aristotle on Constitutional and Legal Reform' (2019) 40: pp. 381–404. Chapter 6 contains material from 'Aristotle and Natural Law,' *The Review of Politics*, (2020) 82, © The University of Notre Dame, published by Cambridge University Press. Section 2 of Chapter 7 contains material from 'The Aristotelian *Spoudaios* as Ethical Exemplar in Finnis' Natural Law Theory,' *American Journal of Jurisprudence* (2013) 58: pp. 183–204. The following journals have also kindly granted permission to draw on forthcoming work: *Ancient Philosophy* (Chapter 1), *Classical Quarterly* (Chapter 2), *Classical Philology* (Chapter 3). I am particularly grateful to Natalie Cole, Christoph Horn, Pavlos Kontos, Thornton Lockwood, Mark C. Murphy, Lars Vinx and Simon Weber for their encouragement and/or helpful comments on drafts. Michael Mitchell provided excellent assistance with the index.

Note on the Text

I follow the Oxford Classical Texts (OCT) versions of the *Nicomachean Ethics*, *Eudemian Ethics*, *Politics*, *Rhetoric*, *Metaphysics* and *Physics*. Translations, where not my own, follow Bartlett and Collins or Reeve (*Nicomachean Ethics*), Inwood and Woolf (*Eudemian Ethics*) and Lord or Reeve (*Politics*).

Abbreviations

Aristotle

APo.	*Posterior Analytics*
APr.	*Prior Analytics*
Cael.	*De Caelo (On the Heavens)*
Cat.	*Categories*
DA	*De Anima*
EE	*Eudemian Ethics*
GA	*Generation of Animals*
GC	*On Generation and Corruption*
HH	*History of Animals*
MA	*Movement of Animals*
MM	*Magna Moralia*
Met.	*Metaphysics*
NE	*Nicomachean Ethics*
PA	*Progression of Animals*
Ph.	*Physics*
Pol.	*Politics*
Rh.	*Rhetoric*
SE	*Sophistical Refutations*
Top.	*Topics*

Plato

Grg.	*Gorgias*
Philb.	*Philebus*
Prt.	*Protagoras*
Rep.	*Republic*
Smp.	*Symposium*
States.	*Statesman*

Introduction

Aristotle does not propound a systematic legal theory in the modern sense. While the *Nicomachean Ethics* and the *Politics* contain several memorable statements on *nomos*, at no point in the practical works does Aristotle purport to provide a scientific account of law as an autonomous system or an analysis of the necessary truths about law that explain it.[1] The absence of a systematic legal theory in Aristotle cannot, moreover, simply be attributed to the dictum that an educated person should only seek as much precision as a subject matter allows (*NE* I.3, 1094b24–5). That such a conclusion would be premature may be seen by a comparison with Aristotle's treatments of justice and the constitution. These two concepts frame Book V of the *Nicomachean Ethics* and Book III of the *Politics* (if not the *Politics* as a whole) respectively and their explanatory value is confirmed when they are deployed to elucidate other important political phenomena such as stability and change. By contrast, Aristotle's tendency is to deal with *nomos* in the context of an examination of more fundamental political concepts. Law accordingly seems to have a derivative explanatory status.

The absence of a 'science of jurisprudence' in Aristotle's practical thought is itself a point worthy of greater reflection.[2] One might even venture the initial hypothesis that what is most illuminating about Aristotle's treatment of *nomos* from a contemporary perspective is its subordination of law to prior explanatory concepts from his political science, insofar as this militates against both the abstraction of law from its wider practical context and the temptation to idealise 'the rule of law'.

Interpretative obstacles to an investigation of Aristotelian *nomos* are nonetheless formidable. Aristotle's thoughts on *nomos* are fragmentary and dispersed. Instead of a dedicated treatise, as with surviving works in the *Corpus Aristotelicum* on ethics,

1 Kelsen (1967) and Raz (2004: 324).

2 In light of the predominant influence of Roman law on later European legal thought, one can compare Aristotle's approach with the historical development of Ulpian's claim (*Digest* 1.1.10.2) that 'practical wisdom in matters of right' (*iuris prudentia*) is properly to be considered a *scientia*. According to the medieval *Glossa Ordinaria*, legal science is not only an 'art', but also a distinct domain of knowledge. See Lee (2016: 20).

politics and rhetoric, there are brief discussions and gnomic utterances scattered throughout the practical works.[3] This provides challenges to the interpreter even greater than those normally associated with the Aristotelian corpus, with its uncertainties of composition and transmission.[4] It is thus far from self-evident that an Aristotelian 'theory of law' is viable, even taken as a self-consciously reconstructive project.[5]

These complexities are one plausible source of the partial neglect of Aristotle's thought on *nomos* in recent Anglo-American literature, despite the resurgence of interest in the *Politics*.[6] Legal themes are prominent enough in the practical works. Aristotle ascribes a significant, albeit difficult to interpret, role to the architectonic legislator (*nomothetēs*) in both the *Nicomachean Ethics* and the *Politics*. The *Nicomachean Ethics* features well-known investigations of justice (Book V) and the role of law in the inculcation of virtue (Book X.9). Book III of the *Politics* includes discussions of both the relativity of law to constitutional regimes (*politeiai*) and the merits of the rule of law relative to the rule of the best man. The *Rhetoric* also considers several legal topics, within the context of forensic rhetoric and beyond. The amount of direct attention Aristotle dedicates to *nomos* is nonetheless modest and appears to belie its centrality to the human good.[7] Aristotle, it seems, prefers to

3 Diogenes Laertius' catalogue of Aristotle's works lists a three book extract from Plato's *Laws*, four books of laws and a 'laws of the mess-table', but no philosophical treatise dedicated to *nomos* as such. DL V.1.22–7. Diogenes does, however, attribute to Aristotle's successor Theophrastus a one book treatise on laws (*Peri nomōn*) and also texts on the legislator (three books) and illegalities (in addition to collections or epitomes of laws). V.2.44.

4 See Shute (1888), Shields (2012) and Lord (2013).

5 On a reconstructive approach to Aristotle's practical thought see Miller (1995: 21–2). Rosler (2005: 7) distils the central assumption of this methodology as follows: 'texts should be understood not only in their own terms but also by applying external concepts and theories *when they do justice to the text itself*' (italics mine).

6 On the 'unprecedented resurgence' of interest in Aristotle's political thought, see Lockwood and Samaras (2015: 1). The last monograph in English which attempts a survey of Aristotle's philosophy of law is Hamburger (1951). Darren Weirnick's 1998 PhD thesis is the closest approximation to a recent comprehensive book-length treatment dedicated to law in Aristotle. There are several illuminating article-length treatments of Aristotle's legal thought, including Shellens (1959), Schroeder (2003), Lisi (2000), Miller (2007) and Horn (2013). Brooks and Murphy (2003) collects a number of important article-length pieces in one volume.

7 Although the legislator (*nomothetēs*) and legislative expertise (*nomothetikē*; *nomothesia*) feature prominently in Book I of the *Nicomachean Ethics* (1094b5, 1102a11, 1103b3), and reappear at significant junctures in Books II (1109b34), III (1113b23) IV (1128a30–2) and VIII (1155a23 and 1160a13), references to *nomos* and *nomoi* are relatively scarce (nine instances according to the Bywater OCT version) outside of Book V and X.9 (Book I: 1094b16 and 1102a10, Book III: 1113b34 and 1116a19, Book VI: 1141b32 and 1144a15, Book VII: 1152a21–4, Book VIII: 1161b7, Book IX: 1164b13). The terms *to nomimon* and *to nomikon* also feature at important points in Book V, as Chapter 4 examines. While the legislator and legislative expertise play a pivotal role in the *Politics* (particularly in Books I and II) the *Index* of the Ross OCT edition of the *Politics* lists only seven instances of *nomos* in the singular and plural (1954: 278). If the common books are excluded, the *Eudemian Ethics* mentions the legislator and legislation twice (1226b38 and 1235a3) and *nomos* on only two occasions (1229a29 and 1243a8). The Aristotelian *Magna Moralia* refers to the legislator at 1187a13–17, 1189b3 and 1199a21, but otherwise does not engage directly with the topic of *nomos* outside of the thematic discussions of justice in Book I.33 and equity in

view *nomos* through the lens of other central concepts in the philosophy of human affairs. And it is understandable that contemporary interpreters have followed this lead. Influential recent treatments of Aristotle's political theory examine legal themes such as constitutional types, the justification of authority, distributive justice, natural law and the existence of a theory of rights.[8] The same applies to edited collections on Aristotle's ethics and politics, which frequently engage with legal topics.[9] In one sense, it is the 'embeddedness' of law within Aristotle's practical thought which explains the relative lack of dedicated scholarly treatment. On closer examination, the claim that *nomos* has been partially neglected might even reflect a misunderstanding of the ethically and politically situated character of Aristotle's thoughts on law.

There is much truth to this. And a closely related point, alluded to above, is that there is a danger of potential anachronism in the treatment of *nomos* as an independent domain of investigation in an Aristotelian framework. Obviously enough, Aristotle's *explanandum* differs from a modern municipal legal system, with its hierarchy of laws and administrative apparatus of application and adjudication. There are nonetheless more subtle forms of anachronism. It is initially tempting, for example, to assimilate the *Nicomachean Ethics* X.9 discussion of the role that *nomos* plays in the inculcation of virtue to contemporary variants of perfectionism which emphasise our status as rational and autonomous agents seeking to order our mutual relations through law. Yet X.9, when examined in detail, suggests that the majority of citizens lack the capacity to develop true virtue and must be subject to coercive measures which operate principally on sub-rational motivations.

Likewise, Aristotle's well-known dialogical presentation in *Politics* III of the law's universality and rationality relative to the arbitrary authority of human rulers cannot straightforwardly be understood in terms of current notions of the rule of law. This can be seen by considering the following representative statement of the aims and benefits of law in a liberal-democratic order:

> Law provides the conditions in which each person's freedom as independence can be secured: its primary task is to define individual domains of liberty, protected from coercive interference ... by governmental authorities. The rule of law preserves the sovereignty of individual choice and action by allowing each person to pursue his own purposes, free from domination either by state officials or overbearing fellow citizens.[10]

While Aristotle also views the function of law as to provide enabling conditions, these conditions are understood in terms of what is conducive to the virtue and

Book II.1–2. References to *nomos* are more prevalent in the *Rhetoric*. This is discussed further in Chapter 6.

8 Miller (1995), Kraut (2002), Rosler (2005) and Keyt (2017) are some notable examples.

9 Recent collections are Deslauriers and Destrée (2013), Polansky (2014) and Lockwood and Samaras (2015).

10 Allen (2016: 204–5).

flourishing of both the individual and the community, rather than as instrumental to the protection of a sovereign domain of individual choice and action. Indeed, Aristotle is so far from such a view of freedom that laws are asserted to be (both descriptively and normatively) determined by a conception of the good life and justice which is reflected in the 'political' choice for a certain kind of constitutional structure.

An instructive starting point for reading Aristotle's account of *nomos* on its own terms is to acknowledge that it simultaneously ascribes to law both an extensive reach and a derivative status. As an exercise of true political expertise, legislative science (*nomothetikē*) has, in at least one crucial sense, principal responsibility for realisation of the human good (*NE* I.2, 1094b7). Law is derived from practical rationality and directed proximately to the common advantage beyond partisan interests and ultimately to virtue (*aretē*) and wellbeing (*eudaimonia*). From this perspective, Aristotle has an expansive view of the scope of law and this entails its extension into domains seen as protected by individual liberty in modern liberal orders. From an alternative perspective, however, *nomos* is always understood by Aristotle as determined by the ends of particular political regimes, the vast majority of which are unjust and defective. Even within the horizon of the philosophy of human affairs – which is to say even apart from its deficiencies in relation to nature – *nomos* is dependent upon conceptions of the good life which tend to be corrupted in actual political communities.

It is important at this juncture directly to confront the well-known fact that the range of denotation of the term *nomos* includes customs, traditions and social norms and is hence broader than the English term 'law' as used to denote positive laws.[11] Ostwald's painstaking analysis of the concept of *nomos* up until the end of the fifth century BCE identifies as many as thirteen related yet distinct meanings, including way of life, the normal order of things, an authority issuing norms, authoritative social customs and religious practices.[12] These different meanings share the underlying sense of an order (*taxis*) that is, or at least ought to be, 'generally regarded as valid by the members of the group in which it prevails'.[13] Such a definition clearly captures a wider array of social norms than positive law in its contemporary sense. Indeed, it has been questioned whether it is even accurate to speak of Greek law as such, because the diverse legal arrangements of different *poleis* during the archaic

[11] Gagarin and Woodruff (2007: 7).

[12] Ostwald (1969: 20–54).

[13] Ostwald (1969: 54) and Heinimann (1965: 65 and 89). Kraut (2002: 105) points to a crucial difference between *nomos* and later concepts of law nourished by Christian influences: 'The noun *nomos* is cognate to the verb *nemein*, one whose sense is "to believe." Whatever conduct a community believes to be fitting – its proper and customary way of doing things – constitutes the *nomoi* (plural of *nomos*) of that community. There can be no such things as *nomoi* in which no one believes; for a *nomos* to exist is for it to be recognised and observed by a group of people. Our own term "law" lacks this feature. It is not an impossible use of this word to say that moral laws exist whether or not people recognise their validity or obey them.'

and classical periods never developed into an autonomous system like that of Rome, let alone of the kind that is found in modern nation states.[14]

Some of the difficulties which the broad scope of the term *nomos* presents the interpreter can be seen in Aristotle's striking statement, with respect to the prohibition on suicide, that what the law does not allow, it forbids (*ho nomos, ha de mē keleuei, apagoreuei*) (V.11, *NE* 1138a7). According to an influential line of interpretation, Aristotle cannot be referring to positive law in this passage, but appeals rather to custom, given the difficulties associated with the view that law prohibits all activities that it does not explicitly permit.[15] Although this reading has been challenged, it does raise the wider question as to whether, and when, other occurrences of *nomos* should be understood as denoting customs or 'mere' social norms rather than positive law.[16] When Aristotle juxtaposes unwritten and written laws (*nomous … tous agraphous kai tous gegrammenos*) in *Politics* VI.5, for example, should one take him to be referring implicitly to custom and positive law or rather to be including within a single category of positive law both unwritten and written norms?

Conversely, although *nomos* is broader in meaning than positive law, it also had a narrower range of denotation from a perspective internal to Greek legal language and conventions. In the first instance, *nomos* was never used as an overarching term, like the Latin *jus*, to refer to all aspects of Greek legal substance and procedure.[17] While *nomos* replaced *thesmos* as the main expression for substantive written and publicly promulgated legal norms in the fifth century BCE, procedural aspects of the legal system, including in particular judicial processes, were generally described by the term *dikē* and its cognates.[18] Second, and here Aristotle follows and reports customary usage (*NE* V.10, 1137b13–33), the Athenians distinguished within the category of legal enactments between *nomoi*, which are universal insofar as they are intended to apply to many particulars, and *psēphismata* (decrees), which are by contrast edicts that are restricted to discrete circumstances.[19]

A sound initial conclusion to draw from all of these points is that an analysis of Aristotle's thought on law must attend to the wide range of meaning of the term *nomos* and its cognates and avoid the anachronism of assuming an invariable reference to positive written laws. One need only consider the education norms proposed in Book VIII of the *Politics* to see that *nomoi* were understood to pertain to a wider range of activity

14 On the unity or otherwise of Greek law see Gagarin (2005: 29–40).

15 Grant (1885: 141), Stewart (1892: 533), Lockwood (unpublished: 17).

16 Van Johnson (1938: 351–56) argues persuasively that this reading is undermined by the fact that Aristotle elsewhere states that the laws pronounce on everything (*hoi de nomoi agoreuousi peri hapantōn*) (*NE* V.1, 1129b14–15) and are required for the whole of life (*peri panta ton bion*) (*NE* X.9, 1180a4). Van Johnson attributes (335) the misinterpretation to the view that 'the state is a necessary evil' which cannot trespass on individual rights.

17 Gagarin and Woodruff (2007: 32).

18 Gagarin and Woodruff (2007: 20).

19 MacDowell (1978: 43–6) and Kraut (2002: 106). On the role of decrees (*ta psēphismata*) in Athenian law see also Todd (1993: 18) and Ostwald (1986: 97). As Ostwald notes, in fifth century Athens a decree was regarded as a particular 'form' of legal statute.

than modern statutes. A less obvious, but equally significant, consequence of the broader meaning of *nomos* is the need for caution with respect to the project of reconstructing a general Aristotelian theory of the 'nature' or 'essence' of law. As an achievement or 'product' of *phronēsis*, *nomos* is never regarded in complete abstraction from practical considerations. Although this does not prevent Aristotle from providing a definition of *nomos* in X.9 of the *Nicomachean Ethics*, it is surely significant that this definition is offered in the context of an inquiry into the capacity for legislators to educate the citizens of a political community in virtue.

Despite all these complicating factors, it is nonetheless possible, with appropriate interpretative caution, to approach Aristotle's account of law on the assumption that there is considerable overlap between the concept of *nomos* and our own concept of positive law. In the first instance, as Gagarin has argued in relation to Greek law, it is plausible, and at the very least helpful as an analytical assumption, to differentiate legal systems from pre- and proto-legal systems by reference to the existence of public written legal rules (in addition to legal procedures).[20] Greek political communities, including Crete and Epizephyrian Locri, began to enact written laws from the middle of the seventh century BCE. In the case of Athens, the laws of both Draco (which were enacted around 620 BCE) and Solon (enacted early sixth century BCE) were inscribed on wooden tablets (*axones*) and hence publicly accessible to all citizens.[21] The shift from more spontaneous forms of dispute resolution to written law not only reflected an increased sense of a unified political community, but also contributed to the development of that sense. Solon's laws in particular, Gagarin argues, 'led to greater control of the polis over its inhabitants'.[22] The written and publicly promulgated character of the laws of Greek cities, including Athens, allow them to be regarded as forming a system of norms relatively distinct from social customs and mores.[23]

What can also be determined with a relative degree of certainty is that by the end of the fifth century BCE, and into the fourth century, the primary use of *nomos* in political contexts was to refer to a written and publicly promulgated positive law or 'statute'.[24] The key development here is commonly regarded to be the shift from conceptualising laws as *thesmoi* imposed from above operative during the time of Draco and Solon to a more democratic notion of *nomoi* as norms that are held valid by a community.[25] As part of the democratic legal reforms led by Cleisthenes in 507 BCE, the normal way for a law to come into force was by vote of the *Ekklēsia* or assembly of all citizens, subsequent to consideration by the *Boulē* or Council.[26] The

20 Gagarin (1986: 8–9).
21 MacDowell (1978: 43).
22 MacDowell (1978: 140).
23 This explains the use of the plural term *hoi nomoi* to refer to the laws of a polis considered as a relatively coherent set of norms. See Gagarin and Woodruff (2007: 20) and Todd (1993: 18–19). Cf. Demosthenes 25.15–16.
24 Ostwald (1969: 58) and Gagarin and Woodruff (2007: 7).
25 Ostwald (1969: 9–55) and MacDowell (1978: 44).
26 MacDowell (1978: 44–5).

Athenian legal reforms of the late fifth century (403–402 BCE) also sought to impart greater coherence to the law in the direction of what we would think of as a legal code or system.[27] By the end of the fifth century, then, not only did the term *nomos*, as employed in political contexts, generally refer to positive laws (primarily those enacted by an assembly), but there was a significant degree of coherence to the legal code.

The practical works of Aristotle, situated in the fourth century BCE, were framed against this historical background. While Aristotle does employ *nomos* to mean customs as well as positive laws, moreover, there are passages which suggest an awareness of the distinction. In his *Politics* VI.4 discussion of the worst form of democracy, for example, Aristotle states that it is not well-composed either in its laws or its customs (*mē tois nomois kai tois ethesin eu sunkeimenēn*) (1319b3–4). The contraposition of law and custom is also found in *Politics* VII.2, where Aristotle notes (employing the *men/de* construction), in the context of a discussion of aggressive foreign policy, that nations prescribe many things in the interest of domination, some of them by law, and others by custom (*ta men nomois kateilēmmena ta de ethesin*) (1324b22). As will be explored in more detail in Chapter 1, Aristotle's most sustained discussion of law in X.9 of the *Nicomachean Ethics* also seems to assume a distinction between *nomos* and *ethos*, according to which the role of *nomos* is precisely to influence *ethos*, to the greatest extent possible, in the direction of virtuous activity.[28]

Even granting that the dominant fourth century BCE meaning of *nomos* in political contexts was positive law, the analysis above might be thought to neglect the term's philosophical content. From a history of ideas perspective, the fifth century development of a dichotomy between *phusis* and *nomos*, and the use of *nomos* to denote widely held, yet conventional or false, popular opinions, is undoubtedly an important part of the intellectual background for both Plato and Aristotle.[29] One consequence of the dichotomy is that a broader use of the term *nomos* to refer to regularities in natural-scientific explanation is paradoxical from a Greek perspective. Yet although the sophistic influence gave *nomos* an 'awkward penumbra' when used of statute law, the term's primary meaning in the fifth and fourth century remained a positive legal norm held as binding.[30]

27 See MacDowell (1978: 47): '[T]he Athenians declared this year, 403/2 . . . to be the start of a new era, as far as the legal code was concerned. No law passed before 403/2 was valid henceforth unless it was included in the new inscriptions made in the years from 410 to 403; no uninscribed law was to be enforced; no decree could override a law; and no prosecution could be brought henceforth for offences committed before 403/2.'

28 Susemihl and Hicks (1894: 163) also make the important point in this context that unwritten customs and usages, while more sacred, were also 'regarded as if each of them could be derived from a definite lawgiver'.

29 Heinimann (1965: 89).

30 Gagarin and Woodruff (2007: 20).

In sum, despite the fact that *nomos* indeed differs from our own concept of law in several respects, there is sufficient overlap to justify the attribution to Aristotle of an account of positive law which is both theoretically accessible to the modern interpreter and can speak to our own concerns.

Aristotle's seemingly diffuse statements on the topic of *nomos*, I contend, are unified by a commitment to its status as an achievement of practical rationality. This commitment has multiple aspects, including the derivation of the content of law from *phronēsis*, the role of the architectonic legislator as a privileged exponent of political science (*politikē*) (understood as the same disposition as *phronēsis*), the relativity of law to a constitutional regime established by a founding law-maker, the subsumption of both the naturally just and the legally just within political justice, the indispensability of political stability to the effective functioning of law, and the privileging of the equitable judgement of a practically reasonable agent over a strict legalism. Underlying these features of Aristotle's treatment of *nomos* is an equivocality, although this should not be regarded as the result of either confusion or inconsistency. On the one hand, the status of law as an achievement of practical reason entails that it has a universal content which serves to alleviate the worst features of partisanship in the political domain. On the other hand, law is always enacted relative to a particular constitutional regime and hence determined by a particular *political* conception of the good life (which is also reflected in the views of a community regarding justice and the common advantage). In this sense, politics is 'constitutive' for law. Aristotelian law-making (*nomothetikē*) in the central, focal or truest sense is a 'part' or 'sub-branch' of political science (*politikē*) and the law's rational guidance of conduct is always determined by a particular conception of the good that is reflected in the preference for a regime of a certain type. This, it should be noted, does not entail that law is *reducible* to the beliefs of the most powerful or authoritative members of a polis. Aristotle acknowledges a best constitution by nature, natural right and the capacity of law to mitigate partisan interests. A significant question in the background of this study is the reconcilability of regarding laws (in the central case) as universal norms derived from practical reason and the constitutional relativity of positive legal enactments.

The discussion in the previous paragraph might at first glance seem to rest on an ambiguity or failure to clarify the multiple meanings of the expression 'politics', both in the context of Aristotle's work and more widely. It is true that Aristotle distinguishes between politics in a broad and a narrow sense (*NE* VI.8, 1141b29–34).[31] In the broadest sense, *politikē* or political expertise encompasses the philosophy of human affairs in its entirety, from reflections on the ends of human life and the

[31] One must hence be attentive to context in analysing Aristotelian *politikē*. See Pellegrin (2012: 559): 'At least three meanings of the term "politics" are ... available: it may refer to the whole sphere of the human good, and in this sense it includes ethics; it may also refer to the wisdom of the politician par excellence, viz. the legislator; and, finally, it may indicate the specific skill of one who partakes in the administration of the city.'

virtues to the different types of constitution. By contrast, narrow *politikē* (roughly identifiable with 'ordinary politics') covers the deliberative expertise (exercised in the assembly) and judicial expertise (exercised in the law courts) involved in the governance of a polis.[32] It is the responsibility of broad *politikē* to promote the overall human good and its privileged instrument is legislation (*NE* I.3, 1094b4–7). The architectonic legislator is the principal exponent of *politikē* in the broad sense and is also plausibly, precisely for this reason, to be regarded as the primary intended audience of the Aristotelian practical works.[33] An architectonic legislator differs from an 'ordinary' legislator by virtue of the fact that they do not merely enact laws, but play a 'founding' role in the establishment or reform of a constitution (*politeia*) (like a Solon or Lycurgus) (*Pol.* II.12, 1273b31–5).

Aristotelian political expertise (*politikē*), inclusive of legislative expertise (*nomothetikē*), is the same disposition (*hexis*) as the intellectual virtue of prudence (*phronēsis*), although it differs 'in being' (*NE* VI.8, 1141b24–5). It is accordingly important to clarify, in a preliminary manner, the scope of the expertise or 'science' of politics. Political phenomena may appear to be inappropriate objects of scientific explanation, given their contingency and dependence on human agency. One must attend, however, to Aristotle's distinction between sciences in the strict or unconditional sense and a broader sense of a science which holds of things for the most part (*hōs epi to polu*) (*Top.* II.6, 112b10–11). An Aristotelian science is a state or disposition of the soul rather than 'a body of propositions in a textbook', although the 'state does involve having an assertoric grasp on a set of true propositions' (*NE* VI.3, 1139b14–16).[34] In Book I.2 of the *Posterior Analytics* Aristotle defines science in the unqualified or unconditional sense (*epistēmē haplōs*) as a cognitive condition in which we are able to grasp the causes of necessary states-of-affairs that cannot be otherwise (*APo.* 71b9–16). This conception of science applies only to a narrow range of strict theoretical sciences, such as mathematics, astronomy and theology. It does not apply to natural sciences, such as physics and biology, which deal with matter and what only holds for the most part (*Met.* VI.1, 1025b25–1026a30). Even the natural sciences are not sciences in the strictest sense, therefore, since they deal with what rarely fails to happen rather than eternal necessary truths. And in *Metaphysics* VI.1 Aristotle employs a broader notion of science (*epistēmē*), according to which it denotes a specific domain of intellectual enquiry and is inclusive of practical and productive sciences.[35] This broader notion of science is what seems to inform the assumption in the practical works that political and legislative expertise (not to mention subordinate forms of knowledge falling under them, such as generalship and household management) are sciences or capacities (*dunameis*) (*NE* I.2, 1094a27–b10). These practical sciences are also best understood as featuring both

32 Keyt (2017: 212).
33 Pellegrin (2012: 561), Bodéüs (1993: 45), Keyt (2017: 166).
34 Reeve (2017: xxi).
35 For discussion see Henry and Nielsen (2015: 2).

a universalist component (akin to a theoretical science in the looser sense that natural sciences are sciences) and a particularist 'experience-based knowledge' of how to apply that universalist component.[36] This is consistent with Aristotle's definition of law as rational speech (*logos*) derived from practical wisdom (*phronēsis*) and intellect (*nous*) (*NE* X.9, 1180a21–22). A 'product' of the political mode of *phronēsis*, pre-eminently that exercised in architectonic law-making, Aristotelian *nomos* in the focal sense is an achievement of the practical reason of the prudent statesperson.

It is instructive at this point to contrast and compare some features of ancient and modern constitutions. According to an influential contemporary view, a constitution (written or unwritten) is a fundamental legal norm in a hierarchical system of legal norms.[37] This assumption is quite foreign to Ancient Greek political thought in general and Aristotle in particular. The *politeia* – the central concept of Aristotle's political science – is an ordered arrangement (*taxis*) of ruling offices (*Pol.* III.6, 1278b9–10), which can also be identified with the governing or authoritative element (*politeuma*) (1278b10) of the polis and its way of life (*bios*) (IV.11, 1295a40–b1, VII.8, 1328b1–2).[38] The *politeia* is fundamental in the sense that it determines the laws of a political community and reflects its overall 'ethical' outlook.[39] Yet the Aristotelian *politeia* is not itself a legal norm, albeit one that occupies a fundamental place in the hierarchy of norms. Aristotle's commitment to the thesis that laws (*nomoi*) are, and should be, enacted relative to different *politeiai* or regime-types (*Pol.* III.12, 1282b8–13, IV.1, 1289a14–22), points back to the derivation of law from political expertise and the ends (*teloi*) directing a legislator's arrangement of positions of authority and ruling offices, not the dependence of the validity of lower legal norms upon higher. Ultimately, in fact, the Aristotelian *politeia* is political in the broadest sense of designating a formal ordering (*taxis*) of relations of power that is determined by a conception of the good for both the individual and a polis.

Aristotle's commitment to the constitutional relativity of law needs to be distinguished from the plausible argument, made by historians of Greek law, which asserts that 'politics and law were at Athens ultimately indistinguishable'.[40] This thesis refers primarily to the functioning of Athenian judicial procedure, according to which jury verdicts were

36 Here I follow Reeve (2013: 3) and (2017: xxi–xxxii).

37 See, for the paradigmatic version of this position, Kelsen (1945) and (1967).

38 Aristotle both presupposes and demonstrates the centrality of constitutional regimes (*politeiai*) to his political science when he alleges that Plato's *Laws* deals mostly with laws and has little to say about the *politeia* (*Pol.* II.6, 1265a1–2). The *politeia* frames the *Politics*: Book II discusses previous accounts of the best *politeia*, Book III the relativity of citizenship, political justice and law to the *politeia*, Books IV and V kinds of *politeia* and what preserves and destroys them, Book VI varieties of *politeia* and political institutions and Books VII and VIII core features of the best *politeia*. For the predominance of the concept of the *politeia* in classical Greek political thought more generally see Schofield (2006: 33) and Harte and Lane (2013).

39 Newman (1887: I. 209–11) remains an insightful commentary on this aspect of Aristotle's practical thought.

40 Todd (1993: 29).

understood as articulations of the opinion of the polis and most prosecutions were brought by individual citizens.[41] The claim that politics is constitutive for law referred to here by contrast points to legislative norms as achievements of the practical reason of an architectonic legislator guided by a conception of the human good that is made concrete in the political decision for a particular form of constitutional arrangement.

A further meaning of 'political' is 'factious' or 'partisan'. As implied above, this is a difficult area of terrain in the interpretation of Aristotelian *nomos*. Laws enacted by a practically reasonable legislator should be directed to the common advantage (*Pol.* III.7, 1279a18–39) and hence alleviate partisanship. Practically reasonable law can also be regarded as universal in its application to citizens, impartial, transparent and fair (*Pol.* II.8, 1269a9–12, III.15, 1286a17–19; *NE* V.10, 1137b11–24; *Rh.* I.1, 1354a32ff). Aristotle's typology of constitutions, moreover, postulates not only a distinction between correct and defective regimes, but a best regime by nature (*NE* V.7, 1134b25–31). It remains the case, as Chapters 4 and 5 discuss, that the predominant regimes of democracy and oligarchy are radically defective in their acceptance of unjust conceptions of merit and promotion of partisan interests. Indeed, even the architectonic Aristotelian legislator is guided by a particular conception of the good life – a conception that is 'political' in the broad sense at least – when enacting laws.

This preliminary discussion of law's derivation from practical reason reflects the assumption that it is generally possible to demonstrate the coherence of Aristotle's account of law and overcome apparent inconsistencies by appealing to considerations internal to the practical works. There are nonetheless some important features of Aristotle's thought on *nomos* that can be clarified by reference to contemporary legal theory. In particular, Aristotle both anticipates and serves as an instructive point of comparison with recent work in jurisprudence which has sought to demonstrate the centrality of practical reason for understanding the nature of law.[42] Aristotle's derivation of law from the practical rationality of the architectonic legislator is distant from contemporary accounts of constitutionalism framed around the assumption of popular sovereignty, yet it also provides a distinct perspective on the attempt by recent legal theorists to explicate law as a social practice intended to regulate conduct by providing 'reasons for action' or serving as a 'rational guide to conduct'. Insofar as Aristotle has an expansive view of the reach of law over conduct, however, the purpose of law-making is elevated to concern for virtue and wellbeing. This contrasts with liberal views of the aim of law as setting limits on action to preserve peace and allow maximal freedom for individuals to pursue their own conceptions of the good.

From a methodological perspective, this study proceeds 'on the basis of the principle of charity, a strong but defeasible presumption of consistency and coherence' and the privileging of 'rational explanations of real and apparent theoretical problems' over appeals to sociological or psychological phenomena.[43] As Riesbeck

41 Todd (1993: 68 and 91).

42 Examples are Hart (1994), Raz (1986), Murphy (2006), Finnis (2011) and Shapiro (2011).

43 Riesbeck (2016: 15).

suggests, it is nevertheless important to keep in mind Aristotle's alterity, and at various points in the chapters which follow I seek to provide some wider historical context where it is useful for understanding the role of *nomos* in the practical works.

This study does not rest any of its major claims on developmental theses of the kind associated with the scholarship of Jaeger.[44] My approach in this respect is best illustrated by considering the right way to resolve the apparent disharmony in Aristotle's constitutional analysis between the putatively 'realist' Books IV–VI of the *Politics* and the more 'idealistic' or normative presentation of Books III and VII–VIII. The claim, for example, that laws are and should be enacted relative to constitutional forms (*Pol.* III.11, 1282b8–13, IV.1, 1289a14–22) initially seems (given the prevalence of defective regimes) to clash with the use of the common advantage as a normative criterion for correct and deviant regime-types and their laws (*Pol.* III.6, 1279a17–29). Rather than appeal to changes in Aristotle's views over time, I follow Rowe and Lockwood in pointing to the different levels of constitutional analysis that are explicitly formulated within the text of the *Politics*.[45] This approach does not of course rule out the thesis that Aristotle's views developed over the course of his philosophical career, but rather seeks to resolve apparent inconsistencies or tensions by reference to textual (and contextual) considerations that can be more easily verified.

With respect to scope, my subject matter is not every aspect of Aristotle's thought on law that could be considered relevant to jurisprudential enquiry. I have little to say, for instance, about the implications of Aristotle's thought for criminal liability, tort law or contract. Although Aristotle's account of voluntary and involuntary action in III.1–5 of the *Nicomachean Ethics* is justifiably seen as a major contribution to the development of the concepts of moral and legal responsibility (not to mention reasonable foreseeability), it is dealt with briefly here only in the broader context of equity. Rather than provide a comprehensive overview of everything Aristotle said on law, this study rather concentrates on *nomos* as a concept of Aristotle's practical philosophy. My focus, that is to say, is upon Aristotle's political account of law's function in the guidance of human affairs.

Relatedly, I employ, and assume that Aristotle also at least implicitly employed, the methodological device of 'central case analysis' (or focal meaning).[46] This device can be elucidated through the example of friendship. I am someone's friend in the focal sense if I feel genuine goodwill towards them, on the basis of some good quality they possess, and if both of us are known to each other to reciprocate these feelings

44 Often persuasive critiques of Jaeger's (1948) arguments for the disunity of the *Politics* – based on attributions of early Platonic influence – are found in Lord (1981), Rowe (1991) and Pellegrin (1996).

45 Rowe (1991) and Lockwood (2017).

46 Finnis (2011: 1–15) provides the canonical recent defence of focal meaning methodology. The use of focal meaning in the practical domain is not identical with the use of *pros hen* homonymy in metaphysical enquiry, where it applies to terms (such as being or *to on*) that are 'said in different ways' or across different genera. On Aristotle's use of *pros hen* homonymy see Hardie (1968: 59–60, 63–5) and Irwin (1981: 522–44).

(*NE* VIII.2, 1156a1–5). This definition serves to identify the central case of friendship from the perspective of a practically reasonable agent. There are nonetheless degrees of friendship, ranging from the focal sense just discussed to less satisfactory forms based upon instrumental benefits or pleasure. Likewise, when Aristotle refers to the legislator as concerned with the overall human good (*NE* I.2, 1094b7), it is to be assumed that he refers to the architectonic practically reasonable law-giver, not merely any law-giver. Central case analysis also allows, to provide one more example, for a cogent interpretation of the otherwise puzzling statement that all lawful things are somehow just (*hoti panta ta nomima esti pōs dikaia*) (*NE* V.1, 1129b12). Aristotle's intention here, central case analysis suggests, is not to say that anything legislated in a polis is just (hence the indefinite adverb), but that the focal sense of law is just law.

My translational choices are for the most part conventional and self-explanatory. One choice is, however, worth stating explicitly. A *politeia*, as discussed above, is an arrangement (*taxis*) of offices, and is also identified with both the ruling element and the way of life that prevails in a polis. The concept of the *politeia* accordingly has both similarities with, and significant points of difference from, the concept of a constitution in the modern sense, particularly insofar as this is understood as a written fundamental or 'highest' law. While no single English word comes close to capturing the complexity and range of the concept of the *politeia*, the translations 'constitution' and 'regime' do both capture aspects of the concept. I have thus chosen to employ them interchangeably, and sometimes as a compound ('constitutional regime') dependent on context.[47]

Finally, I treat the *Rhetoric* with significant caution as a source of Aristotelian doctrine. In the most recent monograph in English dedicated solely to Aristotle's views on law, Hamburger argues that the *Rhetoric* provides a more satisfactory treatment of central topics such as justice and equity than other practical works.[48] Indeed, Hamburger goes so far as to say that 'the *Rhetoric* contains the consummation of Aristotle's legal philosophy and theory'.[49] My approach to the *Rhetoric* is more circumspect.[50] Although the *Rhetoric* is indeed a valuable resource for Aristotle's thought on *nomos* and related concepts, one must also keep in mind that it often presents alternative legal strategies with an apparent tone of neutrality regarding their relationship to the ethical good. Whether Aristotle's statements in the *Rhetoric* are his own considered views, or rather represent competing sides of a question or tropes useful for deliberative, forensic or epideictic rhetoric, must be decided from context in each case.[51] This approach is justified in more detail in Chapter 6.

47 Whereas Keyt (1997) and Reeve (2017) elect for 'constitution', Simpson (1998) and Lord (2012) employ 'regime'. I examine Aristotle's concept of the *politeia* in more detail in Chapter 3.

48 Hamburger (1951: 65).

49 Hamburger (1951: 65).

50 Shellens (1959) offers persuasive arguments in favour of this interpretative approach.

51 I also occasionally draw on the *Athenian Constitution* and *Magna Moralia*. My assumption is that these are authentically peripatetic in their orientation, if not necessarily authentic works of Aristotle. For authorship and use of the *Magna Moralia* to illuminate Aristotle's practical thought see Cooper

It remains to outline the structure of the book. Chapter 1 engages in a close reading of Aristotle's discussion of *nomos* in the Book X.9 transition from the *Nicomachean Ethics* to the *Politics*. This transitional passage characterises *nomos* in intellectualist terms as a form of rational speech (*logos*) deriving from practical wisdom (*phronēsis*) and intellect (*nous*). Aristotle's definition of *nomos* thus seems to emphasise the universality and rationality of law and even favour an association of its function with ethical perfectionism. A feature of Aristotle's analysis of *nomos* that has received less attention, however, is the necessary role of force and compulsion in the use of the law to habituate citizens towards the development of 'a small part of virtue'. When read in the context of Aristotle's statements on the virtues of the ruler and citizen, X.9 in fact suggests that while law is indeed a guide to conduct, its content derives from the practical wisdom of the legislator, and need not be apprehended by subjects *as rational*. Close consideration of the mutually dependent relationship between reason and force in the effective operation of *nomos* serves as a useful point of orientation for considering Aristotle's views on the benefits and limits of law in the rightful ordering of a polis and the debate between the partisans of the rule of law and the rule of the best man in *Politics* III. The final section brings the strands together by considering the role played by education laws in the best regime of *Politics* VII–VIII.

In Chapter 2 I examine the role of the law-maker and legislative expertise in Aristotle's practical thought. Aristotle's intriguing treatment of legislation presupposes the centrality of the figure of the practically wise constitutional founder prevalent in the classical Greek conceptualisation of political ordering. The attribution of a necessary causal role to the legislative founder nevertheless appears in tension with some of the core tenets of Aristotle's more famous political naturalism. My attempted resolution of this tension builds on the argument, found in recent scholarship, that Aristotle's claims for the status of the polis as natural rest on an extended concept of nature, by contending that the exercise of practical rationality is itself a function of distinctly human nature.

Chapter 3 then turns to Aristotle's firmly stated commitment to the relativity of laws to particular constitutional forms. The chapter begins by arguing in favour of the claims that the theory of explanatory causes is applicable to Aristotelian political science and that the constitution should be regarded as a formal cause. I then demonstrate how recognition of these claims can help to clarify Aristotle's contention that laws are not only enacted relative to particular regimes, but should be enacted to reflect the political commitments, or conceptions of the good, embodied in diverse forms of constitutional ordering. While this commitment may seem in danger of reducing the content of the law to the articulation of partisan or sectional interests, Aristotle's nuanced evaluative scheme for assessment of constitutional

(1973: 327–49) and (1975: xi). On similar questions in relation to *The Athenian Constitution* see Rhodes (1981).

forms, which privileges the best constitution and constitutions oriented by the common advantage, prevents the constitutional relativity of law from culminating in a stance of neutrality. From an Aristotelian perspective, I suggest, it is both the case that laws, and the rule of law more generally, are relative to particular political orderings and that such forms can be assessed as to their goodness from a normative point of view.

One of the most well-known features of Aristotle's constitutional theory is its differentiation of forms of political ordering by reference to the common advantage. In Chapter 4 I consider the relationship between the motivational and normative aspects of the common advantage and its implications for the laws falling under different constitutional regimes. Aristotle's identification of the common advantage with political justice also presupposes an association of 'universal' justice, or complete virtue in relation to others, with the lawful. Far from advocating a form of incipient legal positivism, Aristotle's discussion of the just and the lawful assumes a method of focal analysis according to which justice is always understood both in political terms and against the overarching natural standard of what is truly good from the perspective of a practically reasonable agent.

Chapter 5 considers Aristotle's justification for the cautious attitude towards the reform of constitutions and laws that is evident throughout both the *Nicomachean Ethics* and *Politics*. The chapter argues that Aristotle's circumspection regarding legal reform reflects both the importance of habituation to the effective functioning of law and a recognition of the limits of law's capacity to promote virtue and human flourishing. In the first part of the chapter, I engage in a close reading of Aristotle's treatment of the advantages and disadvantages of legal reform in the *Politics* Book II.8 discussion of Hippodamus' legislative proposal to honour innovation. I then examine Aristotle's account of constitutional change and stability in light of his theory of ethical virtue, before turning to political obedience and its dual justification within the practical works.

Chapter 6 considers the much-disputed question of Aristotle's status as a natural law theorist. An adequate approach to this topic, I assume, must set out from a detailed examination of Aristotle's contention that the just by nature and the just by convention are both 'parts' of political justice (*tou de politikou dikaiou to men phusikon esti to de nomikon*) (*NE* V.7, 1134b18–19). While Aristotle conceptualises positive law within a political horizon, he also provides determinant normative criteria for an assessment of just and unjust norms. With this conclusion in place, I then turn directly to the topic of natural law. My central claim is that, once some historical ambiguities are clarified, it is possible to identify several natural law commitments that are anticipated by Aristotle's account of *nomos*. In particular, Aristotle's emphasis upon the status of law as an achievement of practical reason and qualified acceptance of the thesis that law is a rational guide to conduct his views in close proximity to certain strands of the natural law tradition.

Aristotle's account of equity is widely recognised to be one of his most significant contributions to legal thought. In Chapter 7 I examine Aristotle's account of the equitable person and equitable judgement as a response to the potential for the universality of the law to culminate in rigid applications. Section 1 argues that Aristotle's theory of equitable judgement overcomes the threat of arbitrariness through appeal to the rational content of law derived from the practical wisdom of the expert lawmaker. In Section 2, I critically examine the status of the *spoudaios* (mature practically reasonable agent) as an ethical exemplar. Aristotle's privileging of the mature practically reasonable agent is defended against the reproach of decisionism by reference to the appropriate methodology in the philosophy of human affairs. In closing, I suggest that the normative point of law, on an Aristotelian view, only fully comes to light when considered from the perspective of a practically reasonable agent guided by an intelligent grasp of the human good.

Perhaps the greatest challenge for the current work is that, in one sense, Aristotle does not have a philosophy of law. While there is no attempt in Aristotle to demarcate law as an autonomous system existing independently of politics, his statements on *nomos* nonetheless have unity and coherence. While it could be argued that Aristotle's approach closes off certain questions of general jurisprudence, or constrains the capacity to ask questions of interest to us regarding the status of the law as an independent discipline or domain, this stance also means that the origins of law and the reasons for having it, its normative point, always remain in sharp focus. It is in this sense that viewing politics, in a distinctively Aristotelian way, as constitutive for law is instructive.

1

Law As Rational Constraint

In this opening chapter I closely examine Aristotle's most sustained and direct discussions of the topic of *nomos* in *Nicomachean Ethics* X.9 and *Politics* III.15–16. These passages contain famous statements which associate law with rationality, the promotion of virtue, universality and impartiality. A selective reading of these statements can suggest a picture according to which law is strictly identifiable with reason. As a corrective to such a one-sided intellectualist reading, I seek to place the rationalism of Aristotelian *nomos* in its broader political context. This requires engagement with Aristotle's acknowledgement of the law's necessary use of force and constraint over resistant passions in its attempt to guide citizens towards a state of virtue or at least quasi-virtue. While Aristotle undoubtedly regards good law as both an achievement of the architectonic legislator's practical reason and as rational in its content, its effective political application does not presuppose that the majority of citizens grasp the reasons for its directives. It is in this context that Aristotle asserts that true opinion (*doxa alēthēs*), not practical wisdom (*phronēsis*), is the virtue of one ruled by another (*archomenou*) (*Pol.* III.4, 1277b25–7). Aristotle's conception of *nomos* thus resists easy assimilation to the intellectualist view that a political community's laws are a set of reasons for action directed to autonomous rational agents. Section 1 sets the scene for this argument by considering the major passages which have led many interpreters to propose readings of Aristotelian *nomos* with an intellectualist slant. In Section 2, I closely examine the terms of Aristotle's informal definition of law in Book X.9 of the *Nicomachean Ethics*. Section 3 then situates this definition in the broader frame of X.9 in order to demonstrate the role of *nomos* as a constraint on desire and the implications of this for the ideal of the rule of law articulated in the dialogical context of *Politics* III.15–16. Finally, Section 4 discusses education laws as a privileged example of the interplay of reason and compulsion in the political applications of *nomos*.

SECTION 1 LAW AS A RATIONAL STANDARD

Aristotle is justly regarded as an important precursor for a long line of subsequent legal thought and practice which strongly associates law with reason. This conception of law is perhaps most readily identifiable with the natural law tradition, from the Thomistic definition of law as rational order (*rationis ordinatio*) to more contemporary views according to which 'part of what it is to be good law is to be a rational standard'.[1] The idea of law as a reflection of 'right reason' (*ratio recta*) was also decisive, to cite one more obvious example, in the development of the English common law tradition.[2]

A conception of law as rational order and right reason is indeed articulated in important passages in Aristotle's practical works. When Aristotle provides an informal definition of *nomos* in *Nicomachean Ethics* X.9, it is as rational speech (*logos*) derived from practical wisdom (*phronēsis*) and intellect (*nous*) (1180a21–2). Aristotle's famous characterisation of law in the *Politics* III.16 as 'intellect without desire' (*aneu orexeōs nous ho nomos estin*) (*Pol.* 1287a33) seems to corroborate this rationalist understanding of *nomos*, as do both the frequent identification of law with a kind of order (*taxis*) (*Pol.* VII.4, 1326a30 cf. II.5, 1263a23 and III.16, 1287a18) and the attribution of a significant causal role to the practical reason of the lawgiver in the establishment of constitutions and laws (*Pol.* I.2, 1253a33, II.12, 1273b31–5).

Aristotle's identification of *nomos* with reason, when read with his statements on law's role in the inculcation of virtue in *Nicomachean Ethics* X.9 and *Politics* VII–VIII, can easily suggest a rationalist perfectionism. On one version of this view, the laws of a polis would be rational standards or norms which promulgate ethical truths about virtue.[3] The citizen of a just political community with good laws could, on this reading, attain virtue by internalising the propositional content of its legal norms.

While this reading contains truth, it is also one-sided because it understates both Aristotle's emphasis upon law's use of compulsion and its limited capacity to inculcate virtue.[4] This much can be seen, indeed, by attending closely to Aristotle's informal definition of law in X.9, which is framed by references to law's compulsory power, use of command to resistant subjects and restraint of impulses:

> But the law does have a compulsory power (*ho de nomos anankastikēn echei dunamin*), it being rational speech (*logos*) that proceeds from a certain practical wisdom and intellect (*tinos phroneseōs kai nou*). And though people hate those other human beings who oppose their impulses, even if the latter are correct to do so, the law is not invidious when it orders what is equitable (*tattōn to epieikes*) (1180a21–4).

1 ST I-II 90.4 and Murphy (2013: 5).

2 Cromartie (2008: 12).

3 A view like this seems at least implicit, for example, in Ernest Barker's claim that for Aristotle 'law is one with reason … [and] the moral code' Barker (1959: 321).

4 Recent scholarship does, of course, acknowledge the role of force and compulsion in Aristotelian *nomos*, but devotes much more attention to its rational aspect. The relative amount of exposition given to the rational and compulsory aspects of law in the surveys of Lisi (2000: 29–53) and Miller (2007: 79–110) is representative.

Aristotle's definition of *nomos* in X.9 thus emphasises in equal measure the significance of law's rational content and its use of coercion and force. A correct understanding of Aristotle's account of *nomos*, I argue in this first chapter, thus requires attentiveness to both its rationalist and coercive aspects. While Aristotle indeed understands the function of law as *aiming* to make citizens good, its effectiveness in this aim is at least as dependent upon a non-discursive constraint of the passions as it is upon the cognitive apprehension of justified legal norms by autonomous rational agents.

Before I further examine the significance of Aristotle's statements regarding law's use of constraint, however, it is first necessary to do justice to the rational dimension of *nomos*. In the remainder of this section, I accordingly consider some important context for the X.9 definition of law as *logos* and enumerate some potential implications of the association of law with reason. Section 2 then unpacks in more detail the terms of Aristotle's definition of *nomos* as *logos* derived from practical insight.

As a starting point, the *Nicomachean Ethics* X.9 definition of *nomos* is instructively read in conjunction with Aristotle's presentation of the position of an advocate of the rule of law in *Politics* III.16:

> One who orders law to rule (*ton nomon keleuōn archein*), therefore, seems to be asking god and intellect alone to rule (*archein ton theon kai ton noun monous*), while one who asks man (*anthropon*) adds the beast (*thērion*). Desire (*epithumia*) is a thing of this sort; and spiritedness perverts rulers and the best men (*aristous andras*). Hence law is intellect without appetite (*dioper aneu orexeōs nous ho nomos estin*) (*Pol.* 1287a29–33, cf. III.15, 1286a18–20).

The association of *nomos* with the divine and intellect (*theon kai ton noun*) in this passage must be approached with caution, insofar as it is presented dialogically as one side of a debate on the merits of the rule of law and the best man.[5] The characterisation of law as *nous* nonetheless echoes the X.9 definition, which can presumably be attributed to Aristotle with more confidence. The characterisation, moreover, has strong Platonic resonances, which are worth briefly outlining here.

A significant Platonic antecedent to the view of the advocate of the rule of law in *Politics* III.15–16 is found in the Book X preamble to the law against atheism in the *Laws*. The Magnesian atheism legislation is a response to those (the young, certain prose writers, and poets) who employ a sharp dichotomy between *phusis* and *nomos* to argue that human law and ethical standards are merely conventional (888e–890b) and that the correct way to live is 'according to nature' i.e. dominating others without regard for lawful constraints (890a). The Athenian Stranger counters that it is necessary for the law-giver (*nomothetēn*) of even the slightest merit to defend the view found in ancient laws (*tō[i] palaiō[i] nomō[i]*), according to which there are gods and that laws are by nature (*phusei*) (or at least something not inferior to nature)

5 On the dialogical context of *Politics* III.15–16 see in particular Yack (1993: 175–208) and Bates (2003: 171–82).

and also the offspring of intelligence (*nou*) (890d). In support of this claim, the Athenian Stranger insists that the cosmos is guided and directed by a divine soul (899b, 901d–903c) and that law is divine and godlike (cf. 645a, 713a, 762e, 957c). On this view, law is to be regarded as 'the product of the same divine mind that creates order in the universe'.[6] Now it is important to note that Aristotle *compares* the activity of human law-making with the intelligent ordering of the divine rather than deriving, as in Platonic political theology, human law directly from a divine source. For Aristotle, *nomos* is nevertheless conceived as a rational limit imposed by the most divine part of the soul – *nous* – which places a necessary restraint upon desires and appetites with a view to the promotion of the political common good, virtue and human flourishing.

As will be explored in Section 2, Aristotle derives the rationality of law not merely from *nous*, but also *phronēsis*. In *Politics* VII.4, Aristotle asserts that law is a certain sort of order (*ho te gar nomos taxis tis esti*) and that good governance of necessity involves good order (*kai tēn eunomian anankaion eutaxian einai*). The weighty task of constituting political order falls to the true politician and law-giver and requires the sort of divine power *(theias gar dē touto dunameōs ergon*) which holds together the whole (*to pan*) itself (*Pol.* 1326a30–4). While its connotations of authority and command are significant, Aristotle here employs *taxis* to denote the constitutional and legal *order* which has its origins in the practical reason of an architectonic legislator (*nomothetēs*) (*Pol.* II.5, 1263a23 and III.16, 1287a18).[7]

Aristotle characterises legislative expertise or *nomothetikē* as a part of true political expertise (*politikē*) (NE X.9, 1180b31). As noted in the Introduction, *politikē* is a branch of practical knowledge (VI.8, 1141b29–32) and it deals with contingent actions which admit of less precision than the objects of a strict science like mathematics (I.3, 1094b12–27): it is the same disposition (*hexis*) as the intellectual virtue of prudence (*phronēsis*), although it differs 'in being' (VI.7, 1141b23). Like the 'natural' sciences, practical sciences are concerned with what happens for the most part (*hōs epi polu*), rather than exceptionless necessary truths. Aristotle nevertheless implies that *politikē* is akin to the stricter sciences in that it involves an understanding of principles (X.9, 1180b20–5).[8] This explains the further suggestion that an exponent of *nomothetikē*, in order to enact good laws, should possess universal knowledge of what is good for people (X.9, 1180b13–16) if they are to perform their function effectively (see NE III.1, 109b32–5, cf. I.13, 1102a19 and *Pol.* VII.2, 1324a20). A legislator must possess experience and sound practical judgement concerning the application of universal rules in order to identify the laws appropriate for communities and individuals (*NE* X.9, 1180b27; cf. *Pol.* VII.7, 1327b20–38).[9] The function of

6 Stalley (2007: 71).

7 The verb *tassō* can signify the ordering of troops or other parts of a corporate whole and also the appointment of a person to an office. See Liddell and Scott (2000: 793).

8 See Reeve (2014: xxi–xxxii). I return to the 'scientific' status of *politikē* below and in Chapter 2.

9 Although positive laws are stated in universal form, they are intended to govern the members of a particular polis, rather than humankind as a whole. See Kontos (forthcoming: 5–7) and note 10 in this chapter.

the legislator is hence to enact laws concerning the kinds of conduct citizens of a polis are to engage in and refrain from with a view to the promotion of virtue (*aretē*) and well-being (*eudaimonia*) (*NE* I.2, 1094b7). This requires at least practical insight into what sort of legal norms genuinely promote the human good.

The primary source of political order for Aristotle is hence the practically wise legislator (*nomothetēs*). Political expertise is thus also, as Chapter 2 explores, constitutive for law-making and law. Recognition of the source of *nomos* in the prudent legislator entails that all laws are in one sense contingent artefacts of a particular political community. Yet this does not preclude the law containing rational content. Insofar as the rational content of legal directives derives from the activity of practical wisdom and intellect, it draws on universal truths about human flourishing and its preconditions. In the case of the best constitutional order, the content of the law will be pre-eminently rational. Even in less than perfect constitutional orders, there will be rational content embedded in the law to whatever extent it draws on practical truths, holding for the most part, about virtue and wellbeing. Aristotle's analogy with the activity of a divine power imposing order upon the material of the cosmos thus suggests that *nomos* enacted by a good legislator is indeed a rational standard derived from practical reason.

It is necessary to untangle, however, the diverse senses in which just and reasonable law can be regarded as a rational standard. These senses include that law is a rational standard insofar as it (1) derives from the practical reason of an architectonic lawgiver; (2) articulates rational judgements about the human good; (3) *would* be endorsed and followed by a citizen exercising right reason; (4) is grasped intellectually by citizens as a source of reasons for action. A close analysis of Aristotle's definition of *nomos* in *Nicomachean Ethics* X.9 – the focus of Section 2 – sets the scene for my argument in Section 3 that although Aristotle assumes the truth of (1), (2) and (3), he regards (4) as a possibility that is actualised only in rare circumstances and is often unnecessary for law's effective functioning.

SECTION 2 DEFINING *NOMOS*

Aristotle characterises *nomos* in X.9 as reason (*logos*) derived from intelligence (*nous*) and practical reason (*phronēsis*). This informal definition reflects Aristotle's attribution of law to the practical rationality of the true architectonic legislator. In this second section, I unpack in detail the key terms of the X.9 definition in order to arrive at a more precise grasp of the rational dimension of *nomos*.

The derivation of *nomos* from intellect (*nous*) has, as noted above, Platonic resonances. Aristotle's discussion of *nous* in X.7 – close in proximity to his X.9 characterisation of law – describes *nous* as the best and most divine element in us (*NE* 1177a12–18) and as that with which we are most to be identified (1178a2–8). The activity of the intellect is the most self-sufficient (1177a27–b1, 1178a23–b7) and pleasurable (1177a22–7, b20–1) activity of which we are capable and it is the only activity worthy of choice for itself alone (1177b2–4). It is the virtue of the intellect or *nous* which constitutes complete (*teleia*) *eudaimonia* and this is contemplation (*theōretikē*). Aristotle nonetheless employs the term *nous* in a multifaceted way in the *Nicomachean Ethics*, exemplified by its use within Book VI in a narrower (VI.6) and more general sense which includes both theoretical and practical thinking (VI.2). In VI.6, Aristotle does not define *nous* directly, but rather defines wisdom (*sophia*) as the combination of *nous* and science (*epistēmē*) (1141a20). *Nous* is to be understood here as an intellectual grasp of indemonstrable first principles (1141b3; *APo*. II.19, 100b10–17) and is contrasted with practical wisdom insofar as *phronēsis* is concerned with the contingent and particular (*NE* VI.8, 1142a23–30). In VI.2 Aristotle analyses practical choice (*prohairesis*) as intellect (*nous*) informed by a certain desire (*orexis*) or as desire marked by thinking (1139b4–6). Complicating things even further is the difficult passage relating *nous* to practical matters, rather than scientific demonstrations, in VI.11. Here *nous* (in contrast to *logos*) is concerned with the ultimate things – both first defining boundaries and ultimate particulars – in both directions. While *nous* pertaining to demonstrations grasps the unchanging first defining boundaries, intellect in matters of action grasps also the ultimate particular thing that admits of being otherwise. The ultimate particulars grasped by *nous* are the principles of that for the sake of which one acts and the universals arise from the particulars (V.11, 1143a35–b5). This practical application of *nous* involving intellectual grasp of particulars, yet allowing for ascent to universals, is developed through experience (1143b6–9).

The fact that the rational activity of the legislator is an exercise of political expertise (*politikē*), and hence a mode of *phronēsis*, suggests that when Aristotle derives *nomos* from *nous* he has in mind a true law-maker legislating on the basis of practical knowledge and experience. The law-maker would thus primarily engage the more practical sense of *nous* which grasps ultimate particulars, but in such a way as to allow for an ascent towards universal propositions. Law is necessarily framed universally, albeit about matters which hold only for the most part and cannot always be dealt with adequately in universal terms (*ho men nomos katholou pas, peri eniōn d' ouch oion te orthōs eipein katholou*) (*NE* V.10, 1137b13–14). Aristotle defines universals as predicable of, or common to, a plurality of things or particulars (*Int*. VII, 17a39; *Met*. VII.13, 1038b11–12). In the case of laws, the most relevant particulars are human actions, which fall under kinds of conduct. A law is a universal norm intended to govern kinds of conduct and the instances of action falling under it.[10] Consider, for example, a law against violent assaults: 'any person who intentionally commits a violent assault, will be subject to … '. This law is framed in universal

[10] Kontos (forthcoming: 5) argues that Aristotelian laws should be regarded as 'particular universals'. As Kontos suggests, laws are particular not simply because they are applied to many different circumstances, but also because the practically astute law-maker must frame laws suited to the 'material' of their own polis. While the law-maker must attend to particular circumstances of their polis, however, this does not entail that the content of some kinds of laws would not be valid in any well-governed community. I return to this point in Chapter 6.

terms and applies to a certain kind of conduct, under which fall in turn particular actions.[11] The formulation of a law is accordingly to be understood in Aristotelian terms as an achievement of practical insight, arrived at on the basis of experience, into the ethical correctness and the political consequences of kinds of conduct. Legislative expertise, therefore, is charged with establishing laws which serve as rational guides to conduct in the realm of practical affairs, and it does this by deriving from a grasp of particulars universal propositions which serve the end of both individual and communal flourishing.[12] The principal exercise of *nous* engaged in law-making – understood as a branch of political expertise – is thus best interpreted as involving an ascent from a grasp of particulars to universal legal propositions, which in turn govern particular actions.

Aristotle's concomitant derivation of *nomos* from *phronēsis* is what speaks most strongly in favour of this interpretation of law-making *nous*. The role of *phronēsis*, as an exercise of the 'calculative' (*logistikon*) part of the soul (*NE* VI.2, 1139a12–13), is to deliberate about the way to attain a good end (VI.4–5, 1140a24–1140b30) and to issue orders with regard to what should or should not be done (VI.10, 1143a9–10) in contingent circumstances. This last formulation, with its reference to commands and normative directives of the kind articulated in laws, recalls the *Nicomachean Ethics* VI.13 discussion of the status of *phronēsis* as authoritative (*kuria*). Aristotle here points out that *phronēsis* should not be regarded as authoritative over wisdom (*sophias*), when it issues commands towards the ends set by virtue. While medicine also issues directives, it does not issue these commands *to* health, but commands in order *to promote* the end of health. Analogously, while the political art (*politikē*) and architectonic legislation (*nomothetikē*) issue commands and directives as modes of prudence, they are to be regarded as serving the higher ends (*NE* VI.13, 1145a4–11) of individual and communal virtue and flourishing.

This treatment of prudence – and its directives – as instrumental to higher ends raises the question as to whether the true law-maker's exercise of practical reason involves an understanding of the overall human good or is restricted to the calculation of means based on a prior grasp of the good attained through other intellectual faculties.[13] Aristotle's various statements on law-making entail both that the true

[11] The formulation of such a law of assaults plausibly depends on a prior practical or ethical truth that can also be stated in universal terms i.e. 'violent assaults are wrong, because detrimental to the well-being of the individual and community'. I consider in detail Aristotle's connections with the natural law tradition in Chapter 6.

[12] As will be explored in Chapter 2, this does not mean law-making is unable to draw on insights of theoretical *nous*. As Shields (2015: 237) notes, 'precisely because correct action requires a correct understanding of the ends of action, practical science will sooner presuppose theoretical understanding ... rather than preclude it'.

[13] For critique of the so-called 'Grand End' view of *phronēsis* see Broadie (1991: 46). A convincing recent defence of the 'Grand End' view is found in Inglis (2014: 263–87). From a 'Grand End' perspective, there is no reason to deny that *phronēsis* can both assume and rely on the operation of other intellectual faculties, including *nous*, which also grasp the ends of action. See Bodéüs (1993: 30–6) for further discussion of this point.

legislator must have a correct conception of the end of human life in view and that good laws presuppose a knowledge of the true ends of action and not simply the instrumental activities that are necessary means to attain those ends. It is worth recalling in this context that *phronēsis* is defined as a practical state, involving true reasoning, concerned with what is good and bad for a human being (*NE* VI.5, 1140b4–6). The fact that *phronēsis* achieves ends set in advance by correct dispositions is, moreover, consistent with the claim that an understanding of the human good is constitutive for legislative practical wisdom. Aristotle thus contends that the *phronimos* (and hence by implication the true law-maker) deliberates nobly about what is good or beneficial, not in particular respects such as what promotes health or strength, but what promotes living well as a whole (*NE* VI.5, 1140a25–8).[14] The thesis that law-making in the architectonic sense presupposes a grasp of the overall human good is also consistent with the obvious fact about legislative enactments (in contrast to decrees) that they operate at the level of universal judgements about forms of conduct and in so doing must also engage with proximate ends (which as proximate are also instrumental to the higher end of flourishing).

It remains to determine what, for Aristotle, is the nature of the rational account (*logos*) identified with *nomos* and proceeding from intellect and practical wisdom. In the first instance, Aristotle considers (*NE* VI.13, 1144b25–30) *phronēsis* as the disposition which exercises the 'right reason' (*orthos logos*) definitive of ethical virtue. In this guise, *phronēsis* discerns what is appropriate i.e. neither deficient nor excessive from the perspective of the mean (II.2, 1103b31–4 and VI.1, 1138b18–34). As will become apparent in the debate between the advocates of the rule of law and the best man discussed in Section 3, one of the salutary aspects of law is its impartiality and reasonableness in relation to the passions. From this perspective, the rationality of law serves to moderate the most unrestrained human desires.

One can also approach the status of *nomos* as a form of *logos* by reference to the association of *phronēsis* with the 'calculative' (*logistikon*) reasoning capacity. In Book I Aristotle divides the soul into rational and non-rational parts (*NE* I.13, 1102a27–8), with these two parts further subdivided.[15] The non-rational part of the soul is divided into the vegetative capacity, which does not share in reason at all (1102a32–3), and the part with the capacity for desire and emotion, which is able to listen to and obey (*peitharchikon*) reason (1102b30–1103a3). The rational part of the

14 Aristotle's claim that practical thinking involves both reason (*nous*) (*NE* V.2, 1139a18) and desire (*orexis*) does not compromise the status of *nomos* as 'reason without desire'. Although desire must be 'correct' in advance for sound practical reasoning to occur, for an agent with virtue desire pursues what reason asserts (1139a21–6). The 'rule of reason' thus ensures that when practical judgements about the good have been articulated in *nomos*, then it is the law's rational content, rather than the motivating desire, which finds expression.

15 This differs from the later division of the rational part of the soul in Book VI. Here the first rational subpart is that by which we contemplate (*theōroumen*) beings whose principles cannot be other than they are, whereas the second is that by which we contemplate those beings that can be other than they are (*NE* VI.1, 1139a6–9).

soul is also divided between the part that possesses reason with authority (*kurios*) and the part (the desiring part of the soul) which does not itself possess reason, but is capable of listening to reason (1103a2–3). Importantly, then, the lower parts of the soul can listen to reason and obey in the same way that someone can listen to their parents or a friend and obey without possessing reason in the full sense (1102b30–5). An agent in which the desiring part of the soul seeks to prevail is thus able to follow 'right reason' by obeying the directives of another without themselves being practically wise or having attained genuine virtue. This explains why the law can still serve as the rule of reason for an agent lacking mature practical reasonableness insofar as it distils in an accessible way the content of correct judgements about the human good.

The other sense of *logos* salient for Aristotle's understanding of *nomos* is that set out in Book I of the *Politics* as part of the argument that humans are by nature political animals. Aristotle emphasises that humans alone among the animals have *logos* (*Pol.* I.2, 1253a10). Although other animals can indicate to each other the pleasant and painful, rational speech can reveal the advantageous and harmful and hence also the just and unjust (1253a10–14). It is this capacity to determine the good and the bad and the just and unjust which grounds the establishment of a political community (1253a16–17). Insofar as laws function as expressions of particular views of justice (*NE* V.6, 1134a30–2), the *nomoi* of a political community can be understood as an articulation of its beliefs as to the just and unjust, good and bad.

In light of this analysis, it is instructive to return to the four different senses of the rationality of law enumerated at the conclusion of the previous section. What emerges from the discussion is that while Aristotle's definition of *nomos* as a kind of *logos* entails that the law (1) derives from a rational source and (2) articulates reasonable judgements about the human good, it does not directly address the questions whether its rational content (3) would be endorsed by right reason and (4) must be understood by citizens as rationally justified to perform its political function. While it seems reasonable, given the discussion of right reason or *orthos logos* above, to take the truth of (3) as a corollary of (1) and (2), moreover, the same does not apply to (4). This is particularly the case insofar as Aristotle insists, in an important passage of *Politics* III.4 which distances him from the notion of a community of fully rational agents, that true opinion (*doxa alēthēs*), not practical wisdom (*phronēsis*), is the virtue of one ruled (*archomenou*) (1277b25–9). When read in conjunction with the emphasis upon the need for law to compel the many towards action *in conformity with* virtue – my focus in Section 3 – this passage militates against the unequivocal truth of (4) from an Aristotelian perspective.

Before I return to X.9, however, it is worth considering the implications of (4). If (4) is not an Aristotelian thesis, or is one only once appropriate qualifications are made, then this places in question the application to the practical works of recent work in the philosophy of law which understands the role of legal norms as providing those who are subject to its directives with 'reasons for action'. A particularly instructive example is Rosler's reconstruction of an Aristotelian theory of political obligation by reference to Raz's theory of practical authority.[16] Raz's theory grounds an account of practical authority and political obligation in the relationship between authoritative reasons for action and the first person practical reasoning capacities of subjects.[17] According to Raz's theory, I can act rationally, and even autonomously, by following the directives of a practical authority, which directives are intended to 'exclude' other reasons for action I may possess, if those directives allow me to act better on the reasons that apply to me than I would otherwise be able to do.[18] Rosler, in his Razian reconstruction of the *Politics*, argues that the concept of an exclusionary reason for action is implicitly at work in the Aristotelian claim that the flourishing of individuals within a political community depends upon reciprocal relations of ruling (hence issuing directives) and being ruled (hence being subject to the directives of another) through law.[19] While Rosler's reconstruction denies neither the role of constraint in the actual functioning of the law, nor the possibility that law can effectively operate on subjects in the absence of a rational grasp of the law's content, the analysis which follows suggests that its reliance on assumptions regarding a rational justification of the law from the perspective of a subject presents a misleading and one-sided picture of Aristotelian *nomos*.[20]

SECTION 3 LAW AS CONSTRAINT OF THE PASSIONS

The *Nicomachean Ethics* X.9 definition of *nomos* as a rational standard (*logos*) is situated within a broader discussion of the indispensable role of law in providing order to the political community through the imposition of constraint on otherwise unlimited passions. In this third section, I contend that Aristotle's definition of *nomos* in X.9 must be read against the background of his realistic assessment of the capacity for those subject to the law to engage with its directives as practically reasonable agents. Aristotle's acknowledgement of a necessary element of constraint

16 Rosler (2005: 101–12).

17 Raz (1986: 97). The core of Raz's service conception of authority is found in the conjunction of the Dependence Thesis and the Normal Justification Thesis (NJT). The Dependence Thesis asserts that the directives of an authority should reflect reasons which apply to the subjects of those authoritative directives independently of the directives. The NJT asserts that 'the normal way to establish that a person has authority over another person involves showing that the alleged subject is better likely to comply with reasons that apply to him (other than the alleged authoritative directives) if he accepts the directives of the alleged authority as authoritatively binding and tries to follow them, rather than by trying to follow the reasons that apply to him directly'. Ibid. 47 and 53.

18 By substituting the directives of a practical authority for my own first-order reasoning about the reasons for action that apply to me, Raz claims, it is 'possible to act contrary to the balance of reasons without thereby acting contrary to reason'. Ibid. 97.

19 Rosler (2005: 101–12).

20 Rosler (2005: 102–5), for example, notes both Aristotle's penchant for military language and claim that commands (*epitaxeis*) are characteristic of political office (*Pol.* IV.15, 1299a26–7 and VII.4, 1326b14), but interprets this in Razian terms by reference to the capacity of subjects to recognise the justification for the commands.

and force in the effective functioning of the law, moreover, differs in important ways from influential modern accounts of coercion. In the second part of the section, I turn to the implications of this assessment for the debate between the advocates of the rule of law and of the rule of the best man in *Politics* III.15–16.

It is far from accidental that Aristotle's most sustained treatment of *nomos* in the *Nicomachean Ethics* is in the closing transition to the *Politics*. Despite the centrality of the figure of the legislator, and the connections between the themes of justice and law examined in Book V, references to *nomos* in the *Nicomachean Ethics* are relatively sparse.[21] The topic of *nomos* is thematised most explicitly in the transition to an investigation of constitutions and the political conditions for human flourishing.[22]

Once he has established that the best and happiest life is one of theoretical activity, Aristotle asks whether the task of the practical discourses has now come to an end (*NE* X.9, 1179a35). Even allowing for the truth of the previous analysis, he avers, rational discourses (*logoi*) are limited in their capacity for the sort of character formation which would make people decent and equitable (*epieikes*). While *logoi* may help to inculcate virtue in the well-born or the well-educated, they are incapable of exhorting the many to nobility and goodness (*tous de pollous adunatein pros kalokagathein protrepsasthai*) (1179b5–11). The many live according to passion, pursuit of pleasure and avoidance of pain, and are not by nature obedient because of reverence (*aidōs*) or shame (*to aischron*), but rather because of the fear of the pain of vengeance (1179b11–15). What is truly noble and pleasant is inaccessible to the many, who have little or no direct experience of such goods. Given these facts about human motivations, *logoi* (at least when not backed by force) are of little use in the education of character. All that is possible for the many, on this view, is a small share in virtue (1179b15–20). Yet even a small share in virtue presupposes effective habituation and good character formation. Without this, at least for those not divinely blessed, speeches will be of limited use. Someone guided by the end of passion will not be deterred from bad courses of action through speeches and may not even be comprehending of their rational content and justificatory foundation. Compulsion is also necessary because passion seems to yield to force rather than to speech (*ou dokei logo[i] hypeikein to pathos alla bia[i]*) (1179b20–32).

It is at this point that *nomos* enters the scene. A moderate way of life is unpleasant to the many, especially in their formative stage of life. Appropriate laws are therefore required to ensure the correct habituation of the young and for life as a whole

[21] See note 7, Introduction.

[22] Aristotle's discussion of *nomos* in X.9 is more general than in the *Politics* and in one sense incomplete, insofar as it considers law without direct reference to its determination by particular constitutional forms. There is no need to postulate inconsistency, however, between X.9 and Aristotle's statements regarding law's constitutional relativity in the *Politics*. In X.9 Aristotle introduces *nomos* in the context of the question of human flourishing, while pointing forward to the explanatory priority of constitutional theory. For an argument along similar lines, see Vander Waerdt (1991: 231–53). I am grateful to Thornton Lockwood for discussion of this point.

(*peri panta ton bion*) (1179b32–1180a3). The many, once again, obey the governance of necessity more than speech and fear the pain of punishments more than they pursue what is noble (*hoi gar polloi anankē[i] mallon ē logo[i] peitharchousi kai zēmiais ē tō[i] kalō[i]*) (1180a4–6). This is why some thinkers (most obviously Plato) insist that while those already with a sense of how to live nobly may be amenable to speeches, it is necessary to impose punishment and inflict pain on those who are motivated by pleasure (1180a6–12). Even for those motivated by the lower pleasures, it is possible to be good in a qualified sense through effective habituation, so as to live in accordance with intellect and order (*bioumenois kata tina noun kai taxin orthēn*), but on the proviso that habituation through rational norms is backed by strength (*echousan ischun*) (1180a15–19).[23]

Aristotle considers whether rational guidance backed by strength could derive (in most cases) from paternal authority. Yet the authority of an individual lacks the compulsory power of the law (*ho de nomos anankastikēn echei dunamin*) (1180a22–3). One major advantage of law is that, because it does not appear to be an imposition by an individual, it is less invidious to those whose pleasures it restrains, at least when equitable (1180a22–5). The law, that is to say, arouses less resentment than the directives of a person in authority because it has the appearance of fairness. Despite the benefits of law with respect to habituation in virtue, Aristotle observes that it is only among the Spartans (and perhaps a few other communities) that *nomoi* have been enacted by the legislator (*nomothetēs*) so as to deal with the whole regimen of human life. In most cities, such concerns have been neglected and men live – akin to the Cyclops – by laying down their own law (1180a25–8). While it is certainly salutary if individuals seek to encourage virtue in their children and friends, a more systematic approach is hence required. And the goal of promoting human excellence is best actualised by the practically reasonable person becoming a skilled legislator (*nomothetikos genomenos*) (1180a33–5), thus suggesting the line of enquiry pursued in the *Politics*. In the transition to the *Politics* Aristotle concludes by discussing the falsity of the sophists' claim to possess such a legislative art. The sophists demonstrate their ignorance of the true expertise of law-making by reducing legislation to rhetoric and thinking it possible to attain the requisite understanding through mere collections of constitutions and laws (1181a12–18).[24]

23 This is a point recognised by Aquinas in his *Nicomachean Ethics* commentary on this passage: *Quod quidem non contingit nisi vita hominis dirigatur per aliquem intellectum, qui habeat, et rectum ordinem ad hoc quod ducat ad bonum, et habeat fortitudinem, idest vim coactivam ad hoc quod compellat nolentes* ('This is possible [that a man refrain from evil] only when a man's life is directed by some intellect that has both the right order conducive to good and the firmness, i.e., the coercive power, to compel the unwilling'). Aquinas (1993: 642). Significantly, Aquinas attributes intellect to the law-giver, not to 'the ruled', or those who are subject to legal coercion.

24 Isocrates' *Antidosis* is a likely target of this critique. See Kontos (forthcoming: 31) and the references cited there. Aristotle's claim that his predecessors left the theme of legislation unexamined (1181b12–15) has puzzled many commentators and even led some (e.g. Susemihl and Hicks (1894: 69)) to postulate an interpolation. As Vander Waedrt (1991: 239) argues, a more plausible interpretation is that Aristotle is

X.9 read in its entirety thus offers a realistic assessment of the extent to which the law serves as a rational standard for most citizens in actual political regimes. It is not just that ethical discourses (*logoi*) are insufficient for virtue, and that law, as a kind of *logos* deriving from practical insight, is unable to promote virtue without support from compulsion, inclusive of punitive measures, which work directly on the passions through manipulation of incentives of pleasure and pain. The more significant point is that the efficacy of the law does not require that most citizens grasp the content of the law *as a rational standard*. From an Aristotelian perspective, the claim that law is a rational guide to conduct is thus true in a sense rather than absolutely. Good law is a rational guide to conduct insofar as it derives from a rational source, articulates rational judgements about the human good and is *capable* as serving as a standard in an agent's practical reasoning. The effectiveness of the law is, however, independent of citizens grasping the content of the law, and certainly does not presuppose that citizens engage with the content of the law as justified norms directed to a community of autonomous and rational agents.

This view of the operation of the law is consonant with Aristotle's wider teaching regarding the ethical virtues. For Aristotle, the correct ends of human action are set by the right character dispositions (*NE* VI.12, 1144a34 and VII.8, 1151a15–19) working in conjunction with *phronēsis* rather than autonomous rationality. The development of the right character dispositions requires that one's passions and the desire for pleasure are appropriately habituated. A central function of law is thus to create conditions for the cultivation of 'affect' such that practical reason can deliberate consistently with human flourishing. And it is only insofar as law is backed by compulsory force, including the threat of punishment, that it is effective in providing the requisite ethical habituation. The necessity of law is accordingly in large part a function of human limitations with respect to virtue and its recourse to violent compulsion is also a reflection of those same limitations.

A clear recognition of the role of compulsion in Aristotle's account of *nomos* need not undermine the claims regarding the rationality of the law made in the previous section. At the level of the law-maker and the practically reasonable citizen, the rational content of the law allows its directives to serve as reasons for action and guides for conduct. Even at the level of the less than practically reasonable citizen, the law can promote conduct that is *in conformity with* right reason. In particular, in cases where the law forbids certain actions with a view to the wellbeing of citizens, it can function as a form of 'enabling constraint' which empowers a subject to 'engage in a more valuable set of actions' by preventing them from 'performing a different and less valuable set of actions'.[25] Here the rational content of the law, as formulated by the practically reasonable legislator, influences the conduct of a citizen who may

seeking to highlight the originality of his theories of legislative science and constitutional types (the themes of the next two chapters).

25 Rosler (2005: 187). Rosler takes over the concept of 'enabling restraint' from Yack (1993: 206–8).

or may not fully be able to understand the reasons why certain actions are or are not permitted according to the norms of the political community. The identification of *nomos* with reason and its necessary use of compulsion to restrain the passions are from this angle perfectly compatible.

The compatibility should nevertheless not lead one to overlook the sub-rational domain in which *nomos* must operate in to be effective, both psychologically and politically. This restraining role of *nomos* in relation to the passions is particularly evident in Aristotle's *Rhetoric* I.8 discussion of tyranny:

> Monarchy is, as the name suggests, where one person is authoritative overall all (*eis hapantōn kurios estin*). It is kingship (*basileia*) if it is subject to order (*taxin*), and tyranny if it is unlimited (*aoristos*) (1366a1–3).

A kingship is a regime ruled by one person and governed by lawful order (*taxis*), whereas a tyranny is unlimited in the sense that the passions of the ruler are unconstrained by the normative and coercive force of the law. This definition of tyranny in terms of the 'unlimited' (*aoristos*) should be read in light of the claim that a monarchy is a tyranny when the monarch rules unaccountably (*anupeuthunos archei*) over people who are similar to him or better, with an eye to his own advantage, not that of the ruled (*Pol.* IV.10, 1295a18–21). The two accounts of tyranny are complementary in the sense that 'the introduction of accountability would render the rule *horistos*, limited; and any true limitation would come with some accountability'.[26] The tyrant rules in his own interest because of a lack of limitation on desire, which renders him unable to look to the advantage of his subjects. From this perspective, the primary function of *nomos* is to impose a limit on the unrestrained desires of the tyrannical soul.

This discussion of tyranny recalls an important passage in Book IX of Plato's *Republic*. According to Socrates, the tyrannical soul is dominated by an *eros* which was restrained by paternal authority and law in the formative stages, but became anarchic and lawless (*en pasei anarchia kai anomia*) once set free from such limits (574d–e). This picture of the absence of the limiting force of law in the tyrannical soul in the *Republic* is supplemented by the definition of *nomos* provided in the *Philebus*. Here *nomos* is characterised as a limit on limitless pleasure. More precisely, Socrates points out that the Goddess (most likely heavenly Aphrodite, in contrast to vulgar Aphrodite, consistently with *Symposium* 180c–181a) imposes the limit (*peras*) of law and order (*nomon kai taxin*) on our pleasures and their fulfilment (26b). Without such law and order, the Goddess recognises, our tendency to excess (*hubrin*) and wickedness (*ponērian*) means that we would seek, to our overall detriment, pleasures without limit.

Aristotle's account of tyranny thus both corroborates and clarifies his suggestion in X.9 that *nomos* is the rational imposition of order upon otherwise limitless desire.

[26] Hoekstra (2016: 49).

The claim that there is no natural limit to desire is stated or implied by Aristotle on several occasions in the *Politics* (I.8, 1256b32, I.9, 1257b40, II.7, 1267b1). The licence to do whatever one wishes, Aristotle also notes, leaves us defenceless against what is bad in each human being (VI.4, 1319a1). It is thus the 'negative' role of *nomos* to limit the passions and facilitate the individual and community order necessary for the development of virtue.

This X.9 account of the role of constraint in the effective functioning of the law differs in illuminating ways from prominent modern variants of the thesis that coercion is necessary for any legal order. A particularly instructive example is Ripstein's Kantian argument that 'each person's entitlement to be his or her own master is only consistent with the entitlements of others if public legal institutions are in place'.[27] On this view, legal institutions and the authorisation to coerce are necessary conditions for the 'consistent exercise of the right to freedom by a plurality of persons'.[28] The normative foundation of this account is that 'each person is entitled to be his or her own master' in the sense of not being subordinated to choices regarding the human good made by other persons.[29] Aristotle's account, by contrast, assumes that in the central case a law-giver has framed laws conducive to the human good and that constraint is necessary in order to promote the development of the ethical virtues necessary for the wellbeing of the individual and the community. Rather than freedom of choice, the ground of Aristotle's argument for the necessity of lawful coercion is human flourishing.

The constraining role of *nomos* in relation to the passions explains why it is true to say for Aristotle that 'law enforces a behavior which only emulates the one recommended by rational autonomy'.[30] Although the constraint of law may indeed be enabling in relation to the development of partial forms of virtue, Aristotle's emphasis upon the need for force and punishment, particularly in relation to the many given their limitations, precludes an interpretation according to which the primary subject of the law is a practically reasonable agent apprehending its rational content *as* enabling. While the content of the law may indeed be rational, when the law habituates the passions it need not persuade as to the good reasons for having law, or for having particular laws, in order to fulfil its function. In terms later developed by Augustine, *nomos* can perform its political role by addressing subjects in the mode of authority (*auctoritas*) rather than reason (*ratio*), but as an *auctoritas* that is nonetheless ultimately informed by the *ratio* of the law-giver.[31] In closing this section, I will now demonstrate how attentiveness to the indispensable role of compulsion in

27 Ripstein (2009: 9).

28 Ripstein (2009: 9).

29 Ripstein (2009: 4).

30 Horn (2013: 235). See also Kraut (2018: 174): 'a large portion of the citizenry of any city can acquire good habits even though they will fall short of full virtue . . . [t]hey will act well not out of a reasoned understanding of the human good and all the virtues, but because they willingly accept certain norms of behavior'.

31 See Lütcke (1968: 13–62).

Aristotle's X.9 account of *nomos* can clarify the debate between the partisans of the rule of law and of the rule of the best man in *Politics* III.

Recognition of the dialogical character of the debate between the partisans of the rule of law and the best man in *Politics* III.15–16 does not preclude the attribution to Aristotle of a qualified acceptance of the desirable features of law deriving from its rational source and content. Foremost among these features are universality and impartiality. The fact that law is framed in universal terms (*to katholou*) offers obvious advantages over particular decrees (*psēphismata*) or the arbitrary commands of a ruler (*NE* V.10, 1137b11–24; *Pol.* II.8, 1269a9–12; cf. *Rh.* I.1, 1354b1ff). Foremost among these advantages are that 'citizens can learn what the laws require, adapt their behavior to them, and acquire the habit of obedience'.[32] The universality of law also entails that it is relatively unaccompanied by the passionate influences which corrupt human rulers (*Pol.* III.15, 1286a17–19). Humans are apt to make poor judgements due to passions (*en pathei ontes*) and the law provides impartiality by establishing a just mean (*ho gar nomos to meson*) (1287b5). As noted above, Aristotle also points in X.9 to the fact that authoritative pronouncements from a seemingly 'objective' source are less likely to arouse resentment (1180a22–5). This, it is worth stating, is the case even though all laws derive from a legislator and accordingly reflect the preference for a particular regime-type and conception of the human good.

The dialogue between the advocates of the rule of the laws and the rule of the best man must also be read, however, in light of Aristotle's discussion of the view that a person truly outstanding by excess of virtue is no longer part of the polis (*Pol.* III.13, 1284a8). There is in one sense no law for such a person – they are themselves a law (*autoi gar eisis nomos*) – because law pertains to citizens who share a relation of equality (1284a11–14). From this perspective, Aristotle suggests that where a person or family has outstanding virtue, they should have authority simply and not only as part of a reciprocal relationship of ruling and being ruled (III.17, 1288a15–30). It is in light of the possibility of such agents with outstanding virtue that one can point to the limitations of law in responding to contingent circumstances and addressing different members of the community in their particularity.

The advocate of the rule of the best man reprises several insights from Plato's *Statesman*. Here Socrates suggests that in the best regime – one where rulers have genuine expertise and insight – it is much better for a king with (practical) intelligence (*phronēsis*) rather than the *nomoi* to rule (294a). The universality of law means that it is unable to adapt to particular circumstances. On account of the variance between human beings and of situations, a law is incapable of comprehending what is best and just for all (294b). In addition, law-givers – in a manner analogous to physical trainers – may be unable to attend to the needs of each individual and must accordingly enact laws which suit the majority (293e–295b). The proviso that a ruler

[32] Miller (2007: 81). See also Kraut (2002: 105–6, 276, 449–50 and 453).

should not be bound (295b–296a) by the inflexibility of law only applies, however, in a case where the ruler genuinely has expert knowledge. *Nomoi* – understood here principally as written instructions serving as rational guides to conduct – thus appear as the necessary second-best option for the vast majority of political communities and their citizens.

Aristotle presents the advocate of the rule of the best man as subscribing to these Platonic views regarding law in the broad sense that matters of deliberation are resistant to comprehensive legislation (*Pol.* III.16, 1287b15–22). In the first instance, laws speak of the universal only and do not command with a view to particular circumstances (III.15, 1286a10–11). Asking the law to rule is equivalent to asking a doctor to tend for sick people by employing a written set of instructions without proper regard for the nature of the circumstances of the individual patient (1286a12–15). On this basis, the best regime (*politeia*) would not be one that is based on written rules and laws (1286a12–15).[33]

In the best regime all citizens are educated towards virtue. X.9 assumes that the existence of such a regime would be an extraordinary occurrence. A regime ruled by a person with a divine intelligence would certainly be preferable to a law-governed regime, but the absence of law in actual political communities tends rather to tyranny. If one assumes that the virtue of citizens is incomplete or non-existent, the same arguments regarding the limitations of the universality of law would apply to human rulers (*Pol.* III.15, 1286a17), insofar as they also rely on universal rules. More decisively, while humans possess the passionate element, this is not the case with laws (1286a18–20).[34] Among those who are similar and equal, it is neither advantageous nor just for one person to have authority over everyone, whether one acts under laws or as a law unto themselves (III.17, 1288a1–2). Viewed from this perspective, Aristotle implies, laws are in one sense inherently democratic insofar as an arrangement for citizens to rule and be ruled in turn is already an ordered and law-governed political community (*touto ēdē nomos. hē gar taxis nomos*) (III.16, 1287a16–17). This implication suggests the further point that in most actual communities law has an inescapably demotic aspect which reflects the prevalence of vice, albeit that its constitutive aim remains to promote virtue to the greatest extent possible.

As is the case with Plato, laws emerge as a necessary second-best given human nature and the limits of political communities. Law is both constituted by politics

33 I return to these points regarding the universality of law, and its attendant shortcomings, in Chapter 7.

34 Aristotle associates, at this point in the discussion, the rule of law with the rule of the many. While the judgement of an individual is corrupted when it is dominated by anger or another emotion, it is difficult for the many as a whole to become angry at the same time (*Pol.* III.15, 1286a30–5). What is many is also more incorruptible (1286a31). The many may be composed of inferior individuals, on this line of reasoning, and yet the political ordering of a city composed of persons can be considered in an analogous way to a feast where each person brings a contribution (1286a29–31). The dialogical context of this discussion needs to be kept in mind when assessing its relevance for contemporary democratic arguments. See, for example, Waldron (1995).

and mitigates some of its realities. Although law is limited in its capacity to promote virtue, the lawless rule of a person is much more likely to be tyranny than benevolent kingship given the nature of the human soul. It thus seems plausible that Aristotle's actual view – arrived at on the basis of the discussion between the advocates of the rule of the laws and the best man – is that the ruler must necessarily be a legislator and laws must exist, and that they must generally be considered as authoritative, but that they also must not be considered as authoritative when they deviate from (what is right) (*Pol.* III.15, 1286a22–4). It is this claim, indeed, which leads Aristotle to the consideration of whether the best person or the many should step in where the law is unable to be authoritative (1286a24–6). The discussion of political benefits of the lawful rule of the many, then, assumes that *nomos* is a necessity for actual political communities, while constrained in the role that it is able to play in the inculcation of genuine virtue.

SECTION 4 AN EDUCATION IN VIRTUE

Aristotle's commitment to the thesis that *nomos* has a significant part to play in the promotion of virtue makes his work an obvious source of inspiration for contemporary theorists critical of the view that 'laws designed to uphold public morality are inherently unjust'.[35] As the previous section has demonstrated, however, Aristotle sees the law's attempted inculcation of virtue as operating principally through subrational habituation. This habituation of citizens certainly has the capacity to lead to the development of the right character dispositions and virtue, but in the majority of cases the law does not reach as far as the rational agency of its subjects and only incompletely realises its aim. In this final section, I develop these claims by reference to Aristotle's statements on education laws. Only in rare circumstances, namely where laws are enacted relative to the ends of a non-defective constitution and addressed to the practically reasonable citizen, could one retrospectively point to the function of law in promoting genuine virtue. The patterns of conduct promoted by good education laws are nevertheless beneficial in allowing imperfectly rational citizens to approximate human excellence through conformity with just norms. Rather than offering a perfectionist account of law in a fulsome sense, then, Aristotle's more modest claim is that by force of habit the law can give the citizens of a political community the potential to develop a small share of virtue (*NE* X.9, 1179b18–20).

It is because law operates, at least initially, at the level of habits and external behaviour that education laws are so privileged for Aristotle. Virtue and good character require habituation (*Pol.* II.5, 1263a23, II.8, 1269a20; *NE* II.1, 1103a14ff) and the legislator's role is hence to accustom (*ethizontes*) the citizens to become good (1103b3–4). A person learning virtue should be prepared for rational discourses

[35] George (1993: 1).

and teaching by habits in the way earth receives a seed (*NE* X.9, 1179b20–6). The right habits are necessary to ensure a person enjoys and hates nobly (*to kalōs chairein kai misein*) and good laws allow for a correct upbringing (*agōgēs orthēs*) which instils these appropriate habits of enjoyment (1179b20–35). Through the inculcation of correct habits, law allows the many to live in accordance with rationality and order (*bioumenois kata tina noun kai taxin orthēn*) (1180a18) to the extent possible, even when they lack genuine virtue. Education laws of the focal kind contemplated in X.9 are, however, Aristotle openly acknowledges, also exceedingly rare (*NE* I.13, 1102a7–12, V.2, 1130b26–9, X.9, 1180a24–9).

Aristotle's insistence on the importance of education laws in X.9 is consistent with the prominence given to *paideia* in the best regime of *Politics* Books VII–VIII. Whereas the programme of physical education targets the development of the virtues conducive to the common advantage, musical education promotes communal order through patterns of behaviour to be imitated as exemplars. Such a regimen of education, and the legislation by which it is established, are common insofar as they pertain to activities and goods shared within a polis (*Pol.* VIII.1, 1337a26–34). The relevant contrast is with private education, whereby each person teaches their children what seems best to them (1337a24–6; *NE* X.9, 1180a26–9).[36] This presentation of education in the best regime thus echoes X.9, where Aristotle states that it is best that there is common care for upbringing and practices (1180a29–30). Yet while all systems of law should and do *aim* at making people attain virtue, not every political community succeeds in this end (*NE* V.2, 1130b25–9). Most political communities have defective constitutions and equally inadequate systems of education, which reflect flawed conceptions of virtue and wellbeing.

As will be discussed in detail in Chapter 3, Aristotle asserts that laws (*nomoi*) both are and should be enacted with a view to the constitution or regime (*politeia*) (*Pol.* III.12, 1282b10–11, IV.1, 1289a11ff). One important feature distinguishing correct constitutional forms (kingship, aristocracy, polity) from their defective counterparts (tyranny, oligarchy, democracy) is that the former are established to promote the common advantage, whereas the latter aim at the sectional or private advantage of the rulers (III.6, 1279a18–39). Good constitutions, it follows, will serve to inculcate good habits (*NE* II.1, 1103a31–b6) and promote education and virtue (*Pol.* III.13, 1283a24–6; *NE* X.9, 1180a24–9). And in the same way that the laws of a political community reflect its conception of justice and the ends of human action, as manifested most obviously in a choice for a particular constitutional form, ultimately the education laws of a polis also reflect its prevailing understanding of excellence and flourishing.

Now a corollary of these points is that the capacity for the laws to inculcate anything approximating genuine virtue are highly constrained in most political

[36] This, of course, does not entail that the *oikia* has no role to play in ethical habituation. See Weirnick (1998: 28).

circumstances. Aristotle states clearly in *Politics* IV.11 that the majority of actual regimes will either be democratic or oligarchic (*Pol.* 1296a22). It might seem to follow that the laws of these defective regimes would necessarily promote vice rather than virtue, yet Aristotle's approach to constitutional analysis does allow this statement to be qualified.

Aristotle's method of constitutional analysis allows laws falling under particular forms of regime to be evaluated by reference to their own internal assumptions and also the best regime as such.[37] In defective regimes, like democracies and oligarchies, where sectional interests prevail over concern for the common advantage, it is thus possible to assess the relevant laws both from the perspective of their own 'hypotheses' and the correct interpretation of the good (*Pol.* II.9, 1269a32, IV.7, 1293b3, V.8, 1309a3, VII.9, 1328b38). One can, for example, consider the virtues possible and prevalent in a democratic regime and assess democratic laws by reference to those criteria. This allows for recognition of the secondary or civic forms of virtue that are promoted by education laws in a deviant regime form. In the case of constitutions which fall short of the best, the laws can nonetheless establish order in the polis so as to facilitate states of character which may rightly be considered as virtues in a secondary or qualified sense, without attaining to the status of genuine virtues.

Aristotle's discussion of the oligarchical educational regime of Sparta exemplifies this methodology. Sparta is praised for its provision of a public education in virtue (*NE* I.13, 1102a8–11, X.9, 1180a24–30; *Pol.* VIII.1, 1337a31–3), yet this education is also criticised for various shortcomings. In Book II of the *Politics*, for instance, Aristotle disparages the Spartan regime on the grounds that it concentrates exclusively on the courage necessary for war and regards this virtue as instrumental to the attainment of external goods (*Pol.* II.9, 1271a41–b10; cf. *EE* VIII.15, 1248b28ff). Aristotle does not deny that the Spartans possess virtue *simpliciter*. Rather, the Spartans are attributed with 'a certain virtue' (*tis aretē*) (*Pol.* VII.15, 1334b2–3), enabling them to live in an ordered political community that partially realises the form of manly and warlike human excellence they esteem. Ultimately, while the incorrectness of the end (*telos*) of the Spartan constitution from the perspective of genuine virtue means that it falls short in several significant respects, it nonetheless promotes a qualified or partial form of human excellence.[38]

Despite this important qualification, it is nonetheless clear that the already limited capacity of *nomos* to inculcate genuine virtue in citizens only obtains in those rare circumstances where a constitution is non-defective. The optimal role of education laws in most regimes is instead to allow citizens to approximate as closely

37 See Lockwood (2017: 353–79).

38 It is instructive that Aristotle's criticism of the Spartan constitution does not pertain to the wide coverage of the law with respect to education and upbringing. Indeed, while Aristotle discusses the harshness of the Spartan laws, he also criticises the laws for their lack of concern with the virtue of women (*Pol.* II.9, 1269b14–1270b6).

as possible to genuine virtue. Aristotle's discussion in *Politics* V.11 of the mitigation of the worst aspects of tyranny demonstrates that the promotion of a limited virtue even within a regime that is far from the best remains far preferable to complete lack of law or flagrantly unjust laws. Law in most cases encourages conduct which is a semblance of genuine virtue short of the standards required of a *phronimos*. Yet agents who engage in conduct which rests on a totally cynical or corrupt view of human ends will clearly be more deficient with respect to *eudaimonia*.

Even in non-defective regimes, education laws are directed primarily to the young and those lacking *phronēsis* rather than mature practically reasonable agents. The significance of this only becomes fully evident when one returns to the distinction between the virtue of a ruler and the virtue of a subject (particularly of a young subject who is yet to reach the age of mature practical reasonableness). Genuine ethical virtue presupposes practical wisdom. Few possess this and few are capable of possessing it (*NE* V.8, 1142a10–32).[39] Practical wisdom strictly speaking, is, moreover, exercised by legislators and rulers (*Pol.* III.4, 1277b26). As noted above, this leads to the conclusion that true opinion (*doxa alēthēs*), not practical wisdom (*phronēsis*), is the virtue of one ruled (*archomenou*) (1277b25–7).[40]

The claim that true *doxa* is the virtue of those subject to the law is consistent with Aristotle's broader statements on educational *nomos*. Law directs most citizens at the level of their external conduct and *conformity* with virtue. The law orders (*prostattei*) us to do the *actions* of a courageous man (for instance not to leave the battle-line, or to flee, or to throw away our weapons), of a temperate person (not to commit adultery or wanton aggression) and of a mild person (not to strike or revile another); and similarly requires *actions in accord with the other virtues*, and *prohibits actions in accord with vices* (emphases mine) (NE V.1, 1129b20–4).[41] Importantly, it is not said that the law reaches as far as the inner motivations or the rational agency of a citizen. The sort of virtue inculcated by the law-giver in education laws is not, at least for the most part, or in the first instance, 'the fullblooded virtue' of the *Nicomachean Ethics*. It is rather a form of limited or political virtue (*Pol.* III.9, 1280b5; *NE* III.8, 1116a17–b3) which does not require practical wisdom (*phronēsis*) in the true sense i.e. 'the ability to work out for oneself what to do'.[42] Indeed, if education in virtue required a cognitive grasp of the content of any particular law and its grounds of

39 Broadie (1991: 258) and Rosler (2005: 185).

40 It is true that in an aristocratic polity, of the kind described in Books VII–VIII of the *Politics*, all citizens would possess a high degree of virtue and take turns in ruling and being ruled in turn. I return to this point in Chapter 3.

41 The verb *prostatteō* used here to describe the ordering activity of *nomos* has a strong sense of to rule over or domineer and points once again to the sub-rational compulsory force of law. As Schroeder notes, to 'accomplish its purpose, education must use compulsion to force people to practice the virtues in the hope that those forced to act virtuously when young will acquire the virtues as habits as they mature' (2003: 47).

42 Sorabji (1990: 271).

justification, then it would not be able to get started at the formative stages, even for someone with the potential to become practically reasonable in maturity. For Aristotle, education laws promote the preconditions for developing virtue, but this does not require that the content of the law is apprehended by reason, let alone endorsed as rationally justified.

All of these points place in question the capacity, if not the aspiration, for the Aristotelian legislator to make the majority of citizens good and capable of noble actions (*NE* III.1, 1099b30–2, I.13, 1102a7–10; *EE* VII.1, 1234b22–3, VII.2, 1237a2–3). In most cases, laws seek to impose rational limits on conduct that will not necessarily be apprehended as rational, let alone endorsed by those subject to the law as such. Even independently of the prevalence of defective regimes and the fact that the law operates through compulsion which requires outward conformity, rather than genuine goodness of character, Aristotle unambiguously asserts that the many are severely constrained in their capacity to achieve virtue.

One may wonder at this point about the possibility of citizens developing even a 'small share of virtue'. It is helpful in this context to distinguish between full virtue of character, of a kind that would be realised most in a constitutional regime with the musical education laws set out in Book VIII of the *Politics*, and a 'second-best' option, where the external constraint of the law plays an enhanced role.[43] Aristotelian virtue in the focal sense requires that one is guided by the right internal motivations and not simply external incentives or punishments. Aristotle also allows, however, for a form of civic virtue still operating under the direction of the rule of reason but oriented primarily by the need to restrain the appetites and passions. This secondary or 'ground-level' form of virtue is exemplified by the civic courage which, while motivated by honours rather than the noble or *kalon*, nonetheless is directed to the common advantage of the political community and is preferable to a disposition motivated purely by external goods or fear alone (*NE* III.8, 1116a17–b3).[44] From this perspective, one can even acknowledge the usefulness of a sense of shame in promoting compliance with the law (*Rh.* I.14, 1375a14–17). For insofar as the *nomoi* of a community provide a reasonable or not completely unjust interpretation of what is noble, then the youth can act in conformity with virtue in following the law and being motivated by the shame to which they are inclined by their age (II.12, 1389a29–31). This is true even though in a more thoroughgoing sense shame is inconsistent with the possession of full virtue.[45]

In sum, one may grant that *nomos* fails for the most part to reach the internal motivations necessary for full virtue, yet also recognise that the rational content of the law entails (in the case of good or even minimally decent laws) that 'the actions prescribed by the law are *coextensive* with the actions done by the person with virtue of character'.[46] While law is severely limited in its capacity to promote genuine

43 Hitz (2012: 263–306).

44 Hitz (2102: 272).

45 Weirnick (1998: 29–30).

46 Inglis (2014: 271).

virtue in most cases, it also remains preferable to complete lawlessness, even in defective regimes which fall well short of the best, because it promotes conformity with a rational standard.

Ultimately it is virtue that makes the end correct for Aristotle and good laws facilitate its attainment. An Aristotelian citizen could develop genuine virtue (and hence practical wisdom) by repeatedly doing the right thing, and the law, by making us repeatedly do the right thing, can at least potentially set us on the path towards genuine virtue. An agent who is educated by good laws and able to reflect on the ends and means of human action in the manner of the *phronimos* could also certainly acknowledge both the enabling role of law in their attainment of virtue and the rational standards that the law's universal norms articulate. It remains the case that the main function of *nomos* even in this set of circumstances is to inculcate good habits by training appropriate states of affect through rewards and punishments. One can only become truly good when one has developed a *phronēsis* available at maturity. At the point a practically reasonable agent was truly able to apprehend the rational content of the law, that is to say, then they would no longer need the guidance of the law. And in the vast majority of cases, on an Aristotelian conception, laws are not apprehended by citizens as rational guides to conduct, but rather encountered as obligatory norms which serve indirectly to promote a limited form of virtue through incentives and disincentives, external compulsion and constraint. The objective of *nomos* is to promote virtue, but it is also severely limited in its capacity to promote genuine virtue. In the words of Socrates in the *Minos*, the law wishes to be discovery of that which is (315a).

One central insight implicit in Aristotle's account of *nomos* is visible in what might otherwise appear to be a partial digression on the inadequacy of the sophistic approach to politics and law at the conclusion of X.9. Aristotle's criticism of the sophists pertains primarily to their lack of experience in practical matters and this shortcoming leads to a tendency to identify politics with rhetoric (1181a15–23) i.e. to focus upon the efficacy of *logoi* rather than the exigencies of political life. While Aristotle's account of *nomos* does acknowledge both the law's rational source and content, it also emphasises the limits of the political application of legal rationality to the project of making citizens truly good.

2

The Legislator

For Aristotle, as seen in Chapter 1, the rational content of the law derives from the practical reason of the law-giver. In the central case, the legislator's enactments will be oriented by the ends of virtue and human flourishing. Aristotle's attribution of a decisive role to the practical reason of the law-giver seems, however, to be in tension with better-known aspects of his political thought. In particular, it is far from self-evident that a robust account of legislative agency is in harmony with political naturalism. The famous assertion in *Politics* I.2 that there is a natural impulse to form political communities is immediately contraposed with the claim that the person responsible for their foundation is the cause (*aitios*) of the greatest of goods (*Pol.* 1253a33). Yet if the polis truly exists by nature and humans are by nature political animals (1253a1–2), then the obvious question arises as to why active intervention by the legislator is necessary at all for a polis. Conversely, if the polis is an artefact of the architectonic legislator's practical reason, then the distinction between products of the intellect and natural entities seems to preclude the status of the polis as natural.[1] In light of this apparent tension within Aristotle's account of the origins of political communities, the current chapter seeks to demonstrate their reconcilability.[2] Section 1 considers the architectonic legislator in light of broader Greek assumptions regarding foundational law-making. Section 2 then turns to the status of law-making expertise (*nomothetikē*) as a part of political science (*politikē*) and examines the mode of practical reason exercised by the legislative founder. Finally, in Section 3, and building on recent interpretations which have emphasised that Aristotle operates with an extended teleological conception of nature, I argue

[1] Keyt (1991: 118). For the distinction between products of the intellect and natural entities: *Ph.* II.6, 198a9–10; *Met.* VII.7, 1032a12–13, XI.8, 1065b3–4, XII.3, 1070a6–9; *NE* III.3, 1112a31–3, VI.4, 1140a14–16; *Pol.* VII.14, 1333a22–3.

[2] The tension is widely acknowledged by commentators. Keyt (1991: 118), for example, argues that the tension between political naturalism and legislative agency points to a 'contradiction' at the 'very root' of the *Politics* whereas Miller (1995: 29) notes, more cautiously, that Aristotle's political naturalism is 'muddied' by the strong emphasis upon legislative agency. Kraut (2002: 245) attempts to resolve the tension by appeal to the fact that 'many processes of growth are overseen and influenced by human beings'.

that acts of legislative founding and nature can consistently serve as joint causes of the polis because the 'products' of the practical rationality of the legislator are themselves an expression of distinctly human nature.

SECTION 1 THE ARISTOTELIAN LAW-GIVER IN CONTEXT

The law-maker (*nomothetēs*) is central to Aristotle's practical works. This centrality is perhaps most obvious in the *Politics*, where both the Book II survey of constitutional regimes and the discussion of the best regime in VII–VIII conspicuously adopt the viewpoint of the founding legislator. The attribution of a pivotal role to the law-maker is prefigured, however, by the *Nicomachean Ethics* X.9 transition to the *Politics*, which is a preliminary attempt to answer how one can become a legislator capable of making citizens good (1180a34; 1180b25; 1180b30). In the final passage of X.9, Aristotle claims that prior thinkers have inadequately addressed what pertains to legislation (*nomothesias*) and constitutions (*politeias*), and insists that the completion of the philosophy of human affairs (*hē peri ta anthrōpeia philosophia*) is dependent upon the success of this investigation (1181b14–15). In the opening of *Nicomachean Ethics*, Aristotle elaborates on his argument that political expertise (*politikē*) is the most architectonic and authoritative of the sciences by reference to its function in setting down laws regarding what actions citizens ought to engage in and abstain from (I.2, 1094b5–6). The end of the political expertise of the true statesman (*politikos*) is the ultimate human good and it is pursued through legislation (I.9, 1099b29–32, I.12, 1102a7–25). Consistent with this claim, Aristotle suggests in VI.8 that legislative science (*nomothetikē*) is the architectonic part of the practical wisdom concerned with the polis (1142a24–5). The perspective of the law-giver also features, albeit less prominently, in discussions of the ethical virtues. At the beginning of II.1, for example, Aristotle introduces the principle that we attain virtue by engaging in the activities of virtue with the statement that the aim of lawgivers is to habituate citizens to become good (1103b4). Similarly, in III.1, the theme of the voluntary and the involuntary is framed by reference to its usefulness for law-givers, who must mete out both honours and punishments (1109b34–5).

The Aristotelian law-maker nonetheless raises several difficult interpretative questions. In the first instance, Aristotle seems to present the law-maker in different contexts as a 'theoretical' political scientist, as a doer of political actions and as a 'craftsman' or producer.[3] In X.9, Aristotle portrays the legislator as engaged in a form of political science with access to universals (1180b20–3). This characterisation is consistent with the suggestion in Books IV and VII of the *Politics* that the role of the *nomothetēs* is to study (*theōrēsai*) political communities and constitutions and what is to their advantage (*Pol.* IV.1, 1288b21–30, IV.14, 1297b38–9, VII.2, 1325a7–10).

[3] Kontos (forthcoming: 1).

Aristotle also suggests, however, that the legislator is truly a politician (*alētheian politikos*) insofar as they intend to make citizens good and obedient to the laws (*NE* I.13, 1102a8–10; cf. Pol. III.1, 1274b36–8, IV.1, 1288b27, V.9, 1309b35–6). The legislator in this guise appears as an active practitioner of politics – someone concerned with useful action as well as knowledge (*Pol.* I.11, 1258b9–10; *NE* I.3, 1095a5–6, II.2, 1103b26–9, X.9, 1179a35–b4; *Met.* II.1, 993b20–1) – and not merely a politically inexperienced theorist of constitutions and laws of the kind criticised in *Nicomachean Ethics* X.9 and *Politics* II.12. From this perspective, laws are identified as the works or deeds (*erga*) of the activity of true politics (*NE* X.9, 1181a23). Exponents of true politics have a privileged role in the realisation of the human good, and are plausibly also to be regarded as the primary intended audience of the practical works (*NE* I.13, 1102a8–23, III.1, 1109b34; *Pol.* IV.1, 1288b27, 1289a7, V.9, 1309b35–6, VI.5, 1319b33).[4] Further complicating matters, Aristotle often characterises the legislator in terms (*Pol.* II.7, 1267a18, II.8, 1268b9–10; II.10, 1271b30–2) which strongly imply that law-making is a form of production akin to a craft (*technē*). Viewed from this angle, legislators are craftsmen (*dēmiourgoi*) of constitutions and laws (II.12, 1273b32–3), which are produced out of prior 'political material' including the citizens, territory and population. Law-making thus seems awkwardly to traverse Aristotle's distinctions between theoretical, practical and productive kinds of thought (*Met.* VI.1, 1025b25, XI.7, 1064a16–19; *Top.* VI.6, 145a15–16) and scientific, practical and productive modes of knowledge (*NE* VI.5–6).

The second major and closely related puzzle raised by the law-maker is that the ascription of a decisive role to their legislative agency appears to be in direct tension with Aristotle's distinctive brand of political naturalism. Immediately following the argument that the polis is prior to the individual by nature, Aristotle states the following on the origins of the political community:

> Hence, there is in everyone by nature (*phusei men*) an impulse (*hormē*) towards this sort of community (*koinōnian*). And yet (*de*) the person who first founded one is the cause of the greatest of goods (*ho de prōtos sustēsas megistōn agathōn aitios*). For as a human is the best of animals when perfected (*teleōtheis*), when separated from law and justice (*nomou kai dikēs*) they are the worst of all (*Pol.* I.2, 1253a30–3).

In the Book II survey of constitutional forms, Aristotle proceeds to characterise exemplary founding legislators, such as Solon and Lycurgus, as craftsmen (*dēmiourgoi*) of constitutional orders in a way which suggests that the intentional activity of law-making is both an efficient cause in the political domain and a necessary condition for the formation of the polis (II.12, 1273b31–5). The truth of the *Politics* Book I claim that humans are political by nature and that the polis arises by nature (rather than merely by convention or *nomos*) also seems, however, to preclude the view that the existence of a political community requires the intentional activity, the artifice, of a human law-maker. Aristotle's characterisation

4 See Bodéüs (1993: 45–6) and Keyt (2017: 166–7).

of legislators as craftsmen (*dēmiourgoi*) and of politics as a 'craft' (*Pol.* I.2, 1253a30–1, II.12, 1273b32–3, II.12, 1274b18–19, III.12, 1282b14–16, VII.2, 1325b40–1326a5), noted above, nonetheless seems to entail that the polis is a product of human agency.

Aristotle's employment of the contrastive *men-de* grammatical construction above points to the fact that the attribution of a decisive role to the founder of the polis is in at least apparent tension with the arguments for political naturalism. In this context, it is revealing that Aristotle refers to the founder of the political community as the cause (*aitios*) of the greatest of goods, which is inconsistent with the legislator playing a merely ancillary role. As a consequence, the only two viable options would appear to be either that there is a contradictory 'blunder' at the foundations of Aristotle's political thought, or that the two commitments are in some way reconcilable.[5]

This current section sets the scene for my arguments in the following two sections that (1) law-making is primarily a practical activity and that (2) nature and the constitutional founder are co-operative causes of the polis.[6] In order to resolve the questions above, however, it is first helpful to consider some of the presuppositions of Aristotle's appeal to the architectonic constitutional founder. As becomes clear in Sections 2 and 3, this context is highly instructive for understanding the role of legislative agency in Aristotle's political thought, insofar as it points to the status of the law-maker as an exemplar of a practical rationality and insight which fulfils distinctly human nature.

Aristotle's attribution of a pivotal role to legislative expertise reflects broader influences than the Greek tendency to venerate constitutional founders such as Solon and Lycurgus. The *nomen agentis* compound *nomothetēs* (law-giver) emerged in the fifth century BCE as the term *nomos* became more narrowly associated with enacted legal norms or 'statutes' following the reforms of Cleisthenes.[7] Aristotle's fourth century presentation of *nomothetikē* and the activity of the *nomothetēs* conforms to this fifth century shift in the meaning of *nomos* and its compounds towards a more prescriptive legal sense reflective of a new emphasis upon the role of human agency in the political domain. Whereas uses of *nomos* in the archaic period tended to express the immutability and timelessness of customary practices and ways of life, from the Cleisthenean reforms this usage was 'overshadowed by the idea that human agents now became the authors, formulators, enactors, and enforcers of a *nomos* that could no longer be taken for granted'.[8]

Although Aristotle employs *nomothetēs* to refer both to 'mere' legislators and those responsible for establishing a new constitutional order, it is the latter kind of

5 Keyt (1991: 118). See also Miller (1995: 29–30).

6 For earlier defences of this view, albeit with less emphasis on the distinctive features of the legislative exercise of practical reason, see Barker (1959: 7), Miller (1995: 40–5) and Miller (2000: 328).

7 Ostwald (1986: 92). Ostwald cites Antiphon 5.15 and Thucydides 8.97.2 for early uses of *nomothetēs*.

8 Ostwald (1986: 92).

law-maker which is privileged. Aristotle distinguishes between mere craftsmen of laws and constitutional founders as follows:

> Others became legislators (*nomothetai*) – some for their own cities, others for certain foreigners also – and engaged in politics themselves (*politeuthentes autoi*), and of these some were craftsmen of laws only (*hoi men nomōn egenonto dēmiourgoi monon*), but others of a regime (*politeias*) as well, for example, Lycurgus and Solon, who established both laws and regimes (*nomous kai politeias katestēsan*) (*Pol.* II.12, 1273b31–5).

The difference between 'mere' law-makers and constitutional founders is that the latter are responsible for either establishing or altering the fundamental structure or *taxis* of the political community. In the case of Solon, for example, reforms such as the abolishment of loans on the security of persons, the granting of legal redress to non-parties of a dispute, and the right of appeal to the *dikastērion* moved the constitution towards a more popular or democratic form.[9] What is distinctive of the constitutional founder is thus that they establish – hence the use of *sustēsas and katestēsan* in the passage above – a new or different kind of political order (cf. *Pol.* IV.1, 1289a1–4). In most cases a basic political community will exist prior to even a substantive legal reform. As will be examined in Chapter 3, Aristotle's account of the identity conditions for the polis nonetheless entails that a change in constitutional form corresponds to a change in the identity of the political community (*Pol.* III.3, 1276b1–13). It is in this sense that the constitutional founder, or alternatively the art of law-making which directs their architectonic activity, is an efficient cause for a polis.[10] Although *nomothetikē* applies to both ordinary law-making and constitutional founding, therefore, the latter has a privileged and focal status due to its more original and architectonic character.

Aristotle's emphasis on the architectonic *nomothetēs* also speaks to Platonic influence.[11] The regimes of both the *Republic* and *Laws* are presented as foundational acts of constitutional formation. These regimes are designed in rational speech by interlocutors – led by Socrates and the Athenian Stranger respectively – who seek to introduce into politics a level of practical wisdom and insight beyond that which is ordinarily exercised by everyday politicians or 'mere' law-makers. In Book VI of the *Republic*, by reference to the possibility of a polis arising of a philosophic nature, Socrates points to the need for the law-giver (*nomothetēs*) to possess a superior level of rationality (*logon echon*) in order to design a truly good constitution (*Rep.* 497a–c). In the opening of the *Laws*, in a corresponding manner, the Athenian Stranger adopts the perspective of the founding legislator in the design

[9] *Athenian Constitution* 9.

[10] Aristotle's analyses in *Physics* II.3 and *Metaphysics* V.2 suggest that the art of law-making in the foundational sense (*nomothetikē*), rather than the law-maker, is the 'efficient' cause. I return to this point in Chapter 3.

[11] For founding legislators in Plato's *Republic* and *Laws* see Lane (2013: 104–14).

of a regime with excellent laws and states that a worthy law-giver must always enact laws with a view to the greatest virtue (*tēn megistēn aretēn*) (*Laws* 630c).

This architectonic understanding of the constitutional founder is, in certain respects, foreign to the modern understanding of political origins. One distinctive characteristic of the ancient tradition of constitutional design is a tendency to venerate individual founders and architects, like Solon and Lycurgus, who are attributed with rare practical experience and insight.[12] While this tendency remains present in modern constitutional discourse, as evidenced, for example, by the American 'founding fathers', contemporary constitutional design is generally undertaken by assemblies or committees made up of multiple representatives.[13] A central concern in such exercises of constitutional design is the balancing and weighing of competing interests, but the assumption is that these interests are best protected through the advocacy of multiple representatives, rather than mediated through the insightful judgements of a practically wise architectonic law-maker.

This difference in turn speaks to a deeper divergence in assumptions regarding the 'efficient cause' of a political community and its constitutional order. Modern constitutions are generally understood as emerging from the people in an act of constituent power. As Dieter Grimm has argued, concomitant with such a view is a tendency to separate questions of the establishment of a legal order from questions of truth (*auctoritas, non veritas, facit legem*) and to regard the constitution as the outcome of a political decision.[14] Aristotle's account of a constitution as emerging from a legislator's practical grasp of truths about human virtue and flourishing contrasts with this view of constitutionalism as an achievement of a people unified by its decision to be subject to a single source of authority in the interests of their stability, security and prosperity.

For current purposes, the most important point to take out of these contrasts is that ancient constitutional founders were regarded as endowed with exceptional levels of practical wisdom. From an Aristotelian perspective, as I will demonstrate in Sections 2 and 3, the 'products' of this practical wisdom are achievements of distinctly human nature. Before I turn to this point, it is first instructive to consider a few examples of Greek architectonic legislating as practical wisdom.

Between 650 and 550 BCE was a particularly active period for the founding and reform of Greek constitutions. Although these legal codes were not comprehensive regulations of public power akin to modern constitutional orders, they did set out systematically the fundamental norms of the political community.[15] The narratives of Greek constitution-making that have reached us also contain common themes

12 Lanni and Vermeule (2012: 909). Coherence, accountability and efficiency can be identified as merits of the ancient approach. Lanni and Vermeule also note a second unfamiliar feature of ancient constitution-making: the design of constitutions by outsiders or non-citizens of the relevant polis.

13 Lanni and Vermeule (2012: 909).

14 Grimm (2010: 9). See also the discussion of Bodin's critique of Aristotle in Tuck (2016: 1–62).

15 See Szegedy-Maszak (1978: 199–201), Gagarin (1986: 51–2) and Lewis (2007: 41–2).

which are revealing, regardless of exact historical accuracy, insofar as they document the ascription to founding law-makers of an unusual level of practical insight.[16]

Greek constitution-making narratives generally begin with an account of a political crisis or factional dispute (*stasis*), which is subsequently resolved when a uniquely qualified and insightful law-giver enters the scene to establish a new law code. Once the new constitutional order is established, the law-giver frequently leaves the political stage. Despite the esteem attributed to actual or legendary law-givers, it is the laws themselves which are regarded as bringing order and stability to a previously fractious or unstable political community. Narratives of constitution-making thus describe the progress of a political community from a state of *anomia* – or lawlessness – to one of *eunomia* – the state or condition of a well-governed polity.[17] This progression can be seen in the narratives surrounding the constitutional founders of Athens, Sparta and Crete respectively: Solon, Lycurgus and Minos. The main narratives surrounding these legendary law-givers share some common themes regarding the nature and source of their practical wisdom.

The appointment of Solon as a constitutional founder in Athens is attributed by both the Aristotelian author of the *Athenian Constitution* and by Plutarch to the need for a resolution of economic tensions.[18] According to the author of the *Athenian Constitution*, Solon was appointed as a mediator in response to a crisis that developed between the wealthy few, who owned most of the land holdings, and the indebted majority. Solon's broader reforms included the institution of selection for magistracies by lot in accordance with new property classes, the establishment of the Council or *Boulē* of 400 members, the allocation of responsibility as guardian of the constitution to the Areopagus and the introduction of a new right of appeal to the *dikasterion* or popular court.[19] Initially both the wealthy few and poor majority were unhappy with Solon's reforms, but eventually the legal changes came to be regarded as a just and practically wise compromise between the different factions. Despite the fact that Solon held sufficient power to join one of the sides to the dispute and become a tyrant, the author of the *Athenian Constitution* suggests, it was his very outsider (and perhaps middling) status which enabled him to save his political community and provide it with the best constitution possible in the circumstances.[20]

The historical status of Lycurgus of Sparta is uncertain, but more pertinent for current purposes is his putative role in the establishment of the Spartan constitutional order or 'great rhetra'.[21] As in the case of Solon of Athens, the reforms of Lycurgus initially sought to overcome instability caused by disputes between the wealthy and poor.[22] The major reforms instituted by Lycurgus included the

16 Szegedy-Maszak (1978: 208).
17 Szegedy-Maszak (1978: 208).
18 Plutarch, *Solon*, 12.2, 13.2; *Athenian Constitution* 5.2.
19 *Athenian Constitution* 5–13.
20 *Athenian Constitution* 11
21 Gagarin (1986: 59).
22 Plutarch, *Lycurgus*, 8.1.

equalisation of land holdings, the establishment of common meals and the implementation of the *agōgē* or rigorous model of military education undertaken by Spartan children from the age of seven.[23] The reforms of Lycurgus were hence oriented to the promotion of Spartan virtues of equality between full citizens, preparedness for the military and austerity. Narrative accounts of Lycurgus generally attribute his foundational law-making to unusual practical insight. The reforms of Lycurgus were said, for example, to have been based on his extensive travels to Crete, Egypt and Ionia.[24] Lycurgus' laws were also attributed to divine inspiration, with Ephorus suggesting that Apollo gave laws to Lycurgus in the same manner that Minos received laws from Zeus.[25] According to another tradition, when Lycurgus entered the Delphic temple of Apollo, the Pythia asked whether he should be considered a man or a God and greeted him as beloved of Zeus.[26]

Plato's depiction (or the Platonic depiction) of the legendary Cretan law-giver, Minos, contains similar themes. In the *Minos*, which according to its location in the Thrasyllian tetralogies serves as a preface to the *Laws*, Socrates rejects as distorted the view of Minos presented by both Homer and Hesiod.[27] According to Socrates, Minos developed his laws after receiving an education in virtue from his father Zeus (319c–320b). Socrates thus suggests that the laws developed by Minos were grounded in a divine education in virtue and that this has led to the flourishing of the citizens of Crete (and by extension Sparta, which was influenced by the Minoan legislation) (320b). Apart from their divine origin, Socrates points to the stability of the Cretan laws as evidence of the claim that Minos applied insight into 'what is' (320b) in the establishment of his political community.

Although the traditions associated with Solon, Lycurgus and Minos obviously differ in their level of historical reliability, for current purposes what is more relevant is the shared set of assumptions informing the different accounts. In all three cases, the constitutional founders are presented as in possession of a superior level of experience or wisdom, whether this be on account of extensive travel or intercourse with the divine. What emerges is a picture of the constitutional founder as a practically wise person, who does an important service through the enactment of a fundamental set of legal norms which bring stability to the political community as a corrective to disorder.

A constitutional founder, then, of the kind distinguished from ordinary law-givers in *Politics* II.12, is no mere politician, but the exponent of an architectonic practical wisdom. The attribution of practical wisdom to the law-giver in the genuine sense is significant, as I argue further below, for understanding how an act of legislative foundation can be both essential for the existence of the polis and consistent with

23 Plutarch, *Lycurgus*, 8.1.
24 Plutarch, *Lycurgus*, 4; Ephorus ap. Strabo 10.14.9; Hecataeus of Abdera ap. Diod. 1.96. 2–3.
25 Ephorus ap. Strabo 10.4.19.
26 Herodotus, *Histories*, 1.65. Cf. Plutarch, *Lycurgus*, 5.3.
27 See Lewis (2006: 17–53) for the authenticity of the *Minos* and its place in the Platonic corpus.

Aristotle's political naturalism. Before I turn to this argument, however, it is necessary to consider the status of law-making as a part of *politikē* or true political expertise.

SECTION 2 LAW-MAKING AS A SUB-BRANCH OF TRUE POLITICS

Aristotle regards legislative expertise as a part of true politics. This seemingly straightforward statement conceals multiple complexities. In the first instance, Aristotle uses the term *politikē* in different senses, which must be clarified in order correctly to situate law-making expertise as a mode of practical rationality (*phronēsis*). Second, it is necessary to determine more precisely the relationship between the practical and 'theoretical' aspects of the expertise of the 'true politician' (*politikos*) and law-maker. In the current section, I argue that the law-maker's expertise is practical and that this is consistent with the claim that the true politician and legislator must possess knowledge of universals. As will become clear in the final section, it is the distinctive character of the practical knowledge of the prudent legislator – its concern with the ultimate human end (*NE* I.2, 1094b7) – which allows for a reconciliation of legislative agency and political naturalism.

The relationship between political expertise (*politikē*) and law-making (*nomothetikē*) can be reconstructed on the basis of *Nicomachean Ethics* VI.8 and X.9. In VI.8 Aristotle states that:

1. Political expertise (*politikē*) is the same disposition (*hexis*) as practical wisdom (*phronēsis*), although they differ in being (*einai ou tauton autais*)
2. The practical wisdom (*phronēsis*) concerned with the city has:
    a. an architectonic legislative part (*architektonikē phronēsis nomothetikē*)
    b. a practical and deliberative part, concerned primarily with political particulars, which is given the name that is 'common to both parts' i.e. politics (*politikē*).

In X.9 Aristotle characterises law-making expertise (*nomothetikē*) as a part (*morion*) of political expertise (*politikē*) (*NE* 1180b31). This claim is best interpreted as referring back to VI.8, which entails that the sense of 'part' in play is the relation of species to genus i.e. a sub-branch.

Taken together, VI.8 and X.9 suggest that legislative expertise is a species or sub-branch of political expertise (*politikē*), which is the same disposition as practical wisdom, but different insofar as its object is the wellbeing of a political community rather than an individual. A further conclusion to draw from the passages is that legislative expertise, as a sub-branch of political science, needs to be distinguished from politics in the 'everyday' sense, which is concerned with the sorts of matters that are paradigmatically dealt with in decrees (*psēphismata*) (*NE* VI.8, 1141b27) rather than universal laws. This is the domain of 'ordinary politics' and it engages primarily with particulars (if it did not engage with universals at all, then it would lose its status as a form of practical wisdom, as the concluding statements in VI.7 make clear). All these distinctions require elaboration.

Aristotle's analysis in VI.8 motivates a distinction between political expertise (*politikē*) in broad and narrow senses.[28] Considered as a genus, practical wisdom or prudence (*phronēsis*) divides into the three species of individual prudence (*phronēsis* in the specific sense), household management (*oikonomia*) and politics (*politikē*) in the generic sense or political expertise. Generic *politikē* has legislative expertise (*nomothetikē*) as a sub-branch, while the narrower sense of *politikē* is divided into two parts: the expertise of deliberation (*bouleutikē*), exercised in the assembly, and the judicial expertise (*dikastikē*) exercised by the juror (1141b34).[29] As noted above, what distinguishes *politikē* in the generic and broader sense is that it is an architectonic form of prudence, whereas by contrast *politikē* in the narrower sense deals primarily with concrete actions or particulars (1141b25–30). Aristotle thus suggests that the law-giver, in exercising broader architectonic *politikē*, directs those engaged in *politikē* in the narrower sense (through their activities in the assembly and jury) in the way that an architect or master craftsperson directs manual workers (*Pol.* VIII.3, 1325b21–3).[30]

As Aristotle implies in I.2 of the *Nicomachean Ethics*, *politikē* in the broader (and more fundamental) sense thus refers to the architectonic political expertise concerned with the realisation of *aretē* and *eudaimonia* through effective acts of law-giving. The end of law-making expertise is the human good (*tanthrōpinon agathon*) in all its manifestations. This good it seeks to attain by legislating binding norms concerning what activities the members of a political community are to engage in and what activities they are to refrain from (1094b5–7). The exemplary form of *politikē* in the broader sense is hence the expertise necessary to establish, maintain and modify those communal norms promoting virtue and wellbeing. The practically wise law-giver is uniquely responsible for facilitating the conditions (inclusive of 'ethical' education) which allow the citizens of a political community to flourish, both individually and in common.

Aristotle also characterises *politikē* in the opening of the *Nicomachean Ethics* as the most authoritative (*kuriotatēs*) of the crafts and sciences (I.2, 1094a26–7). This does not mean that political expertise is the 'best' knowledge concerned with the most important things; Aristotle privileges theoretical sciences such as theology, mathematics and natural philosophy (*Met.* VI.1, 1026a18–32) when he asserts that humans are not the most serious (*spoudaiotatēn*) thing in the cosmos (*NE* VI.7,

28 See Keyt (2017: 211–15) and Bodéüs (1993: 64).

29 As Keyt (2017: 212) notes, the offices of the juror and the assemblyman are definitive of full citizenship for Aristotle (*Pol.* III.1–2, 1275b17–21) and hence the virtues of *bouleutikē* and *dikastikē* are those of a citizen.

30 Keyt (2017: 212).

1141a22). The status of *politikē* as the most authoritative science requires further elucidation.

Irwin usefully identifies three meanings of *kurios* in Aristotle.[31] First, if X has power over Y, then X may be said to be *kurios* in relation to Y. When one is *kurios* over an event, for example, one determines voluntarily whether it occurs and assumes responsibility for its occurrence. This meaning of the term explains the use of *kurios* to designate a ruler or commander (*NE* III.8, 1116a30–3) and practical authority more generally, including the authority of the laws. Aristotle states at one point, for example, that the laws should be *kurios* except in regard to those matters that cannot be legislated because they are too contingent to fall under universal rules (*Pol.* III.11, 1282b1–5). Second, *kurios* is used by Aristotle to denote importance, in the sense that what is in control of a process can be attributed with pre-eminent significance (*NE* VI.12, 1143b34, VI.13, 1145a6, IX.8, 1168b30 and X.7, 1178a3). Finally, *kurios* can designate the property of being complete, in the sense that a *kurios* F is F most completely, in comparison to things that are only partially F (see *NE* I.7, 1098a6–b14 and I.13, 1103a2). The first two meanings help to explain Aristotle's use of *kuriotatēs* as a superlative describing the status of *politikē* in relation to other arts or sciences. For to say that a form of knowledge X is authoritative over other forms of knowledge Y, Z etc. is to suggest that X governs Y, Z etc., and does so on account of its pre-eminence. Yet this analysis of *kurios* can only get us so far in understanding the claim that *politikē* is the most authoritative of the sciences.

In *Nicomachean Ethics* VI.1 Aristotle identifies the 'calculative' (*logistikon*) faculty with deliberation (1139a12–13) and hence with practical reason (cf. *Pol.* VII.14, 1333a16–26). The part of the soul that possesses authority over the non-rational parts is deliberative, not contemplative, and the role of *phronēsis* is to deliberate about the way to attain a good end (*NE* VI.5, 1140a24–1140b30). From this perspective, *phronēsis* is distinguished by its capacity to issue orders with regard to what should be done (VI.10, 1143a9–10) in particular circumstances. As a complex whole unified by the natural authority (*kurios kata phusin*) of the higher rational part, the soul naturally rules over the material components of living organisms (*DA* I.5, 410b10–15; cf. *Pol.* I.5, 1254a34–6).[32] As noted in Chapter 1, it is because the irrational parts of the soul are capable of listening to reason in the same way that a person can listen to a parent or a friend without themselves possessing reason in the full sense (*NE* I.13, 1102b30–5) that force is not always required in the political domain. Good laws enacted by a legislative expert can serve as rational guides to conduct for citizens ordering their communal life.

Obviously a good legislator must also be able to deal with less than ideal political circumstances and citizens. In *Politics* IV.1, Aristotle compares the skill of the political expert to a physical trainer (1288b10–20). Just as the skilled physical trainer

[31] Irwin (1999: 321).
[32] Miller (2013: 41–2).

should know the training suitable for those with athletic shortcomings, as well as for more gifted athletes, so must the architectonic legislator know what will improve defective regimes, as well as the conditions for ideal political orders. Indeed, Aristotle criticises writers on politics who focus only on the highest constitution or ignore those constitutions that are actually in place (1288b39–1289a1). The reach of *politikē* thus extends beyond ideal and correct constitutions to the effort to improve (and also sometimes to preserve) defective regimes, as Aristotle's constitutional analyses in Books V and VI of the *Politics* demonstrate.

Aristotle's classification of *politikē* in the generic sense as a species of (generic) *phronēsis* suggests that it is a strictly practical disposition and that the same applies to expert law-making or *nomothetikē* as a species of generic *politikē*. Several passages in Aristotle's work, however, indicate that there is a non-practical component to architectonic law-giving expertise and these have even led some interpreters to claim that the legislator is a theorist without an active political role.[33]

As noted above, Aristotle's treatment of architectonic or broad *politikē* entails a contrast between the kind of *phronēsis* exercised in the framing of constitutions and laws and the narrower form of political prudence at work in deliberation about concrete practical affairs. The latter is, plausibly enough, strictly a practical disposition (*NE* VI.7, 1141b26–8). In the case of legislative expertise, by apparent contrast, Aristotle states that those people act in the strict sense, who, like architects, direct the actions of other people by their thoughts (*Pol.* VII.3, 1325b21–3). Rather than construe this as meaning that the legislator is a mere 'political theorist', however, it is preferable to acknowledge that the sort of *practical* activity engaged in by the true legislative expert necessarily draws on universals (and practical truths and principles) in its dealing with diverse particulars.[34]

Confusion can arise because *politikē* abbreviates *politikē technē* or *epistēmē*. Aristotelian *politikē* is clearly not an *epistēmē* in the unqualified (*haplōs*) sense of Book I.2 of the *Posterior Analytics* (the cognitive state by which we grasp the causes of necessary facts that could not be otherwise (*APo.* 71b9–16)) or of VI.3 of the *Nicomachean Ethics* (the faculty of knowledge that draws true conclusions regarding the unchangeable objects grasped by the intellect (*nous*)).[35] One should instead interpret political (and hence legislative) expertise as falling within the broader sense of *epistēmē* found in *Metaphysics* VI.1 (and implied by *Nicomachean Ethics* I.1 and elsewhere), which includes practical and productive 'sciences' and designates an area of enquiry concerned with providing a rational account of the explanatory causes and principles of a particular domain.

Metaphysics VI.1 states that while all sciences deal with causes and principles, these can be determinate or indeterminate (*Met.* 1025b7). In order to understand the status of *politikē* (and hence *nomothetikē*) as practical one must attend closely to

33 See, for example, Stewart (1892: 65). For critique see Kontos (forthcoming: 2–4).

34 Reeve (2017: xxi–xxxii).

35 See Nielsen (2015: 35).

Aristotle's characterisations of *phronēsis* as (1) a true state involving reason, concerned with what is good or bad for a human being and (2) not concerned with universals *alone*, but *also* engaged directly with particulars (*NE* VI.5, 1140b5–6, VI.7, 1141b15–16). Whereas (1) points to the end of *phronēsis* i.e. the human good (2) refers to the diverse sorts of particulars engaged with by different modes of *phronēsis* (individual, domestic, political/legal). On account of the variability of their subject matter, and applied character, political and law-making expertise admit of less precision than theoretical sciences (*NE* I.3, 1094b11–27). Practical sciences are rather, as noted in the introduction, like the natural sciences concerned with what holds 'for the most part' (*hōs epi polu*). Their propositions also, in contrast to those of both theoretical and natural sciences, prescribe human action rather than describe the external world.[36] None of this precludes legislative expertise, as the intellectual virtue of the true politician (VI.8, 1141b29–32), from accessing universals as part of its aim to realise the human good.

Aristotelian political and legislative expertise contain, as modes of *phronēsis*, both a universalist and a particularist component.[37] The universalist component is evident in X.9 of the *Nicomachean Ethics*. A person attempting to become a skilled legislator (*nomothetikō[i] peirateon genesthai*) must proceed to the universal (*epi to katholou*), because the project of making people good through law would best be realised by those who know (*tou eidotos*), as is the case with medicine and whatever else has a certain care and prudence (*epimeleia tis kai phronēsis*) associated with it (1180b20–8). A doctor who only knows anatomy and has no practical experience is unlikely to be effective, and yet one equally expects a doctor to have some universal knowledge of what does and does not work to promote health. In a similar way, the legislator, in exercising a practical disposition, needs to draw on universal practical truths in their law-making activity.[38] This activity also remains directed to particulars, insofar as it enacts laws for a singular political community.

The statement that the law-giver must 'proceed' to universals in order to legislate effectively accordingly does not entail that legislative expertise is a form of non-practical 'political theory'. It rather means that the prudence exercised by the law-maker draws on practical truths about human nature and abiding features of political communities. An example of the sort of knowledge required by the good law-maker can be seen in the claim that the true politician must investigate (*episkopousi*) phenomena such as the experience of pleasure and pain if they are to perform their function effectively (*NE* III.1, 1109b32–5). While it is possible to envisage exceptions, it is a general truth that people will pursue pleasure and avoid pain, and moreover that the sorts of pleasures they pursue and pains they avoid will

36 Reeve (2017: xxvii).

37 See Reeve (2013: 3). Kontos (forthcoming: 25) distinguishes in this context between legislative science and legislative practical wisdom, where the former is the 'universalist' or 'scientific' component of the latter (and also of the other variations of *phronēsis*).

38 See Nielsen (2015: 29–48).

be relatively predictable given human nature. Further examples of truths that would need to be understood by the Aristotelian law-maker include the tendency for the human soul to be influenced by music and other poetic forms, as suggested by the educational programme outlined in *Politics* VII and VIII, and the need to regulate property relations in conformity with human nature discussed in Books I and II. The Aristotelian founding legislator is accordingly a practically wise politician who applies insights from the experience and study of human affairs, understood as informed by regularities, to the establishment of constitutions and laws.[39] These constitutions and laws are directive of the human good, both in the sense that they embed practical principles and truths and in the sense that they govern concrete situations and particulars.

Good laws require insight into particulars. Yet laws are also necessarily universal in formulation, because their prescriptions are supposed to apply to many circumstances (*NE* V.10, 1137b13). A founding legislator must, of course, engage with the distinctive situation of potential or existing political communities (*NE* X.9, 1180b27; cf. *Pol.* VII.7, 1327b20–38). Yet a legislator will be unable to engage effectively with the relevant particulars in the absence of a broader understanding of the human good and the sorts of political and legal structures which serve the promotion of virtue and wellbeing. The activity of legislating is thus confirmed as a mode of *phronēsis* because in its aiming at the good it deals with both universals and their application to particulars. In governing human actions, the law, moreover, draws on practical truths and prescribes universal norms that are intended to guide conduct. Legislative expertise remains practical because it is a true state of reasoning regarding the end of law i.e. the wellbeing of political communities and individuals.

The authoritative status of legislative expertise as a privileged exercise of *politikē* should accordingly be understood as follows. The role of legislation is to provide a framework of norms that are conducive to human flourishing. In this context, Aristotle suggests that good laws presuppose universal knowledge of what is good for people (*NE* X.9, 1180b13–16). Practical truths form the basis for good legislation, insofar as if a person wishes to achieve mastery of a craft or science, they must seek knowledge of the universal (1180b20–3). Experience and sound practical judgement

39 This interpretation of *politikē* as a practically-engaged form of political expertise is consistent with earlier uses of the term. In *The History of the Peloponnesian War* (II.40.2–3 and III.37) Thucydides uses *politikē* in conjunction with *technē* and *epistēmē* to describe the 'art of government'. When Protagoras, who was invited by Pericles to write the constitution for the Athenian colony of Thurii in 444 BCE, attributes the disorder of pre-civic life to the lack of a *politikē technē*, he refers primarily to a form of expertise constitutive of civilised political community (*Prt.* 319a and 322b). Cf. Democritus, DK 68 B 157. It is true that Plato's use of *politikē technē* does not necessarily imply direct practical engagement in the Aristotelian sense. The Platonic critique of the sophists nonetheless suggests affinity with Aristotle's analysis in X.9. When Socrates claims to be the proponent of 'the true political art' (*alēthōs politikē technē*) (Grg. 521d7), this assumes a distance from the pathologies of ordinary Athenian politics. In setting out the regimes of the *Republic* and the *Laws*, Socrates and the Athenian Stranger, at least from an Aristotelian perspective, are also engaged in architectonic practical reasoning about the political conditions for the realisation of virtue and wellbeing.

concerning the correct application of universals to diverse cases is also crucial in the realm of political affairs, as the legislator seeks to determine what kinds of norms and laws are appropriate for diverse communities and individuals. For Aristotle, what differentiates the *phronēsis* of a private person from that of someone regarded as an exemplary statesman, such as Pericles, is that, in the case of the latter, practical knowledge is not restricted to an individual's own good, but rather extends to knowledge of what is good for humans as such (VI.5, 1140b4–11). Legislative expertise, in seeking this good, is hence confirmed as mode of practical rationality.

SECTION 3 THE LEGISLATOR AND POLITICAL NATURALISM

Aristotle's architectonic legislator, the previous section has demonstrated, exercises a mode of *phronēsis* which accesses universals and practical truths in its engagement with particulars. The conclusion that legislative expertise is a practical disposition that draws on universals does not explain, however, why Aristotle also presents it as a form of 'craftlike' production (*Pol.* I.2, 1253a30–1, II.7, 1266b34–8, II.12, 1273b32–3, 1274b18–19, III.12, 1282b14–16, VII.4, 1325b40–1326a5). This feature of Aristotelian law-making is especially puzzling insofar as the claim that the intentional activity of the legislator is both an efficient cause and necessary condition for the polis seems, for the reasons discussed in Section 1, difficult to reconcile with the proposition that the political community is a naturally arising entity. In this final section I argue that Aristotle's commitment to legislative agency as a necessary condition for the polis is in fact consistent with his political naturalism. Legislative agency is required, on Aristotelian assumptions, to complete our natural potential for political life. The establishment of political communities and the enactment of laws both arise out of the capacity humans possess, as practically rational beings, to promote the structural conditions for human flourishing. The establishment of constitutions and laws is, in addition, ordered to the same end – human flourishing – that it is the nature of the practically reasonable agent to pursue.

The designation of the law-maker as a *dēmiourgos* and treatment of *nomothetikē* as a craft both seem to conflict with Aristotle's distinction between practical and productive sciences (*Top.* VI.6, 145a15–16; *Met.* VI.1, 1025b25, XI.7, 1064a16–19; *NE* VI.2, 1139a26–8). An instructive example is the *Politics* VII.5 discussion of the origins of political community. The best regime cannot exist, Aristotle notes, without the appropriate citizens and territory. Just as other craftsmen, such as the weaver or the shipbuilder, need suitable material (*hylēn*) to work on ... so too must the political expert and the legislator (*tō[i]) politiko[i] kai tō[i] nomothetē[i]*) have the proper material in an appropriate condition (1325b37–1326a5). Aristotle's analogy thus suggests that the legislative expert imposes constitutional form upon the material (*hylē*) constituents of a polis such as population and territory. This conforms to the standard model of *poēsis*, whereby the craftsman, or their craft, is an efficient cause and the *telos* an external object (*NE* VI.4, 1140a1–25; *Met.* VI.1, 1025b25).

If law-making is a *technē* and its products (constitutions and laws) external ends which are the outcome of a process of *poēsis* (rather than *praxis*) (*NE* VI.4, 1104a1–23), then this obviously undermines the conclusions of the previous section regarding the status of legislative expertise as a mode of *phronēsis* and as hence genuinely practical.[40] If law-making is a productive science, moreover, then the thesis that nature and the law-giver are 'co-operative' causes of the polis faces insurmountable obstacles. On a 'pure' productive model, the legislator would not only be the efficient cause and necessary condition for the polis (in the same way that a craftsperson of a bed – or the craft of bed-making – is the bed's efficient cause and a necessary condition for its existence), but the constitution would be an artefact external to legislative *poēsis*. Aristotle's opposition between nature (*phusis*) and craft (*technē*) (*Ph.* II.6, 198a10; *Met.* VII.7, 1032a12–13; *NE* III.3, 1112a31–3; *Pol.* VII.14, 1333a23) excludes the possibility that the polis is naturally emerging on this set of assumptions.

Now Aristotle's statements on foundational law-making do imply that legislative activity culminates in a finished product in the sense that the polis – understood as a political community which has a constitutional structure and is governed by law – is the outcome of the imposition of form upon the political matter of citizens and territory. Likewise there is a sense in which laws, particularly written laws, are external and 'public' articulations of the core customs and beliefs of a political community. Yet, as seen above, Aristotle is unequivocal that law-making is a sub-branch of *politikē* and hence a mode of practical rationality. As a consequence, the end of law-making should be understood on the internal model of praxis rather than the external model of productive activity.

Production and practical activity both involve human agency. With *poēsis*, the principle of movement is in the 'producer'. With *praxis*, by contrast, the principle of action is in the 'doer' i.e. the person engaged in the activity as a practically rational being. In this case, 'what is done' and 'what is chosen' through the activity are ultimately the same (*Met.* VI.1, 1025b25–6). In both cases, an agent is responsible for an action, but in the case of a practical disposition the *telos* is the human good, not an external product. As seen in Section 2, the end of political and legislative expertise is none other than the human good (*tanthrōpinon agathon*) in all its manifestations (*NE* I.2, 1094b5). The foundational activity of enacting a constitution is hence not merely a matter of distributing offices and honours and enacting laws, considered as external products, but the establishment of a 'way of life' (*bios*) for the polis (*Pol.* IV.11, 1295b1). In the case of just constitutions directed to the common advantage, legislative activity will at least approximate its *telos*. And this *telos* is in turn

40 Kraut (1997: 67–8) makes the related point in this context that whereas political and legislative science necessarily on occasion employ force, this is not usually the case with productive sciences.

a reflection of our nature as practically rational political beings, such that the ultimate end of law-making is in one sense the same as the end of human flourishing. An explicit conceptualisation of foundational law-making in these terms under Aristotle's model of action is the first step towards a reconciliation of legislative agency and political naturalism.

In order to elaborate on the ramifications of this point regarding the reflexivity of practical activity, it is helpful to rehearse the main tenets of Aristotle's political naturalism. The three tenets are that the polis is by nature (*Pol.* I.2, 1252b30; 1253a2, 1253a25; VII.8, 1328a22), that the polis is by nature prior to the individual (I.2, 1253a19–39) and that humans are by nature political animals (1253a2–3).[41]

Aristotle argues that the polis is by nature because it is 'complete', attains the end of self-sufficiency and exists for the sake of the good life (*Pol.* I.2, 1252b27–30). The polis also exists by nature insofar as it develops from more basic forms of natural association and because it is by participation in political community that humans are best able to approximate perfection (1252b30–1253a4).[42] The difference between a mere association for mutual agent-relative advantage through exchange and contract and the political association in the focal sense is that the polis exists for the sake of the good life i.e. the provision of those conditions necessary for human excellence and flourishing (III.9, 1280a31–1281a5). This explains the import of Aristotle's polis 'priority' claim:

> The political community (*polis*) is also prior (*proteron*) in nature (*phusei*) to the household and to each of us individually, since the whole (*holon*) is necessarily prior to the part (*merous*) . . . that the political community is natural (*phusei*) and prior in nature to the individual (*hekastos*) is clear. For if an individual is not self-sufficient when separated, he will be like other parts in relation to the whole (*Pol.* I.2, 1253a19–28).

For the argument to be sound it is necessary to assume that Aristotle is referring to parts which are not self-sufficient apart from the whole (as with the human hand). There is a sense in which humans lack self-sufficiency suggested by Aristotle's quasi-genetic account of the polis as arising from more basic associations between men and women, masters and slaves, households and villages. Although the importance of this sense of self-sufficiency is not to be underplayed, there is also a teleological sense of self-sufficiency operative in the *Politics* according to which the polis is a natural and complete community (*Pol.* I.2, 1252b26–1253a18) because it enables its members to achieve *eudaimonia* through the virtues. The whole (polis) precedes the parts (citizens) because the full realisation of human nature presupposes circumstances only available in a polis.

Aristotle's political naturalism is thus best interpreted teleologically by reference to the fact that the nature (*phusis*) of a thing, its function (*ergon*) and its end (*telos*)

[41] Keyt (1991) characterises these tenets as the three basic 'theorems' of Aristotle's political philosophy.

[42] See Keys (2006: 77–86); Miller (1995); Miller (2000: 343); Reeve (2009: 512–25).

are 'systematically related': the end of a natural entity is to realise its nature in the performance of its function (*NE* IX.7, 1168a6–9).[43] The natural end of the political community and its purpose is to allow for the actualisation of the human potential to lead a life of virtue and wellbeing consistent with our rational capacities.

The teleological character of Aristotle's political naturalism does not mean that the polis is a natural entity in the strict sense of *Physics* II.1. According to this narrower sense of things which exist by nature, rather than by other causes, natural entities have an internal source of change i.e. each natural entity has *in itself* a principle of motion and rest, whether regarding place, growth etc. (*Ph.* II.1, 192b15–20). Aristotle contrasts this sense of nature explicitly with products of art (*technē*), such as a bed, where there is an external cause i.e. an artisan (*technitēs*) or craftsperson (*dēmiourgos*) who is engaged in the action of producing the bed on the basis of the relevant craft (192b30–1).[44] Aristotle's introduction of his arguments for political naturalism with the statement that 'as elsewhere it is by looking at how things develop naturally from the beginning that one may best study them' (*Pol.* I.2, 1252a24–6) could certainly suggest that he intends to argue that the polis is a natural entity in the strict sense, but such an interpretation is clearly inconsistent with his account of legislative agency. A better approach is accordingly to seek a broader sense of nature that is reconcilable with Aristotle's commitment to the status of the legislator as an efficient cause.

The *Physics* II.8 discussion of why nature is a cause which acts for the sake of something provides the basis for such an extended concept of the natural.[45] Here Aristotle maintains his distinction between natural entities and products of craft. Despite their differences, in both cases the relevant entities are for the sake of their ends and in some cases craft completes what nature cannot bring to its completion (*hē technē epitelei ha hē phusis adunatei apergasasthai*) (*Ph.* 199a9–18). For the natural realm, in addition, there are types of development which cannot be regarded as involving internal principles of change in the narrow sense of *Physics* II.1, yet nonetheless emerge as a result of directedness to an end that is natural. Aristotle thus notes the way in which swallows construct nests and spiders make webs (199a29–30) in order to look after their offspring or pursue the conditions for their sustenance and survival. These 'activities' are a function of natural impulses, rather than a result of inquiry or deliberation, but also involve a sense of the natural that is not strictly speaking classifiable in terms of an internal principle of movement, growth or change.

43 Reeve (2000: 512).

44 In *Metaphysics* V.4 Aristotle distinguishes several senses of nature, which include primary matter, the form or substance which is the *telos* of the process of becoming and substances as such. As Miller points out, however, the sense of nature according to which it is the 'source of the primary movement which is present in each natural entity intrinsically and not accidentally' (2013: 322) seems to be the most basic.

45 A point recognised by Miller (2000: 328) and Reeve (2009: 513) in their discussions of political naturalism.

Physics II.8 thus plausibly points to an extended conception of the natural according to which not all entities with a 'standard' nature find their completion in a purely natural process involving internal principles of change. Applied to the human domain, this would suggest that political activities – pre-eminently law-making – derive from natural impulses and are necessary to complete the work of nature (cf. *Ph.* 199a15–16).[46] Analogous to a spider constructing a web, the activity of the architectonic legislator arises from a natural human impulse to live in well-governed political communities. Insofar as such communities are necessary for a life of self-sufficiency consonant with virtue and flourishing, the impulse of human nature towards the good life serves as a source of the motivation to design forms of political and legal order which promote our natural ends.

Such an interpretation find supports in Aristotle's discussion of the extent to which human virtues are natural. In II.1 of the *Nicomachean Ethics*, Aristotle argues that the virtues arise in us neither by nature nor apart from nature (*NE* II.1, 1103a24–5). Virtues are capacities that require the assistance of habituation to develop fully; hence the well-known claim that one attains the ethical virtues by performing acts of virtue (I.13–II.1, 1103a7–b25). It is also by engaging in good actions and refraining from base conduct that we experience the activities of virtue as pleasurable and the activities of vice as painful (III.4, 1113a22–b2). This applies to justice as much as to courage or moderation.

Significantly, Aristotle offers as evidence for this thesis concerning virtue the activities of law-givers. By habituating citizens, law-givers intend to make them good. As discussed in Chapter 1, it is difficult for the youth to be well-trained in virtue without correct laws (X.9, 1179b31–2). Rational argument alone is inadequate for those raised in bad habits and the soul of the listener must be cultivated to enjoy virtue. Passion is also more likely to yield to force than reason (1179b23–9). As a consequence, the compelling force of law is necessary to ensure that people are raised correctly and habituated so that they at least act in a manner that is in conformity with virtue.[47] The deeds of virtue realise a capacity present in us by nature, but the actualisation of this capacity requires the establishment by practical reason of norms which promote just and equitable conduct.[48] The architectonic activity of the legislative expert is necessary because virtue is not simply naturally emerging. Yet the agency of a law-giver is also far from arbitrary. When a legislator is performing their function well, this activity is ordered towards the enactment of laws

46 Reeve (2009: 513) argues that 'standard natures perfected by craft are not products of craft, since their forms do not flow into them from the souls or minds of a craftsman'.

47 Cf. Nederman (1994: 283–304).

48 Cf. Kraut (2002: 242): 'The city arises out of a feature of our psychology . . . neither chosen nor inculcated by habit, but . . . fixed by our nature – namely our desire to survive, meet our everyday needs, and procreate.' While correct in its focus on human nature, Kraut's reading also understates the significance of the features of practical rationality which allow legislative agency and political naturalism to be reconciled.

which promote the actualisation of human potentialities and our natural impulse to virtue and flourishing.

When Aristotle says that the founder of the political community is the cause (*aitios*) of the greatest of goods, this means not merely that the architectonic activity of the founding legislator is a necessary condition for the formation of the polis. It also means that law-making actualises and fulfils an already existing natural human potentiality. The polis is not simply an external product of the legislative craft, but rather naturally develops from more basic associations through the *practical agency* of a legislative founder imposing constitutional form on political matter.

This reconciliation of legislative agency and political naturalism can be elaborated by reference to a significant difference between the natural 'activities' of animals and the activity of the law-maker in framing laws for a polis. In the case of animals, the construction of a nest or web does not involve art, investigation or deliberation (*oute technē oute zētēsanta oute bouleusamena*) (*Ph.* II.8, 199a21). It rather occurs due to non-rational natural impulse. The formation of political communities through architectonic legislation, by contrast, is carried out on the basis of deliberation and even draws, as demonstrated in Section 2, on universals and practical truths. Conversely, the activity of legislating, insofar as it is an exercise of *phronēsis*, differs from the pure production (*poēsis*) involved in the construction of a bed. It is by considering more closely this latter distinction that one can best see how an extended conception of nature including actions derived from natural impulses is consistent with Aristotle's account of the polis as co-dependent on legislative agency.

Aristotle's claim that humans are political by nature (*Pol.* I.2, 1253a2–3) is the proposition that helps to bring the multiple strands together. The fact that humans are political by nature does not mean that they live, or desire to live, in political communities solely as a function of natural impulses independently of reason and deliberation. It rather means that humans have natural impulses which guide them towards the application of a capacity for practical judgement to the development of political associations.[49] The sense in which humans are more truly political animals than other gregarious animals like bees (*Pol.* 1253a8) points to the active role of reason in the development of political communities and law. Humans are distinct because they have a natural capacity for rational speech (*logos*). This capacity enables humans to express opinions on the expedient and inexpedient and the just and the unjust, in contrast to other animals, which can only express pleasure or pain (*Pol.* 1253a8–14). It is in the development of this natural capacity for rational speech through practical deliberation, choice and action that humans possess a sense of the just and the unjust, the good and the bad, which culminates in the distinctly political association and law.[50]

49 See Yack (1993: 15–33) and Zingano (2013: 199–222).
50 Cf. Cheery and Goerner (2006: 563–85).

For Aristotle the human end is rational activity of the soul in conformity with virtue (*NE* I.7, 1097b22–1098a4). An architectonic legislator, in founding the constitution of a polis and enacting its fundamental laws, is thus engaged in a mode of practically rational activity which is a fulfilment of distinctly human nature. The end of the legislator's activity is, moreover, the human good as such.[51]

The status of humans as naturally political animals thus allows for a distinction between the work of a spider in constructing a web and the activity of a law-maker in designing a fundamental set of laws for a polis. It is the human capacity for deliberation and rational investigation which distinguishes the products of the legislative 'craft' from the products arising from animal impulse. The status of humans as naturally political animals also points, moreover, to clear differences internal to the human domain between founding a political community and the production of a bed. In the case of a bed, considered as the product of the craft of bed-making, the end is external and independent of the craftsman (*NE* VI.4, 1140a1–23). In the case of the polis, at least on the assumption that it is part of our nature to live in political associations, then the legislator is engaged in the practically rational activity of establishing a constitution for the purpose of actualising the human potentiality for virtue and flourishing. Foundational law-making, by contrast with production, has an end contained within the activity that is chosen through that very activity.

Aristotle's reference to the founding legislator (*dēmiourgos*) as a craftsman must accordingly be regarded as an analogy properly speaking in the sense that the activity of law-making has a productive aspect, but is ultimately practical in its ends (see *NE* I.6, 1096b28). Legislative expertise is a function of natural impulses (analogous to the activity of the swallow or spider in constructing a nest or web respectively) and yet differs from the non-deliberative productive work of animals insofar as it exercises a distinctly human capacity and attempts to promote it further in the political domain. While the architectonic activity of founding a constitution and its laws is analogous to the production of a craftsman, it also fulfils the distinctly human natural capacity for rational speech and reflection on the good and the bad, the just and the unjust. The founding legislator, by engaging in the activity of designing political structures and legal norms, hence exercises those very capacities for rational speech and practical deliberation that they attempt to promote. In this sense, there is a reflexive aspect to law-making whereby the exercise of practical reason through constitutional formation aims at the same end – *eudaimonia* – that the activity actualises.

An Aristotelian founding legislator accordingly engages in a form of practical activity that is a realisation of distinctly human nature and in so doing chooses an end – flourishing – that is the *telos* of our specific natural capacities. Now one might

[51] It is this which explains why the origin of the political community can more genuinely be regarded as arising from nature than the formation of other groups such as an athletic team or musical chorus.

of course object that this is a highly idealised conception of constitutional law-making. This would of course be true, but it is completely consistent with the tendency to view foundational law-makers as exemplars of practical wisdom and experience discussed in Section 1. The Aristotelian legislator in the focal sense is no mere enactor of laws, but rather a practically reasonable agent with insight into the human good.

Aristotle's account of the founding legislator and nature as joint causes of the polis therefore rests not only on an extended account of nature, whereby our natural rational faculties allow us to fulfil an innate impulse towards the formation of political communities that are conducive to the development of intellectual and ethical virtues, but also upon a reflexive conception of practical rationality as a faculty whereby 'doing' and the choice for the ultimate human end are the same.

The interpretation offered here is consistent, it is worth noting in closing, with Aristotle's pointed rejection of the stark *phusis-nomos* dichotomy that is associated with the sophistic movement.[52] As discussed in Chapter 1, X.9 seeks to expose the speciousness of the sophistic claim to be able to teach political expertise (*politikē*) and the 'art' of legislation (*NE* 1181a1–b13). It is thus significant that the first mention of *nomos* in *Nicomachean Ethics* alludes to the sophistic teaching on law:

> The noble things and the just things (*ta de kala kai ta dikaia*), which political expertise (*politikē*) examines, admit of much dispute and variability (*pollēn echei diaphoran kai planēn*), such that they are held to exist by law alone and not by nature (*hōste dokein nomō[i] monon einai, phusei de mē*) (*NE* I.2, 1094b15–17).

Aristotle's political naturalism is in part a response to the distortions which arise from an overly sharp opposition between what is by nature and by convention. Undoubtedly a polis is held together by justice (*EE* VII.9, 1241b14–15) and citizens become just, not by nature solely, but by habituation guided by practical reason and law (*NE* II.1, 1103a13–16). On the other hand, practical reason seeks to promote the conditions for distinctly human rational activity directed to the good. While practical wisdom admits of less precision than other forms of knowledge, moreover, there are regularities in the political domain accessible to a practically reasonable person. Aristotle's political science thereby acknowledges the natural tendency to establish communities governed by law, while also recognising the element of intentional activity and habituation necessary for the full realisation of the potential for political life incipient in the more basic forms of association.

It is therefore unsurprising that Aristotle's introduction of the three tenets of his political naturalism is accompanied by several appeals to the necessary role of law in restraining human desires and introducing order to human affairs. In his discussion of the association of the polis out of more basic forms of association – the family and the village – Aristotle thus cites the Homeric passage regarding the Cyclopses

52 See Ambler (1985).

according to which each acts as a law (*themisteuei*) to his children and wives, and pays no attention to the others (*Pol.* I.2, 1252b23).[53] This scattered existence is contrasted with the state of development according to which the formation of political communities, under the guidance of law, allows for the fulfilment of natural human capacities. In asserting that the person who founded a political community was responsible for the greatest of goods – the statement which formed the starting point for the analysis in this chapter – Aristotle thus notes that humans are the best of animals when completed (*teleōtheis*), but the worst of all when separated from law and adjudication (*nomou kai dikēs*) (1253a31–33). The order which law introduces to political communities ultimately derives from the natural tendency that humans possess towards the full realisation of their capacities, but also reflects the need for intentional activity, particularly that of the law-giver, in order to ensure the actualisation of this potentiality.

[53] *Odyssey* 9.112–15.

3

The Constitutional Relativity of Law

The first two chapters have demonstrated that for Aristotle *nomos* in the focal sense is a standard for conduct derived from the practical reason of an architectonic legislator. Legislative expertise, on this view, is a privileged sub-branch of true political expertise and it enacts laws with a view to the human good inclusive of the promotion of the conditions for virtue and wellbeing. The full implications of Aristotle's thesis that law-making is a part of political expertise can only be understood, however, by reference to the claim that legislators should and do enact laws (*nomoi*) relative to the constitution (*politeia*) (*Pol.* III.11, 1282b8–13, IV.1, 1289a14–22). In its simplest sense, the constitutional relativity of law entails that legislators should and do enact laws that are consistent with the priorities of their regime. More fundamentally, the constitutional relativity of law reflects the dependence of law on the explicit or implicit conceptions of the good life which inform alternative arrangements of ruling offices. In this chapter, I argue that the constitutional relativity of law is best interpreted through the lens of Aristotle's theory of explanatory causes. On this interpretation, the *politeia* is the formal cause of the polis and it is structured by the conception of *eudaimonia* prevalent among the dominant political element. Section 1 defends both the general claim that Aristotle's constitutional analysis is informed by his theory of explanatory causes and the specific claim that the *politeia* is a formal cause. In Section 2, I then connect the status of the *politeia* as a formal cause to the different conceptions of *eudaimonia* which determine diverse regime-types and their laws. Finally, in Section 3, I examine whether the constitutional relativity of law entails that all law is necessarily partisan by considering its applicability to the best regime.

SECTION 1 THE *POLITEIA* AS A FORMAL CAUSE

Aristotle's commitment to the constitutional relativity of law reflects the fundamental explanatory role of the *politeia* in his political thought.[1] This first section argues that

[1] For a systematic analysis of the 522 occurrences of the term *politeia* in the *Politics*, see Mulhern (2015). Mulhern identifies four distinct but often closely related senses of the term *politeia*: citizenship,

the explanatory priority of the *politeia* is inseparable from its status as the formal cause of the polis.[2] While Aristotle's analysis of constitutions (*politeiai*) frequently refers to different forms (*eidē*) of political order (*taxis*), there are apparent obstacles to the use of causal explanations in the practical domain. These concerns can nonetheless be overcome and Aristotle's use of the *politeia* to explain both the unity of a polis and its identity conditions supports a non-reductive interpretation of its status as a formal cause. As will become clear in Section 2, recognition of the status of the *politeia* as a formal cause is crucial for understanding Aristotle's claim that laws must be enacted relative to different constitutions.

Miller has provided a suggestive outline of the applicability of the theory of causes to Aristotle's *Politics*.[3] The material cause of the polis, as a composite whole, is its citizens (*Pol.* III.1, 1274b38–41, VII.4, 1326a5). An arrangement of citizens into a composite structure (*sunthesin*) of a particular kind constitutes the *politeia* as the form (*eidos*) of the polis (III.3, 1276b7–10). On this reading, the polis has 'within it a formal principal by which it is organised and governed: its constitution'.[4] The 'efficient' cause of the polis is, as suggested in Chapter 2, either the founding law-maker (*nomothetēs*) responsible for a political regime and its laws (II.12, 1273b32–5) or the expertise of law-making (*nomothetikē*) guiding the legislator's activity. One can complete the picture by identifying the *telos* and final cause of the polis as *eudaimonia* (III.6, 1278b17–24, III.9, 1280b39).

Aristotle's distinctions between types of constitution, citizen and office by reference to differences in kind (*eidos*) provide initial support for granting a non-trivial explanatory role to formal causes in constitutional analysis. The use of the term *eidos* is particularly in evidence in *Politics* III–IV, where not only are different constitutional types regarded as diverse *eidē* (e.g. *Pol.* IV.3, 1290a12–17, IV.8, 1294a26) but these types are themselves broken down into diverse kinds of the same species, with four *eidē* each listed for democracy (IV.4, 1291b31–1292a39) and oligarchy (IV.5, 1292a40–b10).

While suggestive, however, Aristotle's liberal use of the term *eidos* in reference to diverse kinds of political phenomena does not entail that the theory of formal causes – considered as metaphysical principles – have a fundamental explanatory function in Aristotelian political science.[5] In order to defend this explanatory role, it is necessary to examine more closely the concept of the *politeia*.

citizen-body, constitution or arrangement of offices and regime (2015: 84). See also Harte and Lane (2013).

2 The claim that the *politeia* is a formal cause is quite common in recent Anglo-American scholarship, yet has not been developed and defended in detail. Applications of the theory of causes to Aristotle's political theory are found in Miller (1995: 15 and 151; 2011) and Keyt (2017: 178–9). Instructive discussions of the *politeia* as the form or *eidos* of the *polis* are Preus (1977: 354–60) and Bates (2003: 62). For a cautious identification based on *Politics* III.3, 1276b1–9 see Irwin (1988: 254). In his analysis of explanatory causes, Stein assumes that the 'state' and the constitution are formal causes (2011: 700 and 702). See also Neschke-Hentschke (1971: 145–8).

3 Miller (2017).

4 Miller (1995: 15). Miller notes the analogy with the soul as the organising formal principle of the body, citing Plato's *Politeia* and Isocrates *Areopagiticus* 14.1: 'The soul of a *polis* is nothing other than its *politeia*.'

5 On the metaphysical explanatory role of causes (*aitiai*) see Freeland (1991) and Charles (2000: 348–72).

Aristotle's initial characterisation of the polis as a composite whole of citizens (considered as parts) in *Politics* III suggests that both the polis and the *politeia* are best understood through a prior analysis of citizenship and the citizen (*politēs*) (III.1, 1274b39–42).[6] Following the method of breaking wholes down into component parts the focus of *Politics* III.1–5 is accordingly on puzzles raised by citizenship. Aristotle's first, tentative, definition of the notion of *politeia* in the *Politics* is thus as a certain ordered arrangement (*taxis*) of the residents of the polis (1274b38).

The primary ordering (*taxis*) referred to in Aristotle's first definition of *politeia* is between residents (*oikountōn*) of the city who are and are not citizens. This raises doubts as to whether citizenship can have explanatory priority over the *politeia*. As component parts of the polis, citizens may in a sense comprise the polis, but a polis is not a mere collection or aggregate of citizens. Some principle of *unity and order* is necessary to provide a criterion of membership for citizenship in the first instance. Aristotle thus concludes that different kinds of citizen are best explained by reference to different forms of *politeia* (III.5, 1278a15–16) and offers a second definition as follows:

> The *politeia* is an ordered arrangement (*taxis*) of a city (*poleōs*) with respect to its offices (*archōn*), particularly the one that has authority over all matters (*kurias pantōn*). For the government is everywhere authoritative over the polis (*kurion men gar pantachou to politeuma tēs poleōs*) and the *politeia* is the government (*politeuma d' estin hē politeia*). I mean, for example, that in democracies the people (*dēmos*) have authority (*kurios*), while by contrast it is the few (*hoi d' oligoi*) in oligarchies (III.6, 1278b9–15).[7]

This second definition identifies the *politiea* with a particular ordered arrangement of offices and hence the government or the ruling body (*politeuma*).[8] An oligarchy, for example, finds its principle of arrangement in the fact that the wealthy (few) occupy positions of authority and organise the ruling offices to reflect their own (in this case partisan and hence defective) political conception. The second definition, worked out on the basis of Aristotle's dialectical treatment of puzzles concerning

6 Early instances of *politeia* (e.g. Herodotus 9.34) refer more to 'the condition of being a citizen' than a political system or set of foundational laws. See Schofield (2006: 33). Although the concept of the *politeia* as a political system or arrangement – with its attendant laws and customs – is identifiable in Plato's *Politeia* and (pseudo) Xenophon's *Politeia of the Spartans* (c. 394), a close connection with citizenship is retained.

7 Aristotle's identification of government (*politeuma*) with the *politeia* associates citizenship in the active sense with participation in rule. On the distinction between active and passive citizenship see Keyt (2017: 236–7). Passive citizenship (which does not include manual workers, slaves, women and metics) is the citizenship of a free male who is not an active participant in political rule or office (*Pol.* III.5, 1278a16–17).

8 Interestingly, late nineteenth century commentators offer more clear-sighted glosses of this passage than some contemporary scholars. Susemihl and Hicks (1894: 381) suggest that it is 'an emphatic way of stating . . . that the character of the constitution is determined by the holders of . . . power'. Newman (1887: II. 264–5) argues that the expression *taxis* refers here specifically to the distribution of political power.

citizenship, is thus the more authoritative insofar as it points to the fact that it is the dominant group in a political community which determines its institutional structure and its laws.[9]

Both of Aristotle's definitions of the *politeia* identify it with an ordered arrangement (*taxis*).[10] As seen in Chapter 2, for Aristotle the source of the ordering of the parts of the polis in the central case is the *nomothetēs* or architectonic legislator. The constitution in an Aristotelian sense is hence an ordering of offices in conformity with the political commitments of its founder(s) or ruler(s). In the central case, architectonic acts of law-making privilege virtue and wellbeing and the constitutional order will reflect this correct interpretation of the good. In reality, of course, it is the partisan interests of the ruling group which tend to order the constitution. The laws of a polis, in both of these cases, depend upon the form of its constitution as determined by the ends that are privileged among its dominant element.

Aristotle's claim that the *politeia* is, in a way, the life (*bios*) of the city (IV.11, 1295a40) completes the picture.[11] The discussion of *politeiai* in the *Rhetoric* helps to elucidate this claim. Here Aristotle counsels deliberative speakers to pay heed to the *telos* of each *politeia*. This reflects the orientation of different activities, and hence implicitly ways of life, by diverse ends (*teloi*), which are in turn manifested in particular constitutional forms (*Rh.* I.8, 1366a1–15). Democracy is oriented by the end (*telos*) of freedom, oligarchy by wealth, aristocracy by virtue (*aretē*) and tyranny by self-preservation (cf. *NE* V.3, 1131a25–8). As each group pursues participation in happiness in a different manner, Aristotle says in the *Politics*, they also make for themselves different modes of life and constitutions (*tous te bious heterous poiountai kai tas politeias*) (*Pol.* VII.8, 1328b1–2). Pursuit of diverse conceptions of happiness thus determines the different forms (*eidē*) of constitution. The best constitution (*tēn aristēn politeian*) is guided by the best end (*telos*) (VII.2, 1325a14). Each constitutional form has a distinctive character determined by the political commitments – most fundamentally a conception of the good life – prevalent among its authoritative citizens.

9 Simpson (1998: 148) correctly notes Aristotle's identification of the *politeia* with (the arrangement of) a body of persons (rather than a system of 'higher' laws in the modern sense). See also Kraut (2002: 15).

10 See note 7, Chapter 1. The Aristotelian *Athenian Constitution* also employs the term *taxis* liberally in its description of Athenian constitutional history. See, in particular, III. 1 and IV. 1.

11 Aristotle's identification of the *politeia* with the *bios* of the city is not unqualified: it holds 'in a sense (*tis*)'. The assumption that there is a close relationship between the way of life of a polis (in a broad sense incorporating arrangements for the birth and habituation of children) and its constitution is ubiquitous in the earlier *politeia* literature. Apart from the most obvious example – Plato's *Republic* – both Critias and (pseudo) Xenophon in their works *Politeia of the Spartans* focus more on education, women and child rearing than arrangement of political offices. In theorising the best constitution guided by the most choiceworthy way of life (*bios*) (*Pol.* VII.1, 1323a16), Aristotle also speaks of forms of arrangement (*taxis*) for the establishment of agoras, marketplaces, gymnasia and administration of country life (e.g. VII.12, 1331b7–14).

Even if one accepts this analysis of the *politeia*, there are apparent obstacles to the application of formal causes, considered as scientific explanatory principles, to the political domain. In the first instance, the distinction between theoretical knowledge, oriented by truth, and practical knowledge, oriented by action (*Met.* II.1, 993b20; *NE* I.3, 1095a5, II.1, 1103b26–9 and X.9, 1179b2–4) might be taken to entail that principles of causal explanation have a limited role in political science.

As noted in the previous two chapters, Aristotle operates with a broader and a narrower notion of science (*epistēmē*). Political science falls within the broader conception of *Metaphysics* VI.1 and includes both a universalist theoretical knowledge and a particularist 'experience-based knowledge' concerned with applications (*NE* I.2, 1094a27–b10).[12] The practical works assume, as *Nicomachean Ethics* X.9 makes particularly clear, that politics is amenable to analysis of what occurs for the most part (*hōs epi to polu*) and from this perspective there is no principled reason to exclude causal analysis from political science.[13] One must also attend to the distinction between a discipline's proximate and ultimate aims. While political enquiry *ultimately* aims at good action, rather than truth, theoretical knowledge relevant to the philosophy of human affairs can be one of its proximate goals. A correct understanding of the ends of action, for example, presupposes knowledge of the voluntary and involuntary (*EE* II.10, 1226b16–37).[14] Aristotle's discussion of virtue in *Nicomachean Ethics* II.3–6, framed as an enquiry into the *ti esti* or 'what is it?' of virtue (1105a19), is another instructive example. The ultimate aim of this enquiry is good action, but it is nonetheless a search for the essence of virtue. For Aristotle, accordingly, a 'theoretical study extrinsic to some practical activity may inform that activity without even partially constituting that activity'.[15]

A more specific concern is that viewing the Aristotelian *politeia* as a formal cause might be thought inseparable from an implausible organic concept of the polis. Schütrumpf, in this context, has rightly critiqued the view that the polis is a natural substance admitting of a metaphysical analysis in terms of the four explanatory causes.[16] A substance cannot be composed of substances on Aristotelian assumptions (*Met.* VII.13, 1039a3–4, VII.17, 1041a4–5) and the inhabitants of a polis are substances. At most, the polis is a 'quasi-substance' because composed 'according to nature'.[17]

In order to see why attribution of an explanatory role to causes (*aitiai*) in Aristotle's political thought is independent of the view that the polis is a natural substance, it is

12 Reeve (2017: xxvi).

13 Nielsen (2015: 29–48).

14 Henry and Nielsen (2015: 3) and Shields (2015: 237). See also Anagnostopoulos (1994).

15 Shields (2015: 237).

16 See Schütrumpf's critique (1991 i: 104–7) of Neschke-Hentschke's (1971) attempt to establish the explanatory function of the four causes as '*metapolitischen Strukturprinzipien*'.

17 Keyt (2017: 16).

instructive to recall the theory's function. According to Aristotle, one does not have knowledge of a thing without grasping its 'why' or 'because' (*to dia to peri hekaston*) (*Ph.* II.3, 194b19; *APo.* I.2, 71b9–11). The material cause is that 'out of which something becomes' (*to ex hou gignetai ti*) e.g. the bronze of a statue (*Ph.* II.3, 194b24). The formal cause is the form or archetype (*to eidos kai to paradeigma*), which is also the rational intelligibility or essence (and its genera) of a thing (*ho logos ho tou to hēn einai kai ta toutou gene*) (*Ph.* II.3, 194b27–9; *Met.* V.2, 1013a26–9; *APo.* II.11, 94a21–30) e.g. the shape or intelligible structure of a statue or the ratio 2:1 and number as the causes of the octave.[18] A third kind of cause (the so-called 'efficient' cause) is the starting point of change (*hē archē tēs metabolēs*) e.g. as a father is the cause of his child (*Ph.* II.3, 194b30–2). With respect to artificial kinds such as a statue, the principle of change is readily understood as the statue-maker or artisan, although Aristotle suggests it is the expertise which is the real 'efficient' cause (*Ph.* II.3, 195b21–5). The final cause is the end (*telos*) or the 'for the sake of which' (*hou heneka*) something is done in the sense that health can serve as a final cause for someone engaged in the activity of walking (194b34–5).

Aristotle's account is better understood as a theory of 'becauses' in the sense of metaphysical explanatory principles than as a theory of causes in the modern sense.[19] Although the relationship between causality and explanation in Aristotle is tighter than in modern conceptions, the theory of causes is a 'theory about the structure of explanations'.[20] An explanation of the formal cause seeks out the essence of a part of reality by reference to what binds together its constituent parts (see *Met.* VII.17, 1041b5ff). The primary role of formal causes is to serve in metaphysical explanations of the structure of reality by reference to unity-providing structural constituents.[21]

Schütrumpf's critique of the application of the theory of causes to Aristotle's political theory correctly assumes as its first premise the falsity of a strong metaphysical reading of the polis as a natural substance. As suggested in Chapter 2, the most compelling reading of Aristotle's political naturalism is that nature and the legislator are 'co-operative causes' of the polis i.e. the natural impulse to political community

18 The definitions in *Physics* II.3 and *Metaphysics* V.2 refer to the form (*eidos*), the essence (*to ti ēn einai*) or the 'what it is to be' something, the substance (*tēn ousian*) and the whole or synthesis (*Ph.* II.3, 195a20; *Met.* V.2, 1013b22–3). The form is also identified with actualisation of potential such that, for example, in the case of an artificial object the impression of a form upon matter constitutes a synthesis involving the actualisation of intelligible structure. Difficulties with the explication of the causes by reference to the statue example are discussed in Sprague (1968) and Todd (1976), but these are not directly relevant to my concerns here.

19 Annas (1982: 319).

20 Moravcsik (1974: 3). For the links between causality, explanation and necessity see Stein (2011: 2012).

21 Moravcsik (1974: 8–9). Insofar as they feature in *explanations* of the structure of reality, formal causes can also be understood from an epistemological perspective. See Stein (2011, 706): 'The four causes are, from the start, held to be crucial to our knowledge-seeking activity as well as to the structure of the world.'

must be supplemented by human intention (*Pol.* I.2, 1253a30–2).[22] On the one hand, the polis is an ordered whole that emerges from more basic associations such as the family and the village because of natural impulses (1252b30–1253a1). On the other hand, a necessary condition for the establishment of the political association is the expertise of the true legislator (II.8, 1268b34–8, II.12, 1273b30–3, III.12, 1282b14–16, VII.4, 1325b40–1326a5).[23] This picture is consistent, however, with the thesis that *politeia* is a formal cause insofar as Aristotle employs the theory of causes to explain the unity and identity-conditions of artefacts as well as natural substances (*Phy.* II.3; *Met.* V.2).[24] Even an interpretation of the polis as primarily an artefact of human practical intelligence hence in no way precludes the use of formal causes in political science.

The applicability of the theory of explanatory causes to politics cannot be impugned simply because it is implausible to view the polis metaphysically as a natural substance. Indeed, insofar as the function of the theory of explanatory causes is to explain the 'why' or 'because' of particular phenomena, then it may be enlivened on any occasion when we seek knowledge.[25] Such an application of causal analysis to the practical domain is most explicit in *Eudemian Ethics* I.6:

> One should not, even when pursuing politics, consider as superfluous the kind of theory (*theōrian*) which makes clear not only what (*to ti*) something is, but also its cause (*to dia ti*). For such is the philosophical approach in all fields of enquiry. This does, however, require a good deal of caution (*EE* 1216b35–40).

The need for caution, Aristotle implies, follows from the fact that people without practical experience or insight engage in arguments which are extraneous to the matters at hand (1217a3–7). Merely because some theorists (these comments recall the critique of the sophists in Book X.9 of the *Nicomachean Ethics*) apply theoretical principles of explanation to the practical domain in a mistaken way, does not entail that such an application is methodologically illegitimate.

22 Miller (1991: 296).

23 Reeve (2009: 517).

24 The non-coincidence of final and formal causes in Aristotle's analysis of the polis supports its status as at least in part a product of human intention. In the natural realm of 'for the most part' regularities, the final cause is the fully developed form of the thing and hence there can be a coincidence of formal and final causes (*Ph.* II.8, 199a31; *DA.* II.4, 415b10; *GA.* I.1, 715a4ff). In the case of living organisms, for example, the starting point of change (e.g. the father) is a living organism of the same kind, so that the formal, final and 'efficient' causes can coincide (*Ph.* II.7, 198a25). Aristotle's examples in *Physics* II.3 and *Metaphysics* V.2 suggest that the coincidence of different causes is less applicable for artefacts than it is in the natural realm strictly speaking.

25 As noted in the next section, the opening arguments of both *Nicomachean Ethics* and the *Politics* appeal to the good as the final cause of action (*NE* I.1, 1094a1–3; *Pol.* I.1, 1252a1–3). The argument of Book VI.2 of the *Nicomachean Ethics* also suggests that choice (*prohairesis*) is rightly viewed as the 'efficient' cause of action.

With all these points in mind – in particular the methodological acknowledgement of the need to ask the '*dia ti*' question in political science – there is little reason to disregard Aristotle's reference to kinds (*eidē*) in the *Politics* as an application of formal explanatory analysis. In *Politics* V.5, for example, Aristotle asserts the need to theorise political phenomena by reference to the different *form* of each constitution (*kath hekaston d' eidos politeias ek toutōn merizontas ta sumbainonta dei theōrein*) (*Pol.* 1304b19–20). This theorisation of constitutional kinds corresponds neatly with the general account of formal causes outlined above. As an ordering (*taxis*) of citizens and offices, the *politeia* is an archetype which provides a principle of intelligibility to the polis (*Ph.* II.3, 194b27–9; *Met.* V.2, 1013a26–9; *APo.* II.11, 94a21–30). Insofar as the polis is a composite whole made up of different parts, it is a synthesis ordered according to structural principles (*Met.* V.2, 1013b22–3; cf. *Ph.* II.3, 195a20). Considered as the way of life of the polis, moreover, the *politeia* is an organising principle akin to the soul of an organism (*Pol.* III.3, 1276b7–8, IV.4, 1291a24–8). When combined with Aristotle's frequent references in the *Politics* to different forms (*eidē*) of *politeia* (and even different forms of the kinds of *politeia*), then this provides solid evidence that the constitution serves as a formal principle of intelligibility which binds together constituent parts of the polis.

Aristotelian causes are, however, principles of explanation and it is at this level that the fruitfulness of viewing the *politeia* as a formal cause needs to be assessed. One important explanatory role of formal causes is that a rational account of the essence (*to ti ēn einai*) or 'what it is to be' of kinds of entity allows us to fix their identity-conditions. It is telling in this context that Aristotle explicitly invokes the concept of the *politeia* to provide the criterion of identity for political communities.[26]

The question of the criterion of identity for a polis frames the discussion in *Politics* III. Aristotle here introduces the problem of political attribution i.e. whether instances of political action should be attributed to the polis or to the particular form of government that is prevailing in the polis (e.g. Athens or the Athenian democracy) (*Pol.* III.1, 1274b35–6). A related dispute concerns, as discussed above, the nature of the citizen insofar as what constitutes a citizen in a democracy will not be the same as in an oligarchy (1275a3–5). From an explanatory perspective, what is sought in both cases is a principled basis on which to assert that a polis is the same across time and circumstance.

Aristotle's answer to the puzzle is that a polis may be considered the same by reference to its *politeia* considered as a form of the compound. The relevant passage is worth quoting at length:

> For if the polis is a type of community (*koinōnia*), and if it is a community of citizens sharing in a *politeia*, if the *politeia* becomes and remains different in kind (*tō eidei*), it might be held that the polis as well is necessarily not the same (*tēn autēn*). At any rate, just as we assert a chorus which is at one time comic and another

[26] On this point see Newman (1887: I. 211) and Susemihl and Hicks (1894: 380).

> tragic is different even though the human beings in at are often the same, it is similar with any other community and any compound (*sunthesin*), when the compound takes a different form (*eidos*) – e.g. we would say that mode is different even when the notes are the same, if it is at one time Dorian and at another time Phrygian. If this is indeed the case, it is evident that it is looking to the *politeia* (*eis tēn politeian blepontas*) above all that the polis must be said to be the same; the name one calls it can be different or the same no matter whether the same human beings inhabit it or altogether different ones (*Pol.* III.3, 1276b1–13).

In the case of the dramatic form, the identical matter is the humans who make up the chorus. The *teloi* of different genres determine structural differences in the way that the activity of the chorus is organised. The musical analogy is more complex because Aristotle is asserting that the diverse modes are sufficient to establish that we are dealing with different musical kinds, despite the fact that the obvious candidate for the formal cause – the structure of the notes – remains the same. Just as notes are insufficient to provide a principle of identity, reference to citizens – considered as the constituents that make up the polis – cannot provide the necessary identity criteria. As Aristotle notes a little earlier, reference to the territory or location (1276a34–6) in which a polis happens to be situated also does not resolve whether we are considering the same polis or not. In the same way that a pile of bricks and wooden planks is insufficient to constitute a house without a particular end and structure, a collection of people in a particular place is insufficient to constitute a polis. It is therefore the *politeia* which serves as the principle of unity binding together different political parts and it is this which serves as the required basis for accurate attributions of identity.[27]

Aristotle's conception of the constitution as a formal unifying principle of component parts is also evident in his comparison of forms of *politeia* with kinds of animals. All *politeiai* possess multiple parts. It is the combination of these into a structured whole that determines the different species:

> When all the possible combination [of the parts] are taken they will all produce the animal species (*eidē zōou*), and there will be as many species (*eidē*) of the animal as there are combinations of the necessary parts: hence in the same way we also classify the varieties of the *politeia* (*Pol.* IV.4, 1290b35–9).

In 'describing the change and persistence of a political community', Aristotle thus 'relies on something parallel to the particular form that persists through the growth of an organism'.[28] The relationship between matter and form clearly differs for natural organisms and political associations that result from an interplay of nature

[27] Aristotle's use of the *politeia* as the formal principle of political unity may be contrasted with the Bodinian view, concomitant with the rise of modern sovereignty, that what makes a state is 'its common subjection under one and the same *imperium*, an authority supreme over all the others'. See Lee (2016: 172).

[28] Irwin (1988: 254).

and artifice. In both cases the formal cause nonetheless serves as an explanatory principle of unity and identity. The relevant parts of the polis in this comparison are not individuals taken in an aggregative sense, but the different kinds of individuals that make up a polis divided according to their functions in sustaining the community (1290b39–1291a18). The *politeia* as the form of a composite is thus an ordered arrangement of parts.

The explanatory centrality of the *politeia* to political science ultimately rests on its status as a formal principle of unity for the polis. For Aristotle, unity (*to hen*) and being (*to on*) are the same and there are also as many types of being as there are unity (*Met.* IV.2, 1003b23–4). As the critique of Plato in *Politics* II.2 suggests, the polis should be regarded as an articulated unity made up of different parts, rather than something one in the same way as an individual person. The application of formal causes in constitutional analysis allows Aristotle to develop this alternative account of the polis as an articulated whole made up of component parts.

Aristotle's account of the *politeia* seems to be complicated by the identification of different kinds *within* the main regime types.[29] Once one considers the forms (*eidē*) of *politeia* that already exist (*Pol.* IV.1, 1289a8), then there is more than one kind of democracy and oligarchy (1289a10, 1289b14). This plurality follows from the different ways of organising offices even within specific constitutional forms (1289b15–16). There are thus as many forms of *politeia* as modes of arrangement (*taxeis*) of the offices (IV.3, 1290a6–11), even though these structures can be grouped under general constitutional forms in line with diverse conceptions of the practical ends of the regime, justice and the common advantage.[30] In considering the four main forms (*eidē*) of democracy (IV.4, 1291b31ff), for example, Aristotle notes variations in arrangement that nonetheless reflect a common view of justice. The identification of political justice with the form (*eidos*) and order (*taxis*) of a polis – its *politeia* (III.3, 1276a17–b34) – thus explains why different kinds of the main regime-types are nonetheless still governed by an overarching principle of unity.

All of these considerations militate against a deflationary view according to which Aristotle's account of the *politeia* as an ordered arrangement of political elements rests on a loose appeal to the notion of forms or kinds rather than formal causes understood as explanatory principles. Such a deflationary reading overlooks that the theory of causes – as outlined in *Physics* II.3 and *Metaphysics* V.2 – is designed to play a particular theoretical role which it manifestly does play in Aristotle's political science, namely to provide an answer to the '*dia to*' question which culminates in knowledge of the phenomena under

[29] On the implications of this fine-grained analysis for Aristotle's constitutional theory see Riesbeck (2016a).

[30] Elsewhere (*Pol.* V.8, 1308b32–3) Aristotle implies that the particular arrangement of the laws and the administration structures the *politeia*.

investigation. Aristotle's account of the *politeia* as a formal cause explains the identity and unity of political communities and renders intelligible the structure of diverse constitutional arrangements. Given that Aristotle also repeatedly employs the term *aitia* in his discussion of kinds of regime in Book IV of the *Politics* (IV, 3. 1289b26–8; IV.4, 1290b21; 1291b15) a refusal to acknowledge the application of causes to constitutional analysis is unmotivated.

SECTION 2 CONSTITUTIONAL RELATIVITY AND THE ENDS OF THE REGIME

As the formal cause of the polis, the *politeia* is the principle of unity which provides a criterion of identity for particular kinds of political community. In this second section, I demonstrate that the structure of different kinds of *politeia* is determined by diverse conceptions of *eudaimonia*. The constitutional relativity of *nomos* in turn entails that a political community's laws reflect the conception of the good prevalent among its authoritative members or the most powerful participants in the regime. Politics is hence constitutive for *nomos* both in the narrower sense that laws are enacted relative to specific political forms and the broader sense that their content is informed by a particular conception of the good. Aristotle's account of constitutional forms and their derivative laws thus ultimately rests on his teleological theory of the ends of human action.

Aristotle's commitment to the constitutional relativity of law is introduced in the context of the *Politics* III.12 search for the authoritative (*kurios*) element of the polis. Candidates include the best (*tous aristous*), the decent (*tous epieikeis*), the wealthy (*tous plousious*), the multitude (*to plēthos*), one who is best of all (*ton beltiston hena pantōn*), a tyrant (*turannon*) or the laws (*tous nomous*) (1281a11–13, 40–3). Aristotle provisionally concludes his search by stating that the laws should be authoritative when they are enacted correctly, but that rulers should be authoritative over those matters about which law (on account of its universality) cannot deal precisely (1282b1–6). This raises the question as to how we are to assess the goodness or justness of laws, which leads Aristotle in turn to state the following on the relationship between laws and the constitution:

> Laws are necessarily poor or excellent (*anankē tous nomous phaulous hē spoudaios einai*) and just or unjust in a manner similar to the constitutions (*tais politais*) to which they belong: if nothing else, it is evident that laws should be enacted with a view to the constitution (*dei pros tēn politeian keisthai tous nomous*). But if this is the case, it is clear that those enacted in accordance with the correct constitutions (*tas orthas politeias*) are necessarily (*anankaion*) just, and those in accordance with deviant ones, unjust (III.11, 1282b8–13).

As will be considered in detail in Chapter 4, what principally distinguishes correct constitutional forms from their defective counterparts is that the former aim at the common advantage (*to koine[i] sumpheron*) whereas the latter aim at the private advantage of the rulers (*Pol.* III.6, 1279a18–39). Insofar as the common advantage is identified with political justice and a lawful ordering of the polis (III.12, 1282b17–18), then it follows that the excellence and justice of laws depends on the excellence and justice of constitutional forms. Aristotle's commitment to the constitutional relativity of law is hence robust and seems to entail that just regimes *always* enact just laws and unjust regimes unjust laws. The strength of this thesis is only explicable in terms of Aristotle's prioritisation of final causes in his political science, such that the ends of the regime impart excellence and justice (or their contraries) to its laws by a kind of normative transitivity.

In *Politics* IV.2, Aristotle clarifies law's constitutional relativity with the statement that laws should be enacted – and are all in fact enacted – with a view to the constitutions, and not constitutions established with a view to the laws (*pros gar tas politeias tous nomous dei tithesthai and tithentai pantes, all' ou tas politeias pros tous nomous*) (1289a14–15). While consistent with the statement from III.12, this second passage confirms that constitutional relativity is a descriptive claim about the actual enactment (*tithentai*) of laws. In a descriptive sense, laws are enactments regarding correct and incorrect conduct, which ultimately reflect the priorities and commitments of the ruling element of the political community. In a normative sense, just regimes, as noted above, seek to enact laws that are consistent with the common advantage. Even in the case of defective or unjust regimes, as Chapter 5 will examine, it is true in a sense that laws should be enacted consistently with the regime-type, if only from the perspective of an internal consistency with the commitments of the ruling element that is conducive to the secondary political goal of stability.

Aristotle continues this passage by repeating his standard characterisation of the *politeia* as an ordered arrangement (*taxis*) of offices. Crucially, however, the ordering of authoritative positions is here explicitly referred back to the end or purpose of the community (*to telos hekastēs tēs koinōnias*), which varies across diverse kinds of constitution (*Pol.* IV.1, 1289a15–18). This statement should be read in conjunction with the passage from the *Rhetoric*, cited in Section 1, asserting the determination of constitutional forms by different conceptions of the correct human end. For while the human *telos* is commonly agreed to be *eudaimonia* (*NE* I.7, 1097b22), it is pursued in diverse ways. And the pursuit of these ends (pleasure, honour and reason or wisdom) is ultimately the choice for different ways of life (the apolaustic, the political and the philosophic) (1096b23–4):

> Since happiness (*eudaimonia*) is the best thing, and this is the actualisation of virtue (*aretēs energeia*) and a certain complete practice of it (*chrēsis tis teleios*), and since it happens that some persons are able to partake of it while other are able to do so only to a small degree or not at all, it is clear that this is the cause of their being several kinds (*eidē*) and varieties of city and several sorts of regime (*politeias pleious*). For it

is through the hunting for this in a different manner and by means of different things that individuals create ways of life and regimes that differ (*tous te bious heterous poiountai kai tas politeias*) (*Pol.* VII.8, 1328a37–b2).

Politics is concerned with the ultimate human good (*NE* I.2, 1094b7) and it hence stands to reason that alternative conceptions of the best life would inform diverse constitutional arrangements. On the assumption that the *politeia* is a formal cause, and that the final cause in practical affairs is *eudaimonia*, then regimes are ultimately determined by different conceptions of the correct ends of a human life.[31] The dependence of the content of the laws on the commitments of the dominant political element hence reflects the teleological structure of Aristotle's constitutional theory.

The thesis that the final cause of action – *eudaimonia* – is determinative of architectonic legislative activity and the form taken by different kinds of *politeia* is also readily intelligible on Aristotelian assumptions regarding the nature of scientific explanations. Aristotle defends the explanatory priority of final over 'efficient' causes in both the natural and the productive realms (*PA.* I.1, 639b12–640a26).[32] This priority reflects the principle that generation is for the sake of substance (*genesis heneka tēs ousias*) rather than vice–versa (640a18–19). Although the principle paradigmatically applies in the natural realm, Aristotle nonetheless contends that the activity of building a house is only explicable on the basis of the end of building the house (639b27). The same explanatory priority of final causes applies in the realm of practical affairs, as demonstrated most vividly by Aristotle's invocation of the good as the end of all human activities and intentions at the start of the *Nicomachean Ethics* and the *Politics* (*NE* I.1, 1094a1–2; *Pol.* I.1, 1252a1–7). Aristotle's theory of constitutions likewise postulates the *telos* of the regime as determinative of its establishment and structure.

Aristotle notes that some laws 'stand out' (*kechōrismenoi*) as indicative of the ends of the regime and that rulers must particularly guard these from transgression (*Pol.* IV.1, 1289a18–25). This suggests that there is a privileged subset of laws for each constitutional form which conforms to the ends of its authoritative element. One can consider, for example, laws on the appointment to offices and property. Aristotle characterises as paradigmatically oligarchical laws which stipulate the need for elections and property assessments, and as paradigmatically democratic laws which stipulate the selection of offices by lot without property assessments (*Pol.* IV.9, 1294b1–40). In his enumeration of different kinds of oligarchy, Aristotle also notes that rulers proceed from the laws concerning appointment to offices to the enactment of inheritance laws requiring that sons succeed their fathers in order to maintain control of property (IV.7, 1293a25–30). The content of oligarchical laws

31 This, as Kontos (2018: 85) notes, entails that 'deviant constitutions are deviant in that they are premised on a mistaken conception of *eudaimonia* and this mistake renders them unjust too'.

32 See also Code (1997: 127–43).

regarding selection of offices and property thus both reflect and serve to support a constitutional form which is consistent with the interests and the priorities of the wealthy few.

The teleological normative structure of Aristotle's constitutional analysis is further exemplified by the treatment of democracy in *Politics* VI.1–2. Aristotle here identifies freedom (*eleutheria*) as the fundamental assumption (*hupothesis*) at which all democracies aim (*stochazesthai*) (*Pol.* 1317a40–1317b2). Associated with the democratic prioritisation of the end of freedom is a commitment to being ruled and ruling in turn (*en merei archesthai kai archein*) (1317b3), as this participation in rule is viewed as an aspect of liberty (*eleutherias*). Such a commitment matches what Aristotle refers to as a demotic conception of justice (*to dikaion to dēmotikon*) whereby equality (*to ison*) is determined arithmetically rather than according to worth (*kat' axian*) (1317b4). Another aspect of freedom privileged in the democratic constitution is the capacity for a person to live as they wish (*to zēn hōs bouletai tis*) (1317b12). In a constitution structured around the aim of freedom and a demotic conception of justice, the multitude must necessarily be authoritative (*kurion*) (1317b6).

As noted above, different kinds of *politeia* also reflect diverse conceptions of justice (*Pol.* III.9, 1280a8–9).[33] This claim is a corollary of the priority of ends, for it is only the correct regimes aiming at the common advantage which are just simply speaking (*aplōs dikaion*) (III.6, 1279a17–20). One-sided conceptions of justice arise because people make partisan judgements regarding equality and inequality due to their own self-interest. In discussing the extreme forms of democracy, Aristotle hence states that they are determined by a one-sided democratic conception of justice according to which equality is determined arithmetically in abstraction from merit (VI.2, 1318a5–7). Such a view of justice – associated with democratic assumptions about freedom (1317b19–20) – directly shapes laws which are paradigmatically regarded as democratic, including election to offices of all from all, restrictions on the duration of offices and low property qualifications (1317b2ff.). These institutional structures in turn determine the justice or otherwise of the laws.

The determination of diverse kinds of constitution and laws by different conceptions of *eudaimonia* is also applicable in the case of the best regime. In the opening of Book VII of the *Politics*, Aristotle asserts that a theorist seeking to establish the best constitution (*politeias aristēs*) must necessarily engage in a prior investigation of the most choice-worthy way of life (*airetōtatos bios*) (*Pol.* 1323a15–16). Working from a threefold categorisation of goods (1323a27), Aristotle predictably upholds the traditional Socratic ordering, whereby bodily and external goods are instrumental to the true goods of the soul associated with human excellence, and hence less choice-worthy (1323b23). In determining the structure of the best *politeia* it is thus necessary to attend to the axiom that a person is happy (*eudaimōn*) to the extent that

33 Irwin (1988: 449).

they possess virtue and practical wisdom (*aretēs kai phronēseōs*) (1323b22–4). The role of the true legislative expert can here be seen particularly vividly as the enactment of constitutions and laws consistent with the true conception of *eudaimonia*.

Aristotle's *Politics* VII discussion of education further corroborates the dependence of constitutional forms, and their laws, on the *telos* of the regime. The true law-giver should prioritise the correct upbringing of the young above all with an awareness that education norms reflect the ends of a constitutional order. Each constitutional form has its own character (*ethos*) and education should be conducted with a view to each kind of constitution. A failure of the legislator to keep in mind the democratic or oligarchic character of a constitutional order in the formulation of education norms inevitably harms the prevailing regime (*Pol.* VIII.1, 1337a10–18). The ends of a particular constitutional order are in the first instance a function of the characters of its citizens, or the dominant citizens. Yet once a regime is in place, then the dominant class, in order to remain stable in power, must attempt to mould the characters of citizens through habituation in laws reflective of a regime's conception of the good. From the perspective of architectonic legislation, or law-making in the focal sense, legislation should therefore assist citizens to develop virtuous or 'quasi-virtuous' characters consistent with the particular ends of their regime. In the majority of cases, the best the law-maker will be able to do is promote incomplete virtue, through the preservation and improvement of a less than perfect constitutional regime (*Pol.* III.4, 1276b28–34).

There is accordingly evidence across the *Politics* as a whole that it is the choice for different conceptions of *eudaimonia* which ultimately determines each regime-form.[34] This interpretation also further explains Aristotle's qualified identification of the *politeia* with the way of life (*bios*) of the polis in *Politics* IV.11. Aristotelian constitutions are purposeful in the sense that they are directed towards a determinate end (*Pol.* III.6, 1278b23, III.9, 1280b39, IV.1, 1289a17, VII.2, 1324a14).[35] It is fully intelligible, then, that laws within any particular constitutional regime – which is itself a structured unity determined by a *telos* – correspondingly reflect a particular conception of the ends of human life. Laws about what one ought to do and ought not to do, that is to say, reflect a conception of the human good that is derivative from constitutional forms structured by diverse ends. Legislators – both architectonic and 'ordinary' – establish constitutions and enact laws in conformity with their own conception of the good. Once a constitutional form is in place, with its associated arrangement of offices, then the laws enacted under that regime will necessarily follow the authoritative opinions of those in positions of rulership. As Aristotle states explicitly, this is not only the case on a descriptive level, but has a normative

34 Aristotle's thematisation of the dependence of constitutions on diverse views of the good – and the concomitant normative priority of constitutional forms – provides some justification for the otherwise unfair objection in II.5 that Plato's *Laws* focuses too much on laws, and not enough on the *politeia* (*Pol.* 1265a1–2).

35 Fortenbaugh (1991: 229).

dimension. The effectiveness of legislation is dependent upon its consistency with the conception of the good which informs a political community's arrangements for distribution of offices, honours and external or material goods.

The constitutional relativity of law thus entails that those in positions of authority within a regime will enact laws which reflect their own, often implicit, conception of the good of the polis. Or, more precisely, those in correct constitutional regimes will enact such laws, while those in defective regimes will enact laws which suit their private or sectional interests (*Pol.* III.6, 1279a18–39). This could be taken to suggest that all law is necessarily partisan. At the very least, it would seem that Aristotle accepts one part of Thrasymachus' argument in Plato's *Republic* (338c–339a). For Aristotle, as for Thrasymachus, laws are laid down by rulers as occupants of positions of authority and it would be naïve to think that such laws do not reflect particular conceptions of the good and consequent conceptions of political justice. And although a monarchical or aristocratic regime guided by the end of virtue is the best from an Aristotelian perspective, it remains the case that its laws are necessarily relative to a particular conception of the good. Aristotle's view can of course be distinguished from Thrasymachus' by reference to the distinction between regimes guided by the common advantage (*to koine[i] sumpheron*) and those guided by more straightforwardly partisan political conceptions. Yet this does not completely remove the concern regarding partisanship.[36] Undoubtedly, the Aristotelian common advantage serves as a normative criterion for a distinction between better and worse constitutional forms. Even in the case of regimes guided by the common advantage, however, laws reflect a conception of the good that may not be shared by all citizens. In order to determine whether the constitutional relativity of law makes it inescapable that law is partisan, it is helpful to consider its applicability to the best constitution.

SECTION 3 THE BEST CONSTITUTION BY NATURE AND POLITICAL PARTISANSHIP

Aristotle asserts that there is only one constitution that is everywhere according to nature the best (*mia monon pantachou kata phusin hē aristē*) (NE V.7, 1135a5). An obvious corollary of this claim, given the constitutional relativity of law, is that laws enacted in the best regime will also be the best according to nature. Yet although the laws of the best regime serve, on Aristotelian assumptions, as an ideal standard, they also remain determined by a particular conception of the good. This points to a potential ambiguity in the application of the constitutional relativity of law to the best regime. The laws of the best regime are, for Aristotle, clearly determined by the *correct* conception of the human good. The view of *eudaimonia* that is determinative for the best regime and its laws is not, however, widely held given the

[36] Cf. *Laws* (714b, 734e).

propensity of the many to favour an *apolaustic* life (I.4, 1095b20–30). From this perspective, the laws of the best regime are partisan insofar as they reflect an unpopular philosophical view of wellbeing. In this final section, I thus consider the implications of law's constitutional relativity for the best regime and questions of partisanship.

Before I turn to the applicability of the constitutional relativity of law to the best regime, it is useful to outline some interpretative preliminaries regarding the status of the best constitution by nature. Of particular relevance are (1) the specific sort of regime the best constitution is and (2) its role as a normative exemplar for the assessment of both the correct and defective constitutional forms.

Aristotle states that the best constitution most adequately satisfies the two criteria of good regimes: those in authority rule for the sake of the common advantage rather than sectional interests (*Pol.* III.7, 1279a28–31) and participation in political office is granted on the basis of genuine merit or ethical virtue (III.13, 1283b23–40).[37] The best constitution is hence just without qualification (cf. III.17, 1287b37–41). Aristotle's discussions of the best constitution are nonetheless far from uniform across the *Politics*. Books III and IV suggest that the best regime would be either a type of absolute kingship (*pambasileia*) or an aristocracy. Of the six constitutional orders discussed in Book IV, kingship (*basileian*) is said to be the first and most divine (*prōtēs kai theotatēs*) (IV.2, 1289a40). Kingship would be the best regime on the proviso that there was someone who far exceeded all the other citizens in virtue and political expertise (III.13, 1284a3–8). Soon after these statements, however, two constitutions – absolute kingship and true aristocracy – are said to merit the title of the best constitution (IV.2, 1289a30–3). In Books VII–VIII, further complicating matters, the best constitution is presented as an arrangement where many citizens with virtue rule and are ruled in turn. This constitution appears to be an aristocracy with elements of polity (VII.13–14, 1332a34–b27).

There is nonetheless a consistent principle which unifies Aristotle's various statements on the best regime. What the different 'best regimes' share in common is the virtue of the rulers and the allocation of political offices and honours on the basis of merit.[38] The best resolution of the apparent lack of uniformity is hence to note Aristotle's acknowledgement that the prospects for one or a few people arising who exceed other citizens in virtue and goodness in the same proportion that heroes or gods surpass humans are low (*Pol.* VII.14, 1332b20–4). A prudent legislator, even assuming circumstances 'according to prayer' (*kat' euchēn*), should therefore design a best regime where citizens with virtue take turns in ruling and being ruled (1332b27–34). From this perspective, the most viable best constitution is an

37 On these criteria see Miller (1995: 191).

38 See Keyt (2017: 15): 'the one constitution to which [Aristotle] refers must be one in genus, not in species'. Supporting evidence for this view is found in Aristotle's statement at V.10, 1310b32–4 that kingship is ranked with aristocracy, because both are based upon merit. For further discussion see also Miller (1991: 192–3).

'aristocratic polity': it is aristocratic in the sense that the rulers have virtue and pursue the common advantage, but the prevalence of virtue also means that all free citizens can participate, at different stages, in the activity of ruling.[39]

Aristotle's outline of the polis 'according to prayer' and its laws in *Politics* VII–VIII hence allocates citizenship on the basis of virtue accompanied by external means (VII.1, 1323b40–1324a2). Genuine merit or virtue is the principle of distributive justice in this polis rather than wealth (as in oligarchy) or free status (as in democracy) (*NE* V.3, 1131a25–8). The end of the best polis is *eudaimonia* correctly understood as rational activity of the soul (I.7, 1098a15–17) and an actualisation and perfect employment of virtue (*Pol.* VII.8, 1328a37–8). The citizens of the best polis possess the ethical virtues – (including courage, moderation and justice (*Pol.* VII.1, 1323a32–5)) – which thus implies the practical wisdom that genuine ethical virtue presupposes. The citizens of the best polis must also have leisure from necessary material concerns so that they can lead flourishing lives by engaging in activities of virtue (VII.9, 1329a1–2). The statement that leisure is needed for philosophy in the best regime (VII.15, 1334a22–5), when read with *Nicomachean Ethics* X, suggests that Aristotle's account of the best polis in the later books of the *Politics* assumes the status of the theoretical life as the best according to nature. This is consistent with the thesis that the best person and best polis have the same end (*Pol.* VII.2, 1324a5–8, VII.3, 1325b30–2, VII.14, 1333b37, VII.15, 1334a11–13).[40] As the form of the naturally just polis, the best constitution is determined by the true human end and its laws are enacted relative to this correct conception of *eudaimonia* as rational activity.

The best regime according to nature serves as a normative ideal and exemplar for all other constitutional forms, whether they are guided by the common advantage or are truly defective.[41] The main counterargument to this interpretation is that Aristotle's constitutional analyses in Books IV–VI suggest a more 'realist' perspective according to which it is at least equally a concern of the good legislator to ensure the stability of existing regimes. While the analyses of Books I, III, VII and VIII seem to rest on normative claims derived from the ethical investigations, according to which the ultimate aim of the political community is the same as the ultimate aim of an individual, (namely the realisation of virtue and *eudaimonia*), it is not always immediately apparent how the best regime serves as a normative ideal and exemplar in Aristotle's warnings against faction and concomitant recommendations for the preservation of defective regimes in Books V and VI.

The full implications of Aristotle's emphasis upon constitutional stability will be explored in Chapter 5. For present purposes, it is sufficient to recall that the methodological differences in approach across the *Politics* can often be reconciled through considerations internal to the practical works.[42] Aristotle states explicitly in

39 See Miller (2009: 548).
40 Keyt (2017: 181).
41 Kraut (2002: 193) and Destrée (2015: 203).
42 See Kahn (1990), Rowe (1991) and Riesbeck's (2016a) recent critique of Hansen (2013).

the opening of *Politics* IV that it is part of the expertise of the law-giver to study the *politeia* from a range of perspectives including (1) the best constitution one would pray for with no external impediments, (2) the best constitution circumstances allow, (3) constitutions according to their presuppositions (*Pol.* IV.1, 1288b22–8). Just as a gymnastic trainer should be able to provide advice to elite athletes, so they should also be able to offer assistance to those with less natural gifts or ambition (1288b10–20). And in *Politics* Book II, as Lockwood has demonstrated, Aristotle employs at least four levels of analysis.[43] Regimes can be assessed by reference to their cogency and normative desirability relative to existing arrangements (*Pol.* II.2, 1261a8–15), by reference to their conformity with the 'external norm' of the best possible arrangements, by reference to the 'internal norm' of 'the fit between a constitution's laws and its fundamental principle' or 'hypothesis' (*Pol.* II.9, 1269b30–4), and in relation to their overall normative desirability. What emerges is a complex scheme for assessment of constitutional forms.

Aristotle's constitutional methodology thus allows regimes to be judged according to their own 'internal' criteria and against the benchmark of the best regime. This can be seen in the analysis of the Spartan constitution.[44] The greater part of Aristotle's critique of Sparta in II.9 concerns the lack of consistency between the hypothesis of the constitution and its actual constitutional arrangements. Aristotle criticises Spartan inattention to the habituation of women, a neglect which results in licentiousness and conflicts with the fundamental orientation of the constitution by the end of military domination (1271b1–7). Yet *Politics II*.9 also puts forward a more fundamental critique of the end of the Spartan polis that is reminiscent of Plato's reproaches in the *Laws* (625c–638b). From this perspective, the problem with the Spartan regime is that the entire arrangement of the laws is oriented by warlike virtue with a view to domination (*Pol.* 1271b1–5). Not only is warlike virtue a mere part of virtue, but the Spartans are concerned with the external goods won by virtue rather than virtue for its own sake (1271b9–11). Aristotle's advice to tyrants is suggestive of the same point. While tyranny is the worst regime (it does not qualify as a regime properly speaking), tyrants should rule in a more kinglike way (V.11, 1315a41–b4).[45] By ruling in a more kinglike way, tyrants encourage as much virtue in themselves and the citizens as is possible in the circumstances. Even in relation to a tyrannical regime, the best regime serves as a model for improvements that serve to promote a limited virtue and concern for the common advantage.

On Aristotelian assumptions, an adequate analysis of a defective constitution, understood as a deviation from the norm, is accordingly dependent upon an

43 Lockwood (2017: 353–79).

44 Lockwood (2017: 353–79).

45 Admittedly Aristotle also offers a more 'traditional' mode of preserving a tyranny through the prevention of the development of mutual trust among citizens. As Destrée suggests (2015: 219), Aristotle implies that such measures are less successful in the long run than the 'kinglike' strategy discussed above.

understanding of its shortcomings relative to the best regime. The point can indeed also be generalised to correct constitutional forms serving the common advantage (kingship, aristocracy and polity) which remain prior – in an evaluative, rather than a temporal, sense – to the defective forms (*Cat*.12. 14b4–8; *Met*. III.3, 999a13–14).[46] As purposeful, Aristotelian constitutions must be assessed by reference to their success in attaining their end, and the constitution that is best by nature provides this ultimate benchmark.

The status of the best regime by nature as a normative ideal and exemplar means that the laws enacted under that constitution are also the best by nature. Yet the conception of *eudaimonia* as rational activity in conformity with virtue which animates the structure of the best constitution might, as noted above, be considered partisan by a citizen who did not share that conception. While citizens in the best regime would presumably share the same conception of the good, it is worth considering the cogency of a possible reproach from a citizen who did not share this conception and hence regarded Aristotle's best constitution as a 'philosophical regime' in a pejorative sense i.e. as both partisan and unjust from the perspective of democratic equality.

The true founding legislator of the best constitution is presumably Aristotle himself, or at least a practically wise statesperson with an Aristotelian education. The end at which this founding legislator aims is *eudaimonia* as understood throughout the practical works (*NE* I.1, 1094b7), rather than the ends of honour or pleasure privileged in the political or apolaustic lives. Even on the assumption that in the best regime all citizens would have virtue, its status as a normative standard and exemplar thus seems dependent upon acceptance of Aristotle's entire practical teaching.

If this is true, then the laws of the best regime are partisan in the sense that they privilege the 'philosophical' conception of the good life. This much can be seen by reference to the regimen of education set out in Book VIII of the *Politics*. The function of these education laws is to promote virtue, whether, as in the case of physical education, the sorts of virtues necessary for the political common advantage, or whether, as with musical education, the kinds of virtue which facilitate intellectual development. In both cases, the ultimate aim is the formation of character to facilitate a fulfilling life of rational activity. Aristotle's education laws thus exemplify the constitutional relativity of law insofar as they are oriented to the goal of the best constitution. And this constitution again assumes that the philosophical life – as defended by Aristotle – is the best life.

While Aristotle's appeals to the common advantage as the proximate goal of correct regime forms and the rule of law both seem to mitigate this partisanship concern, they ultimately leave the constitutional relativity of law in place.

46 See Fortenbaugh (1991: 23) and Destrée (2015: 208).

Unsurprisingly, only a fully fledged defence of Aristotle's practical teaching can support the natural status of the best regime as in a sense non-partisan.

The common advantage is the advantage of all citizens, not the advantage of each member of a polis (*Pol.* III.5, 1278a32–7).[47] In the best constitution by nature, all free members of the political community are citizens and partake in the best life according to virtue (VII.13, 1332a34–5). Although in one sense the best regime is exclusionary (it denies full citizenship to slaves, women, metics, labourers etc.), in another it is inclusionary insofar as all free citizens are provided with the necessary means to engage in the activity of virtue and motivated by the same conception of *eudaimonia* (VIII.9–10, 1329a17–1330a25). The best constitution is also a regime in which equal citizens take turns in ruling and being ruled and the common advantage is genuinely the good of all citizens. This clearly contrasts with the predominant defective regimes of democracy and oligarchy. While Aristotle characterises democracy and oligarchy in terms of the rule of the many and the few, he later qualifies this in 'socio-economic' terms (i.e. it just happens that the poor tend to be in the majority and the wealthy in the minority (III.8, 1279b34–1280a6, IV.4, 1290b17–20)) and his ultimate criterion is, as the previous section suggested, teleological. Democratic and oligarchic constitutions are determined by the perceived interests of the ruling group (i.e. wealth and freedom respectively), and hence beset by conflict between economic classes. When one recalls that the best regime is a genus, under which falls species of regime which aim at the common advantage, then the best regime is indeed *less* partisan than the predominant defective regimes.

Aristotle's statements on the universality and impartiality of law also serve partly to alleviate the partisanship concern. As discussed in Chapter 1, because it is framed in universal terms (*to katholou*), the law is less vulnerable to the sway of passionate influences which corrupt human rulers (*Pol.* II.9, 1269a9–12, III.15, 1286a17–19; *NE* V.10, 1137b11–24; *Rh.* I.1, 1354b6). People in positions of power are apt to make poor judgements due to their passions (*en pathei ontes*). Legislative enactments by contrast allow for impartiality in application of norms and also the establishment of a just mean between extremes (*ho gar nomos to meson*) (*Pol.* III.16, 1287b3). The impartiality of law also means that it is less likely to arouse resentment, at least when legal norms appear to be equitable (*NE* X.9, 1180a22–5). It is plausible to think that these benefits of the rule of law apply most in the case of the best regime by nature.

These arguments only extend so far, however. In the best regime, laws are rational standards derived from the practical reason of a prudent architectonic legislator. Yet while aristocratic laws may seem equitable and impartial to a good aristocrat, for obvious reasons they will appear less so to an oligarch. Aristotle's ideal king and a genuine aristocracy will both be directed by a conception of *eudaimonia* as

47 I assume both that the common advantage at least extends to 'passive' citizens and that sharing in rule is a matter of degrees rather than 'all or nothing'. For 'passive' citizenship see Keyt (2017: 236–7). For share in rule as a matter of degree see Riesbeck (2016: 179–235). I return to this point in the next chapter.

consisting in rational activity, but this is not the only available conception, let alone the one most prevalent in actual political communities. This is significant in the context of Aristotle's suggestion in *Politics* III.10 that the *rule* of law is itself relative to a constitutional form:

> One might perhaps assert, however, that it is bad for the authoritative element (*to kurion*) generally to be a human instead of law (*nomon*), at any rate if he has the passions that result in his soul (*pathē peri tēn psuchēn*). But if law may be oligarchic or democratic, what difference will it make with regard to the questions that have been raised? (*Pol.* 1281a34–8).

The rule of law is beneficial insofar as *nomos* operates at a further remove from the passions than the orders or decrees of an authoritative person. Yet although law contains rational content derived from the judgements of a legislator regarding what is good and bad for a political community, it is still determined by a particular conception of the correct ends of action. The relativity of (the rule of) law to particular constitutional regimes also obtains for the best regime.

In sum, while the rational content of legal norms within Aristotle's best constitution will be just and promote virtue, these laws will nonetheless be regime-relative. The constitutional relativity of law applies across Aristotle's political thought. Even the best constitutional form retains its status as a kind of political order determined by a particular conception of the human good. It is only that, on Aristotelian assumptions, the conception of the good animating the best regime is the correct conception according to nature, and hence not partisan for one in possession of the practical truth.

Predictably enough, then, the best regime rests on the normative foundation of Aristotle's conception of virtue and *eudaimonia*. The best regime may be considered as partisan insofar as it is determined by a conception of the good not held by all possible citizens. If the Aristotelian conception is truly in conformity with nature, however, then it would of course be much more accurate to say that not every person is able to attain an understanding of the correct human end.

In closing, it is worth noting one further consideration in favour of the natural superiority of the best constitution which can be expressed dialogically from a perspective internal to politics. An argument for the superiority of the philosophical life that is at least implicit in *Nicomachean Ethics* I is that those who are able to partake of a life of rational virtue are also able to experience the other forms of life, whereas the converse does not hold. A person only able to partake of the apolaustic life, or only of the apolaustic life and the political life, thus has a more partisan perspective than someone able to participate in these forms of life and the philosophic as well.

4

The Common Advantage and Political Justice

The ultimate *telos* for an architectonic legislator intending to establish a good constitution and laws, the previous chapters have argued, is *eudaimonia*. As an activity of the soul in accord with the best virtue (*NE* I.7, 1098a17), *eudaimonia* nonetheless presupposes a political community with just laws that are directed to the common advantage. Aristotle accordingly characterises the common advantage (*to koine[i] sumpheron*) as the aim of law and associates it with the promotion of *eudaimonia* in the polis (*NE* V.1, 1129b15–19). The common advantage may thus be regarded as the proximate final cause of legislative activity. Aristotle's account of the common advantage nonetheless seems to equivocate between its status as an instrumental good serving the ends of individuals and as an intrinsically desirable state of affairs. In the current chapter, I seek to resolve this tension by conceptualising the common advantage as both a motivational reason leading individuals to enter the polis and a normative reason – identifiable with the political good of justice – which should guide the enactment of law. Section 1 considers some interpretative preliminaries to a correct understanding of the common advantage. Section 2 then examines the motivational role of the common advantage as a reason for political participation and its relation to instrumental and aggregative accounts of the common good. In Section 3, I turn to the common advantage's status as a normative reason identifiable with political justice. Section 4 then argues for the reconcilability of motivational and normative aspects of the common advantage by reference to the medieval interpretation of the polis as a unity of order.

SECTION 1 THE COMMON ADVANTAGE

The normative significance of the common advantage (*to koine[i] sumpheron*) for Aristotle's account of constitutions and law extends beyond its status, already considered in the previous chapter, as a central criterion for the classification of correct and deviant regimes (*politeiai*) (*Pol.* III.6, 1279a17–29). In the discussion of justice in

Book V.1 of the *Nicomachean Ethics*, Aristotle suggests that the common advantage is in fact the end at which all (just) laws (should) aim:

> The laws pronounce on all things, in their aiming at the common advantage (*hoi de nomoi agoreuousi peri hapantōn, stochasdomenoi ē tou koine[i] sumpherontos*), either for all persons or the best or for those who have authority (*pasin ē tois aristois ē tois kuriois*), either in accord with virtue or in some other such way. As a result, we say that those things apt to produce and preserve happiness (*eudaimonias*) and its parts for the political community (*politikē[i] koinōnia[i]*) are in a manner just (*tropon dikaia*) (1129b15–19).

The common advantage is thus the proximate *telos* of law. While the ultimate aim of all practical action is *eudaimonia*, the common advantage is the proximate end of legislative activity insofar as the promotion of the wellbeing of the community is integral to achievement of the human *telos*.

The proposition that the common advantage is the end of law would seem to entail that it serves as a normative reason providing a criterion for the evaluative assessment of correct and defective regimes.[1] As a normative reason that is shared, moreover, the common advantage would appear to be identifiable with a kind of communal flourishing irreducible to the flourishing of the particular individuals who comprise a political community. Aristotle's famous statement that the polis is prior to the individual by nature (*Pol.* I.2, 1253a19–20) and the outline for the best regime in Books VII and VIII both support such a conception of the common advantage as a shared and distinctive good of the polis. This plausible interpretation is nonetheless undermined by passages suggesting that it is the desire of *individuals* to lead a better life which ultimately motivates them to form political communities and seek the common advantage (*NE* VIII.9, 1160a9–13; *Pol.* III.6, 1278b19–23). These passages point to a more individualistic conception of the common advantage, according to which it is identifiable with the benefits that accrue to each person 'entering' the polis for the purposes of promoting their own individual flourishing.

The Aristotelian common advantage thus appears to confront the interpreter with irreconcilable 'holist' and 'individualist' elements.[2] On a robust holist interpretation, the common advantage refers collectively to a benefit that is attributable to the polis over and above any individual benefits and its end 'supersedes' (takes normative priority over) the ends of each of its members.[3] On the individualist reading, the common advantage refers to the aggregated goods that accrue to individuals engaged in political activities in order to benefit themselves. As Miller suggests, both of these interpretations also come in more moderate forms. On a moderate holist interpretation, the individual is not a mere means to the higher purpose of the polis, yet the

1 As Riesbeck (2016: 202) and Kontos (2018: 88) both point out, even defective regimes tend to aim at the common advantage in some sense; the problem is that they apprehend and pursue it incorrectly.

2 Miller (1995: 194–224). See also Miller (2009: 549–51).

3 Miller (1995: 196).

'political good is a ... good distinct from the good of all the members'.[4] On a moderate individualist reading, 'other-regarding virtuous activity remains an essential part of individual perfection'.[5] All of these interpretations find support in different passages of the practical works.

My primary contention in the current chapter is that one can reconcile the individualist and holist aspects of the common advantage by distinguishing between two diverse yet compatible functions that it performs in Aristotle's practical thought. The common advantage, I suggest, serves as both (1) a motivating reason for individuals to enter the polis and as (2) a normative reason – the political good of justice – which serves as a criterion for assessing not only the correctness of constitutions (*politeiai*), but also the laws enacted under those regimes. Before I turn to the defence of these claims, it is worth setting out some interpretative preliminaries.

Aristotle's principle of inclusion for the common advantage in the VI.1 passage cited above is notably open-ended, referring to all persons, or the best, or those in authority. This open-endedness reflects the divergences between kinds of regime discussed in the previous chapter and also the context-sensitivity of Aristotle's constitutional methodology. Even in the most inclusive regime, however, the common advantage does not extend to all inhabitants of a polis and excludes slaves (*Pol.* III.6, 1278b32–7), resident aliens (*metoikoi*) and foreign visitors (*xenoi*). Some of Aristotle's statements seem to support a distinction between a full or unqualified citizen (*politēs haplōs*) (III.1, 1275a19–23, III.5, 1278a4–5), who would share in deliberative or judicial office, consistent with the *Politics* III.1 definition of citizenship (1275b18–21), and 'passive' or 'second-class' citizens. In a relatively inclusive regime like a democracy, where all free male inhabitants share in rule, these second-class citizens would be youths, women and the elderly.[6] In the less inclusive regimes, a significant proportion of free male inhabitants would also be 'second-class' citizens. The postulation of this broader 'second-class' conception of citizenship addresses an obvious and well-known tension in Aristotle's account of constitutions and citizenship. If only office-holders in the strict sense are citizens and included in the common advantage, then the advantage of a kingship or aristocratic regime would problematically be restricted only to one citizen or a select few respectively. An alternative solution to this difficulty, persuasively argued by Riesbeck, is that the

4 Miller (1995: 200). Miller attributes a conciliatory position to Irwin (1988: 389–438) and Cooper (1999: 356–77). Such attempts to reconcile apparently conflicting tendencies in Aristotle's political thought may be contrasted with the position taken by Nussbaum (1990: 196–9), who claims that we should resolve the inconsistency developmentally by regarding holism as a severable product of early Platonic influence.

5 Miller (1995: 196).

6 As Keyt notes (2017: 149–51), Aristotle's contrast between those 'outside the constitution' and office-holders (V.4, 1304a16–17) supports this view, insofar as the latter group would not include slaves, foreigners or metics. On second-class citizenship, see in particular the discussions in Newman (1887 i: 228–30), Miller (1995: 219), Cooper (1999), Morrison (1999), Collins (2006: 134) and Riesbeck (2016).

ruling body (*politeuma*) and citizen-class are not co-extensive because authority within a constitution admits of degrees.[7] On this interpretation, what is distinctive of an aristocracy, for example, is that the virtuous few monopolise the key deliberative posts, not that the rest of the free population are completely excluded from all offices whatsoever. In any case, whether one accepts either the 'passive citizenship' or 'degrees of authority' interpretation, the scope of the common advantage is best understood as extending to all native free inhabitants.

Aristotle's common advantage has cast a long historical shadow and it is instructive to clarify its relationship with both the Thomistic *bonum commune* and more recent natural law accounts. While the Thomistic *bonum commune* is indebted to the Western 'rediscovery' of Aristotle's ethical and political thought in the thirteenth century, it is not identical in content.[8] In *Summa Theologiae* (1265–1274), Aquinas characterises the *bonum commune* as the justice and peace of a well-ordered polity. Justice refers in this context primarily to the preservation of a certain form of equality or a proper relation among persons.[9] Peace is both the proper ordering of citizens and the absence of strife and discord.[10] Justice and peace are thus conditions of the political community considered as a whole; a just and well-ordered community is a unity of order that is in good condition. While this understanding of the common good has strong Aristotelian resonances, Aquinas treats the *bonum commune* as an analogical concept applicable not only to political communities, but also to the universal good of God.[11] By contrast, Aristotle employs the concept of the common advantage exclusively within the philosophy of human affairs, albeit that the ultimate good is the *eudaimonia* associated with the self-sufficient activity of an agent engaged in 'godlike' contemplation. This is not to deny the usefulness of Thomistic insights for the exposition of Aristotle on the common advantage, only to point to the need for interpretative caution.

It is noteworthy in this context that recent scholars avoid the translation 'common good', except in passages where Aristotle explicitly employs the compound term *to koinon agathon*.[12] Although Aristotle usually employs *to koine[i] sumpheron* in political contexts, his use of *koinon agathon* in Books II and III (II.8, 1268b32 and III.13, 1284b6) of the *Politics* suggests that the terms are more or less synonymous. The translation 'common advantage' is nonetheless preferable given Aristotle's more frequent use of *sumpheron* (with its implication of what is useful, expedient and

7 Riesbeck (2016: 179–235). One point strongly in favour of Riesbeck's interpretation is that the distribution of citizenship is itself, for Aristotle, an important consideration of political justice (*Pol.* III.13, 1283b36–40).

8 On the reception and interpretation of Aristotle's political thought in the thirteenth century, see Martin (1951: 29–44) and Dunbabin (1982: 723–38).

9 ST II-II. q. 57. a.1.

10 ST II-II. q. 29. a.1.

11 For Aquinas' wide-ranging use of *bonum commune* and related terms see Kempshall (1999: 76–129).

12 Lord (2013) and Reeve (2017) both translate *to koine[i] sumpheron* as 'common advantage'. Barnes (1996) elects for 'common interest'.

advantageous).[13] Aristotle's emphasis in the *Politics*, as is appropriate for a practical inquiry, is predominately upon what is advantageous for the members of a political community, rather than good *simpliciter*.[14] The use of the term 'advantage' in addition reflects that the common advantage is not simply a normative concept, but also performs a motivational explanatory role.

The theories of the common good developed by more recent natural law theorists, most notably Finnis and Murphy, can nevertheless help to illuminate Aristotle's concept of the common advantage. Murphy's development of a threefold distinction between instrumental, aggregative and distinctive conceptions of the common good is a particularly useful framework for understanding the Aristotelian common advantage and its broader normative implications.[15]

The *instrumental* common good is 'a set of conditions which enables members of a community to attain for themselves reasonable objectives, or to realize reasonably for themselves the value(s), for the sake of which they have reason to collaborate with each other (positively and/or negatively) in a community'.[16] On the instrumental conception defended by Finnis, the political common good is subordinate to the realisation of basic goods such as knowledge, friendship, health, play etc. at the level of individuals and families.[17] The political common good does not itself instantiate one of these basic goods, but is instrumental to their realisation. Practical reasoning about the common good reveals a wide range of projects, orientations and commitments with respect to the basic goods, none of which can be regarded as definitively superior. This incommensurability causes co-ordination problems, which reflect the diversity of human projects and lead to disputes about the most effective means to realise the basic goods that require authoritative legal resolution.[18] Finnis gives an example of the rival interests of environmentalists and farmers in relation to river pollution to demonstrate the role of the law in addressing co-ordination problems arising out of competing projects and interests.[19] The farmer in this case is confronted with a law on river pollution that goes against immediate economic self-interest, yet also has reason to believe that a general framework of legal obligations provides a range of otherwise unavailable benefits (e.g. protection of private property, subsidies etc.).

The *aggregative* common good 'consists in the realisation of some set of individual intrinsic goods, characteristically the goods of all (and only) those persons that are members of the political community in question'.[20] This conception, defended by

13 Liddell and Scott (2000: 764) note that the primary Latin synonym of *sumpheron* is *utile*.
14 Kraut (2013: 351). *NE* VIII.12, 1162a29 refers to a child as the common good (*agathon*) of its parents.
15 Murphy (2006: 61–90). Morrison (2013: 176–98) also applies Murphy's framework to Aristotle.
16 Finnis (2011: 155). This conception is influenced by Grisez (1983: 850).
17 Finnis (2011: 85–90). See also Finnis (1998b: 82 and 97–8).
18 This sense of a co-ordination problem is to be distinguished from the narrower sense found in game-theory, which Finnis describes as 'emaciated'. See Finnis (1984: 115 37).
19 Finnis (1984: 133–7).
20 Murphy (2005: 136).

Murphy, assumes that the state of affairs in which an agent, A, is flourishing is 'a fundamental reason for political action within A's political community'.[21] If the state of affairs in which an individual A is flourishing provides a decisive reason for political action within A's community, then the state of affairs in which A and another individual, B, are flourishing is an even more decisive reason for action. One generates the normative ideal of the aggregative common good by carrying out this process of inclusion to its limit, including all of the goods of all of the members of a political community. As a result, the aggregative common good 'is that state of affairs in which all of the members of a political community are fully flourishing'.[22] On the aggregative conception, therefore, it is ultimately the good of each and every individual that provides the normative reason-giving force of the common good. The normative core of the aggregative conception is accordingly the claim that 'an individual's good provides *all* members of the political community with a reason for action'.[23]

The *distinctive* common good is 'the obtaining of some state of affairs that is literally the good of the community as a whole'.[24] By contrast with the instrumental and aggregative conceptions, the distinctive common good is identified with a good of the whole community irreducible to the basic goods of individuals. Although not an ultimate end in an unqualified sense, the distinctive political common good derives its normative force 'as a direct consequence of the priority of the whole over the parts'.[25] This priority of the whole over the parts can be understood as referring to the shared end of a community beyond the personal goods of its members.[26] The distinctive common good also refers, however, to a state-of-affairs of just relations between citizens which is an integral component of their wellbeing. The distinctive conception thus differs from the aggregative insofar as it is 'not an addition or multiplication of individual, private goods, but a distinct kind of good to be pursued and enjoyed together by people living in community'.[27]

Murphy's classification might be taken to suggest that three conceptions of the common good are mutually exclusive.[28] A better reading, however, is that different theorists emphasise alternative dimensions of the political common good and give

21 Murphy (2005: 137).
22 Murphy (2005: 137).
23 Murphy (2005: 138). Italics mine.
24 Murphy (2005: 136).
25 Simon (1965: 105).
26 Cochran (1978: 233–5).
27 Cochran (1978: 232).
28 The manner in which Murphy formulates the three candidate conceptions leaves open the possibility that the conceptions are reconcilable, despite his firm advocacy of the aggregative conception. Murphy's discussion of the instrumental conception, for example, seems to entail that this conception is normatively subordinate to the aggregative conception, rather than precluded by it. See Murphy (2005: 139–47).

one conception explanatory or normative priority, without necessarily rejecting the applicability of the other conceptions.

While Murphy's classification is useful for clarifying the normative implications of the Aristotelian common advantage, its dichotomy between intrinsic and instrumental goods also has the potential to mislead. Aristotle distinguishes between (1) things that are good only for the sake of something else, (2) things that are good both for their own sake and for the sake of something else and (3) things that are good only for their own sake and not for the sake of anything else (*NE* I.7, 1097a26–b7).[29] Hence if one were to argue that Aristotle's common advantage is a means to intrinsic goods (such as knowledge), then this would not necessarily entail that it is an instrumental good in Murphy's sense, as it could just as readily fall under category (2) as (1).

Whether Aristotle regards the aim of law as the benefit of individuals engaged in a political association out of self-interested motivations, or as the promotion of benefits for the political community taken as a whole, or as a combination of both, has important implications for his conception of the scope and function of *nomos*. In order to resolve the apparent tensions within Aristotle's account of the common advantage sketched above, I argue in the next two sections, it is necessary to distinguish its motivational and normative aspects. In closing this section, it is worth outlining briefly the concepts of motivational and normative reason referred to below.

A motivational reason explains a particular kind of action by serving in an explanation of the form 'I φ because I have a set of beliefs and/or desires that motivates me to φ'.[30] Motivational reasons thus sit most easily within an instrumental account of practical rationality according to which the principal role of practical reason is to work out the appropriate means to realise ends that have been set by antecedent beliefs and desires. Normative reasons, by contrast, are reasons in virtue of which certain actions may be regarded as good or valuable.[31] An adequate description of the normative reasons for a human action or practice is accordingly an identification of the reasons which allow for a characterisation of that action or practice as good or valuable.[32] On this approach, talk of the normative reason for an action is more-or-less synonymous with talk about its purpose (understood as a final cause), 'value', function or good-making characteristics. What is sought in each case is a reason that explains why engaging in a certain kind of activity would be 'valuable' or good. In what follows, I contend that both of these forms of reason are present, in a manner which is fully reconcilable, within Aristotle's conception of the common advantage.

29 See Irwin (1990: 74–5).
30 Smith (1994: 94–8). See also Parfit (1997: 99–130) and Dancy (2000).
31 Raz (2002: 23).
32 As Raz (2002: 23) suggests, this is the 'classical approach to human agency – a position shared by Plato, Aristotle and Aquinas'. See also Anscombe (1957).

SECTION 2 THE COMMON ADVANTAGE AS A MOTIVATIONAL REASON

Aristotle's use of the common advantage as a motivating reason for individuals to enter a political community is exemplified by the following passage from Book III.6 of the *Politics*:

> A human being is by nature a political animal. That is why, even when they do not need one another's help (*tēs para allēlōn boētheias ouk*), people no less desire (*oregontai*) to live together, although it is also true that common advantage (*to koine[i] sumpheron*) *brings [human beings] together*, to the extent that it contributes some part of living well (*zēn kalōs*) to each (*hekastō[i]*). (*Pol.* 1278b19–23. *Italics mine*)

Even apart from their desire to live together as political animals, human beings would still have a strong incentive to form a polis, because it provides advantages that are distributed to *each* (*hekastō[i]*) *and every* participant. In *Nicomachean Ethics* VIII.8 Aristotle states in a similar manner that the polis is formed from the outset (*ex archēs*), and continues to exist, because people come together (*sumporeuontai*) for a certain advantage (*tini sumpheronti*) (*NE* VIII.9, 1160a9–13). Once more, what motivates entrance into a political community is the advantages that accrue to each from the establishment and maintenance of an association that is privileged because it provides the things conducive to a good life. Both passages thus suggest that the origins and formation of the polis are at least in part dependent upon the motivations of its members to receive benefits.

Aristotle in the statements above identifies the motivational reason for individuals to enter the polis as the benefits – both material and otherwise – that accrue from political participation. There is some abstraction in talking of the motivations individuals have for entering the polis. Citizenship is not, at least in most cases, best understood on the model of voluntary choice. Aristotle, by describing the beliefs of an agent faced with the choice to be part of a polis, nevertheless identifies the principal reason that *would* motivate a decision to partake in the benefits of political association. This is participation in a political life that surpasses bare survival.

In adopting the perspective of a potential citizen, Aristotle seems to presuppose an individualistic conception of the common advantage.[33] This interpretation is supported by Aristotle's use of the dative of interest in these passages, which is indicative of a focus upon the advantages of political association from the perspective of each individual, rather than the community as a whole. Such a reading is, moreover, consonant with Aristotle's further claims that the polis is a composite whole (*tōn sunkeimenōn*) of many parts (namely its citizens) (*Pol.* III.1, 1274b39–40), the critique of Plato's ideal of political unity in Book II (see in particular II.1, 1261a16–22) and the acknowledgement that individuals could exist apart from a polis by chance (I.3, 1253a3–4).

33 Morrison (2013: 178).

These considerations in favour of an individualistic reading of the common advantage support an instrumental or aggregative interpretation of its normative implications. In the instrumental and aggregative conceptions of the common good, the good of each individual has unqualified normative priority over the good of the community as a whole. This normative priority is perfectly intelligible on the assumption that the main ground for entering the polis is the desire-motivated rational belief of individuals that it provides them with a wide range of benefits.

An instrumental interpretation of the common advantage also harmonises with Aristotle's commitment to the status of the contemplative life as the best in *Nicomachean Ethics* X.[34] From the perspective of true human flourishing, engagement in political affairs is not as self-sufficient or satisfying as theoretical activity (cf. *Pol.* V.16, 1334b1–32) and hence subordinate. The political common advantage, looked at from this angle, is not an ultimate reason for action, but a set of enabling conditions, inclusive of just laws, allowing individuals capable of genuine virtue to realise *eudaimonia* through contemplation. Even if one adopts a more conciliatory interpretation, according to which Aristotle's account of *eudaimonia* implies a moderate intellectualism, 'which accords priority to contemplation without denying a place to ethical virtue in the best life',[35] then the political association and its laws are still ascribed an instrumental role in human flourishing. Indeed, all that is required for the attribution of an instrumental conception of the common advantage to Aristotle is the relatively weak claim that the good condition of the polis is a necessary condition and means for individuals to engage in the theoretical activity of true virtue.

Aristotle's discussion of education in *Politics* VII.14 demonstrates this instrumental aspect of the common advantage. The architectonic legislative founder must consider how citizens become good by reference to the end of the best life (*Pol.* 1333a12–16). As noted in Chapter 1, education laws directed towards the development of virtue in the citizenry are a precondition for the flourishing of each individual. A good legislator must look to the different parts of the soul – that which has reason and that which can obey reason (1333a17–18) – in order to enact education laws conducive to the flourishing of the individuals who comprise a political community. Well-framed legislative education norms are thus enacted to promote the common advantage, in turn understood in terms of the enabling conditions for the promotion of individual wellbeing.

Aristotle's use of the common advantage as a motivating reason for individuals to enter a political association is also consistent with an aggregative conception. On the aggregative conception, the common advantage consists in the realisation of the goods of all (and only) those persons that are members of the political community.[36]

34 See, for example, Vander Waerdt (1985: 249–73) and Lord (1982: 196–202).

35 Miller (1995: 237). Other defenders of moderate intellectualism include Irwin (1990: 73–98), Depew (1991: 346–80) and Kraut (2002: 94–6). See also the influential discussion in Hardie (1968).

36 Murphy (2006: 63).

Insofar as all citizens not only desire the material benefits that accrue from living in a political community, but also to lead truly good lives, they share a common goal and hence also desire that their fellow citizens share in the relevant forms of benefit. Despite the emphasis upon individual benefit in the aggregative conception, the goal of living well need not be taken as merely agent-relative. Each member of the community can take the wellbeing of each and every member of the political community as an end (*telos*) and reason for action.[37] Every individual, taken distributively, is thus a beneficiary of the arrangement. And insofar as each member is a beneficiary, the common advantage can accordingly be understood as an aggregate of the wellbeing of all citizens.

The Aristotelian common advantage is therefore instrumental and aggregative in the sense that the polis provides the conditions (not exclusively or even primarily material) that are necessary for individual flourishing. An acknowledgement of the common advantage's instrumental and aggregative aspects does not entail, however, that it is reducible to these conceptions.

A narrow 'laissez-faire' and individualistic instrumental interpretation of the common advantage is of course inconsistent with Aristotle's clear rejection of the sophistic view that the polis exists only for preventing mutual wrongdoing and exchange of goods (*Pol.* III.10, 1280b30–1). On such a conception, the common advantage would consist solely in those conditions that are necessary means for members of a community to realise their own ends, *whatever they might happen to be*. Aristotle unequivocally rejects, however, the view of Lycrophron that the polis is based on an artificial agreement or alliance for the sake of peace and commerce (and implicitly the fulfilment of individual wants), rather than established for the sake of living well and nobly (1280b7–12). This criticism also applies to partisans of oligarchic constitutions, who regard the city as an association designed to protect accumulation and exchange of possessions (1280a25–36, 1280b1–11).

While Aristotle's commitment to the end of the polis as virtue and *eudaimonia* precludes such a narrowly instrumental conception, however, the critique of the sophistic account of political origins does not in itself explain how the normative force of the common advantage can derive from any other source than individual benefit, whether taken instrumentally or aggregatively.

In several important passages of the *Politics*, Aristotle ascribes *eudaimonia* to the polis as such, considered as a whole, rather than simply to each and every member of the political community in an instrumental or aggregative sense. A notable example is found in *Politics* VII.14:

> Next … is the assertion that the best city is happy (*eudaimona*) and acts finely (*prattousan kalōs*). It is impossible to act finely without acting to achieve fine things: but there is no fine deed either of a man or of a city separate from virtue and

[37] Cf. Morrison (2013: 183): 'the happiness of all the citizens stands in a *common* relationship to each citizen, namely, each citizen's happiness is a *part* of the happiness of all'.

> prudence (*aretēs kai phronēseōs*). The courage, justice and prudence of a city have the same power and form (*tēn autēn echei dunamin kai morphēn*) as those things human beings share in individually (*hekastos tōn anthrōpōn*) who are called just, prudent and sound. (*Pol.* 1323b30–6)

This passage attributes virtues and capacities to the polis.[38] On a merely aggregative interpretation, the polis is a collection of individuals, and the common advantage of the polis is ultimately the sum of the benefit that each citizen receives. The passage above suggests, however, that Aristotle has a sense of the flourishing – and even agency – of the polis as a unified whole which obtains in a manner that is irreducible to the wellbeing of its individual members.

More decisively, Aristotle's outline for legislation in the best regime presupposes that the common advantage – understood as the aim of law – cannot be identified solely with the interests of individuals. In the opening of Book VIII, while introducing education as the primary concern of the legislator (*Pol.* 1337a10–34), Aristotle explicitly attributes the need for an education that is common for all citizens to the claim that there is a single end for the political community as a whole (*hen to telos tē [i] polei pasē[i]*) (1337a20–1). While an education in virtue is obviously of benefit to each individual, this is not Aristotle's focus. His argument is rather that for common things, the training too should be common (*koinēn*) and that particular citizens do not belong to themselves, but rather to the polis, for each is a part of the political community (*morion gar hekastos tēs poleōs*) (1337a26–9). Aristotle's concrete legislative proposals in Books VII and VIII are consonant with this claim. The proposed laws regarding marital relations and offspring in *Politics* VII.16, for example, either presuppose the priority of the interests of the community over that of individual citizens or, at the very least, identify the two sets of interests. All of this suggests that it would be one-sided to characterise the Aristotelian common advantage as deriving all its normative weight from individual benefit. The question is whether it is possible to identify a distinctive aspect of the common advantage that is neither disagreeably organicist nor holist.

One way to introduce a distinctive conception of the common advantage that is neither disagreeably organicist nor holist is by reference to civic friendship. Cooper, for example, has argued that civic friendship instantiates the mutual concern for wellbeing found in genuine friendship.[39] In a community with genuine civic friendship, there exists good will and trust such that each citizen 'has a certain measure of interest in and concern for the well-being of each citizen just because the other is

[38] In his discussion of different regimes, Aristotle also refers to cities as 'tyrannical' or 'democratic' (see, for example, *Pol.* VII.2, 1324a10–11) in a manner which suggests that they have a particular character or *ethos*.

[39] Cooper (1999: 370–1). Cooper acknowledges the lack of references to *politikē philia* in the *Politics* and the instrumental character of the civic friendship discussed in the *Eudemian Ethics* (*EE* VII.10, 1242a6–7, b32, 1243b4). Aristotle does refer, in the *Politics*, to *philias kai koinōnias politikēs* (IV.11, 1295b23–4). *Politikē philia* is referred to four times in *Nicomachean Ethics*: VIII.12, 1161b13, IX.1, 1163b34, IX.6, 1167b2 and IX.10, 1171a17.

a fellow citizen'.[40] In addition, because citizens can participate in the good of others, individual goods become communal goods 'shared by all who are members in good standing of the community'.[41] While Aristotle's discussion of friendship sets out from more intimate relations, he also describes friendships in terms of good will and friends wishing their friends' wellbeing for their friends' own sake, neither of which necessarily entails personal intimacy (*NE* VIII.2, 1155b34–1156a5).[42] Without acknowledgement of this sort of friendship, it is also difficult to see why Aristotle would claim that friendship holds cities together or that law-givers, in seeking 'like-mindedness' (*homonoia*), care more about friendship than justice (1155a22–4). In defending this interpretation of civic friendship, which culminates in the claim that citizens are united by pursuit of a common activity 'that is the single life they all jointly live by merging their lives', Cooper identifies a distinctive component of the common advantage.[43]

Mutual relations of goodwill between citizens of a polis are indeed plausibly irreducible to the good of individuals. This is because relations of goodwill between citizens are constitutive of the good condition of the political community considered as a whole, as becomes evident in Aristotle's *Politics* V discussion of the faction (*stasis*) which arises when such goodwill is absent.[44] Aristotle's statement that 'when people are friends, they have no need of justice' (*NE* VIII.2, 1155a26–7) nevertheless cuts both ways in this context. As Section 3 demonstrates, the common advantage is identified by Aristotle with a concept of political justice that is in turn closely connected with law.[45] Political justice and law, however, arise due to features of human nature which suggest both that *politikē philia* in a robust sense is quite rare and that the flourishing of a polis presupposes the more authoritative guidance that is provided by binding legal norms.

Morrison has argued that many of the apparent tensions discussed in this section can be resolved by distinguishing between the common advantage and the flourishing of the polis. Whereas the common advantage is best understood in aggregative terms, the flourishing of the polis is a 'genuinely holistic notion' i.e. a property of the city as a structured whole.[46] On this interpretation, the 'common good is the individualist notion, the individual well-being of every citizen, taken together'.[47] Morrison's reading correctly identifies the individualist and motivational aspect of the common advantage, but does not consider all aspects of its normative role. The identification of the common advantage with the political good of justice, as the next

40 Cooper (1999: 371).
41 Cooper (1999: 372 and 377).
42 Cooper (1999: 371).
43 Cooper acknowledges an aggregative aspect to the common good (1999: 373–4) based on *Pol.* III.10, 1280b33–4 and notes that the 'living well' of a city depends on households and families.
44 See Hatzistavrou (2013: 275–300).
45 Kraut (2018: 186).
46 Morrison (2013: 188).
47 Morrison (2013: 188).

two sections demonstrate, entails that it is irreducible to the promotion of individual goods.

This conclusion has important ramifications for Aristotle's account of law. If the common advantage can be construed in a distinctive sense, then the normative force of law does not derive merely from the good of each individual, but also from the wellbeing of the polis. In what follows, I investigate Aristotle's identification of communal wellbeing with political justice, understood as both a normative reason and a property of the polis as a unity of order. This investigation reveals that the normative force of law does not simply derive from the need to promote individual flourishing, but also from the end of community wellbeing. The acknowledgement of a distinctive aspect to the common advantage with normative force, moreover, strengthens the claim of the law in circumstances where obeying the law may not be in an individual's best interests considered in abstraction from the wellbeing of the community.

SECTION 3 POLITICAL JUSTICE

The common advantage has a motivational aspect that is individualist in orientation and best construed in instrumental and aggregative terms. Aristotle's identification of the common advantage with the political good of justice (*Pol.* III.6, 1279a18, III.12, 1282b17–18; *EE* VII.9, 1241b13–15), nonetheless points to its parallel status as a normative reason irreducible to the promotion of individual benefit. In the current section I examine Aristotle's conception of political justice, which is described as existing in accordance with law (*NE* V.6, 1134b8–15). This analysis reveals that political justice is a state of affairs attributable to the polis as a whole and a shared good in the distinctive sense that it belongs to the community, not just to each of the individual members.

In order to develop the implications of the identification of the common advantage with political justice, it is necessary to set out the multiple senses of justice in *Nicomachean Ethics* Book V. Aristotle's concept of the politically just (*politikon dikaion*) – which includes both universal and particular forms – emerges as the overarching communal justice which obtains between citizens governed by law (*NE* V.6, 1134a30). It is within this framework that the constitutive aim of law can be understood as not simply the flourishing of each and every member of the polis, but the community as a whole.

The initial investigation of justice (*dikaiosunē*) in Book V approaches the concept as an ethical virtue and disposition (*hexis*) of persons according to which they wish to do just things (*boulontai ta dikaia*) (*NE* V.1, 1129a7–9), rather than as a set of principles for the reasonable and fair distribution of benefits and burdens within a political community.[48] After noting that the terms 'justice' (*dikaiosunē*) and

[48] Whereas *dikaiosunē* (justice) generally describes an ethical quality of persons, Aristotle's primary concern in *Nicomachean Ethics* V.6–7 is with 'the just' (*to dikaion*): 'external facts of right which can be viewed in isolation from the acting subject'. See Schütrumpf (2015: 165–7) and Dirlmeier (1974: 404).

'injustice' (*adikia*) are homonymous or employed with different but closely related senses (1129a27–9), Aristotle examines two types of unjust person: the law-breaker (*paranomos*) and the person who grasps for more (*pleonektēs*) in a manner that is unfair or unequal (*anisos*) (1129a32–4). This distinction between types of unjust disposition allows Aristotle to identify the just with what is lawful and equal (*to nomimon kai to ison*) and the unjust with what is unlawful and unequal (*to paranomon kai to anison*) (1129a34–b1). These two senses of the unjust person – one who acts unlawfully and one who grasps for more than is fair and equal – form the basis for the well-known division of justice into so-called universal and particular forms.

The 'universal' sense of justice is described by Aristotle as complete or perfect virtue, not without qualification, but in relation to another (*dikaiosunē aretē men esti teleia, all' ouk haplōs alla pros heteron*) (1129b26–7). A disposition to act the right way in all respects in relation to others is in one sense 'the whole of virtue' (*holē aretē estin*) (1130a10). Although it pertains to the entire ethical realm, justice in the universal sense is not the same in being (*einai ou to auto*) as virtue, because it serves the common advantage (1130a4–6), and not merely the good for oneself. In serving the common advantage, universal justice is identifiable with the lawful (*to nomimon*). Although *to nomimon* has a broader meaning than *nomos*, the context of the following passage – with its emphasis upon legislative expertise – indicates that it here refers primarily to enacted law:

> Since . . . a law-breaker (*ho paranomos*) is unjust and he who is lawful just, it is clear that all lawful things are somehow just (*panta to nomima esti pōs dikaia*). For matters defined by the legislative expertise are lawful (*hupo tēs nomothetikēs nomima esti*), and each of these we declare to be just (*dikaion*) (1129b11–14).[49]

Shortly after, Aristotle notes that the majority of lawful things are those commanded by law (*kōluei ho nomos*) on the basis of the whole of virtue (V.2, 1130b24–5). The laws of a polis are here understood as a shared set of normative commitments that belong to the entire community.

Aristotle's identification of complete virtue in relation to others with the rational content of legislative enactments rests on a presupposition of the inseparability of the ethical and political domains. An agent who acts with complete virtue in relation to another is regarded by Aristotle from a perspective internal to a political community living under shared laws, rather than as an autonomous agent governed by a moral law which transcends institutional politics and positive legal norms. As will be considered in more detail in Chapter 6, such a position does not entail that the

[49] Ostwald notes that in the fifth century BCE, as *nomos* began to be used for legal enactments, the adjective *nomimos* was increasingly employed to refer to customary practices and behavioural norms. By the late fifth century, however, *nomimos* also came to be 'tinged with statutory implications' such that 'an act is *nomimos* when it is consonant with what written treaties or laws stipulate' (1986: 94 and 108).

legislative enactments of all political communities are laws in the focal sense. In his elaboration of the identification of the lawful with the just, Aristotle states that those things productive of justice are all the legislative acts pertaining to what is common (*to koinon*) (V.2, 1130b25–6). The perspective assumed by Aristotle in identifying the lawful and the just is hence that *nomos* in the focal sense must fulfil its normative purpose of serving the common advantage of the polis. In stating that all lawful things are somehow, or in a way, just (*panta to nomima esti pōs dikaia*), Aristotle is not to be taken as proposing an incipient version of legal positivism (the qualification *pōs* is crucial), but rather as asserting that laws in the focal sense have been enacted to reflect reasonable community understandings of virtues such as courage and moderation.

The 'particular' form of justice pertains to pleasures associated with gain i.e. the desire to have more honour, money or security than other members of the polis (1130b1–2). Aristotle divides this form of justice into two kinds.[50] On the one hand, there is the just (*to dikaion*) in the distribution of honour and money and things divisible between citizens (*to en tais dianomais timēs ē chrematōn ē tōn allōn hosa merista tois koinōnousi tēs politeias*) (1130b31–2). On the other hand, there is the just in relation to the correction of transactions (*to en tois sunallagmasi diorthōtikon*) (1131a1–2). This form of particular justice in turn divides up into that governing voluntary commercial transactions, such as buying and selling, and involuntary 'transactions', including covert acts such as theft and adultery and violent acts like assault, rape and murder (1131a3–9).

Aristotle's analysis of distributive particular justice applies a 'geometric' or proportional model whereby a just distribution should reflect merit rather than simple equality. Noting widespread agreement that the just is the equal and that the just in distribution ought to be in accordance with merit (*kat' axian tina dein einai*), Aristotle contends that disputes over allocations of benefit and harm are caused by disagreement over what merit really consists in. Different conceptions of merit, in line with the previous chapter, reflect diverse interpretations of the good and influence the establishment of alternative regimes (V.3, 1131a25–8). A truly just allocation of benefits and burdens would be one where a correct conception of merit determines the proportional distribution. The distribution of honour, money and security within a community (a distribution that is ordered and enforced by law) is here understood in an explicitly political manner as dependent upon the ends privileged in that community: freedom in a democracy, wealth in an oligarchy and virtue in an aristocracy (1131a25–8). Allocations of goods within a polis are hence dependent upon its overarching conception of *political* justice. This explains why Aristotle's exposition of the just in distribution refers explicitly to the allocation of

[50] In V.5–6 Aristotle also suggests that there is a third form of particular justice involving reciprocity. Here the focus is primarily upon economic exchange based on need (*chreia*). For analysis see Miller (1995: 73–4).

finite goods among those who share a constitutional community in common (*tois koinōnousi tēs politeias*) (V.2, 1130b31–2).

In the case of 'corrective' justice, by contrast, an arithmetical model of proportion should be applied in which the law treats people as equals and seeks merely to restore the balance of the unfair gain to one party at the expense of another (V.4, 1132a2–8). Aristotle assumes, reasonably enough, that voluntary transactions are best safeguarded in a political community that is governed by law. With involuntary transactions – criminal offences like theft and murder – the arithmetical correction is relational insofar as it seeks redress of injustices occurring between citizens sharing a life in common. The function of a judge is to consider differences stemming from harm done (1132a5) and this presupposes a common legislation which allows disputes to be resolved through the identification of a middle way between the conflicting parties (1132a22).

Aristotle presents just action (*dikaiopragia*) as a middle term between doing injustice and suffering injustice. In the former case one has more than one should and in the latter less (V.5, 1133b30–3). The just is therefore a certain mean (*mesotēs tis estin*), although not in exactly the same way as with the other virtues, because injustice concerns the extremes (1133b33–1134a1).

Aristotle's discussion of universal and particular forms of justice thus moves from a disposition of an agent to act in a lawful way towards others to an account of the distribution and allocation of benefits and burdens. From this latter perspective, it is possible to apply the language of legal rights and duties to Aristotle's theory. Although the reconstructive application of a Hohfeldian theory to Aristotle's account can offer some insights into the uses of terms such as *to dikaion, exousia, kurion* and *akuros*, however, the use of the language of rights also has the potential to mislead.[51] When Aristotle, in his discussion of 'corrective justice', states that someone who obtains an 'intermediate amount' will get justice (*tou dikaiou*), the primary object of this analysis is a correct allocation of benefits or burdens, considered as an external distribution of 'right', not a 'claim-right' considered as a subjective entitlement of an individual.

Aristotle introduces the just in the political sense (*to politikon dikaion*) in V.6 as follows:

> It must not escape our notice that what is being sought is also the just unqualifiedly, that is, the just in the political sense (*to haplōs dikaion kai to politikon dikaion*).[52] And this exists among those who share a life in common (*epi koinōnōn biou*) with a view to being self-sufficient (*autarkeian*), who are free and equal, either in accord with proportion or arithmetically. As a result, for those for whom this does not exist, there is nothing politically just in relation to one another, but only something just in a certain sense and by way of a similarity. The just exists for those for whom there is

[51] Miller (1995: 87–139). Miller's argument concerning (political) natural rights is considered in Chapter 6.

[52] I take the *kai* here as exepegetical, following Bartlett and Collins (2011: 103).

> also law pertaining to them (*esti gar dikaion, hois kai nomos pros autous*) and law exists among those for whom there is injustice (*nomos d', en hois adikia*). For justice is a judgement about the just and the unjust (*ē gar dikē krisis tou dikaiou kai tou adikou*) (1134a25–32).

The relation of the politically just to the other senses of justice in V.1–5 is not stated explicitly, but several considerations favour the conclusion that it is an all-embracing communal justice which includes both universal and particular forms. Firstly, the politically just is introduced directly after discussion of the other forms of justice. Secondly, the association of the politically just with the just without qualification (*haplōs*) points to its status as a comprehensive form. Finally, Aristotle asserts that justice truly speaking pertains to the citizens of a polis governed by law; other forms of relations between persons (e.g. husband and wife, master and slave) are just only by analogy.

Justice is hence the communal virtue (*koinōnikēn aretēn*) (*Pol.* III.13, 1283a38–9) of those who freely share in a political life. As political virtue, justice is manifested in laws and adjudicative procedures consistent with the universal and particular senses explicated above. The subsumption of both the universal and particular forms of the just within an overarching notion of political justice supports the latter's identification with the common advantage of a polis. In the following passage of *Eudemian Ethics*, Aristotle hence suggests that the prevailing view of political justice in a polis reflects a conception of the common advantage that is in line with its regime-form: 'All constitutions partake in the just (*hai de politeiai pasai dikaiou*), since they are a community (*koinōnai*), and everything that is common (*koinon*) comes about through the just (*tou dikaiou*)' (VII.9, 1241b13–15). Aristotle's treatment of political justice therefore supports the claim made in the opening of the chapter that while the ultimate end of law is *eudaimonia*, its proximate end is the common advantage. It is not simply that the common advantage – identified with political justice – serves as a normative ideal for true legislative experts. A community governed by law should aim to promote virtue and ensure a reasonable distribution of goods and fair allocation of the benefits and harms that arise in transactions. Insofar as a polis governed by law is a unity of order, it requires the mediation of justice to bring the different elements into a state of relative harmony.

The status of political justice as the unqualified justice that obtains between citizens sharing in a constitution and law provides initial evidence for the claim that there is a distinctive aspect to the common advantage. A politically just community is one in a lawful condition or state of *eunomia* (*Pol.* IV.8, 1294a3–7, VII.4, 1326a29–31).[53] This suggests that the just ordering of a community through law is a state-of-affairs attributable to the polis as a whole and a component part of the wellbeing of each member (VII.1, 1323b30–6). Aristotle implies, in this context, that the virtue of *phronēsis* cannot properly be developed outside political activity

[53] I return to the concept of *eunomia* in the next chapter.

and relations of justice (III.4, 1277b1–32).[54] Political justice is irreducible to private interactions of individuals and in the focal sense describes the condition of a community governed by practically reasonable laws directed to wellbeing. The distinctive good of a political community, moreover, does not simply describe the reciprocated affection of individuals, but refers to a prudent and just ordering of the community constitutive for the flourishing of each. In order to elaborate on this interpretation, it is instructive to consider some medieval readings of Aristotle's account of political community.

SECTION 4 THE POLIS AS A UNITY OF ORDER

Aristotle's identification of the common advantage with political justice provides initial support for the claim that the flourishing of a polis is a shared reason for action and distinctive good. More argument is required, however, to justify the normative significance of the common advantage in the distinctive sense as a *telos* determining the activities of legislators and citizens (*NE* VIII.9, 1160a9–13). In this final section I argue, with reference to the late medieval interpretation of the polis as a unity of order, that the distinctive conception of the common advantage plays an important part in Aristotle's account of the obligatory force of law and that the concept's motivational and normative aspects perform complementary explanatory roles.

The ascription of a normative role to the distinctive common advantage is arguably implicit in the *Nicomachean Ethics* I.2 identification of the end of the polis with the human good. Although the good (*agathon*) is the same for an individual and a polis, Aristotle states, the latter is both greater (*meizon*) and more perfect (*teleioteron*) to attain and preserve. And while it is satisfactory to secure the good for one person, it is nobler (*kallion*) and more divine (*theioteron*) to attain it for a people or a polis (1094b7–10). This passage does admit of competing interpretations, yet its full import cannot easily be explicated in simple instrumental or aggregative terms, insofar as it refers to the good of the polis as a whole over and above any mere collection of individual goods.

Aristotle's statement is puzzling because it asserts both the superiority of the good of the polis over the good of the individual and their identity. Albertus Magnus, in his second *Nicomachean Ethics* commentary, attempted to resolve this interpretative difficulty as follows. The good of the political community is a potential whole (present in its parts only in power or virtue) rather than a universal whole that is present in essence in each of its parts.[55] Albertus explains the point by reference to the diverse virtues and powers (fighting, ordering troops etc.) operative in the case of a victorious army.[56] While the victory of an army depends on the virtues of its parts, it is only when all the virtues 'are gathered together and directed towards a single goal

54 MacIntyre (1988: 103–45).

55 Kempshall (1999: 31).

56 *Ethicorum Libri Decem* I.3.

that victory is made complete (*perficitur*)'.[57] As a potential rather than a universal whole, the political common good is a unity which serves as an end (*telos*) of practical action. Individual virtues, on this reading, share in the unity of the good according to their proximity to a common standard.[58]

In his discussion of the Aristotelian common advantage, Albertus Magnus demonstrates the way in which a group can achieve a collective goal that would be impossible for individuals to achieve on their own. In the *Physics*, Aristotle argues against Zeno's claim that if a bushel of millet makes a noise, then every grain making up the bushel must make a proportionate noise (*Ph.* VII.5, 249b27–250a24). Aristotle also notes that a ship hauled by a number of people cannot be moved any distance at all by one individual working independently. In the second commentary on *Nicomachean Ethics*, Albertus applies both of these analogies to the political domain. Human wellbeing, as the supreme practical good, presupposes the existence of the four cardinal virtues. It is the virtue of justice, however, which is represented by the hauling of a ship, the sound of a bushel of millet and the good found in the leader of an army.[59] Justice is a virtue which derives its potential for action from its parts, yet it is present in a way that cannot be reduced to an aggregation of those parts. Like the hauling of a ship and the sound of a bushel of millet, it is a necessary condition for the attribution of the relevant activity to the parts that the activity is attributed to the whole.[60] In this sense, justice functions as a distinctive common good of a political community, because it represents a unity of order attributable to the association as such.

If justice may be regarded as the good order of a polis (*Pol.*I.2, 1253a31–9), then a just polis is one in which a state of affairs obtains that is the good condition of the entire community. The final cause of human flourishing, that is to say, provides a principle for the constitutional arrangement of the political association so that all the parts contribute to the flourishing of the whole, considered as unity of order. This unity is not simple or organic: it is rather the 'articulated unity' that also emerges from the *Politics* II.1–5 critique of Plato. The status of the polis as unity of order, moreover, is consistent with the fact that the common advantage – understood as a motivating reason – has both instrumental and aggregative components. Individuals certainly form together into a distinctively political association because it provides them with the conditions to flourish both individually and in common. Yet the ultimate end for which members of a political community associate also establishes the polis as a unity of order which is more than a set of either instrumental conditions or an aggregate of individual flourishing (cf. *Pol.* III.3, 1276b7–8, IV.4, 1291a24–8). Here the common advantage as justice – understood as a distinctive

57 Kempshall (1999: 31).
58 Kempshall (1999: 32).
59 Kempshall (1999: 38–40).
60 *Ethicorum Libri Decem* 1.6.3.

good of political community – has both priority over individual benefit and its own normative significance.

The account of the common advantage just outlined has close affinities with other medieval interpretations of Aristotle's polis as a unity of order. According to Aquinas, for example, the whole is necessarily prior to the parts in the rank of nature and perfection (*ordine scilicet naturae et perfectionis*).[61] The sense in which the part is destroyed when the whole is destroyed, moreover, is that the part is defined by its activity and the power with which it acts (*pars definitur per suam operationem, et per virtutem qua operator*).[62] This is what ultimately justifies the analogy with the human body in Aristotle's argument for the priority of the polis over the individual (*Pol.* I.2, 1253a19–20). Just as the parts of a body cannot fulfil their function except as parts of a human being, so an individual cannot be self-sufficient and carry out acts of virtue without participation in a political community.[63] Accordingly, the term *proteron* in *Politics* I.2 has the sense of more valuable or important, not priority in temporality.[64] The polis is also not prior by nature to the individual in an organicist sense, but rather because it is perfective of human capacities (1252b28 and 1253a31–3).[65] Indeed, as argued in Chapter 2, the kind of naturalness belonging to the polis requires perfection by craft or expertise (*technē*), which Aristotle acknowledges in frequently referring to the role of politics and legislation in the establishment and maintenance of a polis.

According to Aquinas, the whole constituting a political association is hence a unity of order which is more than the sum of its parts (*habet solam ordinis unitatem*), not absolutely one.[66] A part of a whole can act separately from the whole (as a soldier can act separately from the entire army), but the whole nonetheless has an operation that is not proper to its parts, but rather to the whole (e.g. an assault by the entire army).[67] It is therefore justified to ascribe action to the whole, insofar as it is a unity structured by a common goal. For the political association this common goal is *eudaimonia* and the polis is natural insofar as it allows for its realisation. The polis is thus a collection of individuals who, through participation in a common activity and goal, form an articulated unity. This interpretation maps neatly onto the analysis of the previous chapter, according to which the *politeia* is the principle of unity for the polis – what binds its constituent elements together – and is itself determined by a particular conception of human flourishing.

61 *Sententia Politic.*, lib. 1 l. 1 n. 30. *Cat.* 11 14b4–8 acknowledges 'evaluative' priority. Cf. *Met.* II.3, 999a13–14.

62 *Sententia Politic.*, lib. 1 l. 1 n. 30.

63 *Sententia Politic.*, lib. 1 l. 1 n. 31.

64 See further supporting arguments in Kraut (2002: 265). At *Sententia Politic.*, lib. 1 l. 1 n. 31 Aquinas notes that the whole is not prior to the parts in the order of coming to be.

65 See Miller (2000: 330–1).

66 *Sententia Ethic*, lib. 1 l. 1 n. 5.

67 *Sententia Ethic*, lib. 1 l. 1 n. 5.

As Kempshall has demonstrated, in the background of Aquinas' commentary is Aristotle's *Metaphysics* XII.10 account of the double ordering of a whole.[68] Here Aristotle argues that 'individual parts of a whole are ordered towards other parts in an intrinsic good of order but they are also ordered towards the extrinsic good of the whole'.[69] Aquinas' analysis of the political common good also understands it as a double ordering (*duplex ordo*), which incorporates both the formal cause of order and the final cause of virtue and flourishing. It is plausibly the tendency to jettison or understate this metaphysical framework and the associated terminology of formal and final causes which is one source of the 'thinner' conceptions of the common good that are found in contemporary natural law theory.

The characterisation of the polis as a unity of order sketched above allows for a reconciliation of Aristotle's aggregative statements on the common advantage and his treatment of the polis as a whole subject to predications. As noted in Section 2, Aristotle describes the polis aggregatively as a multitude (*plethos*) of individuals (*Pol.* III.1, 1274b44). This is consistent with the distinction between artificial and natural wholes, which entails that the polis cannot be a substance in the strict sense (*Met.* V.26, 1023b34–6, X.1, 1052a20–5).[70] Yet Aristotle not only attributes *eudaimonia*, but virtues to the polis (*Pol.* VII.1, 1323b30–1 and VII.7, 1327b31–6).[71] The apparent inconsistency can be resolved by allowing that the polis sustains predications as a structured unity of individuals with the same purpose, not as a natural whole (*NE* I.2, 1094b2–13; *Pol.* VII.7, 1327b30).

Aristotle's other 'holistic' assertions support this interpretation. Consider, for example, the claims that one should not think that any of the citizens belong to themselves, but rather that all belong as parts to the one polis, and that the care of each part naturally *(pephukeri)* looks to the care of the whole (*Pol.* VIII.1, 1337a27–30). Interpreted in terms of the claim that the polis is a unity of order, this passage entails that humans are naturally political beings because they are only able to attain virtue, perfection and happiness within a just political community. The polis is natural in the sense that it provides the conditions for *eudaimonia*, which presupposes that the political association is constituted as a unity of order, the flourishing of which is integral to the wellbeing of all. As a corporate entity that has a distinctive form of unity, a just polis is accordingly the end of a natural inclination for each individual insofar as they are a practically reasonable agent.

This interpretation of the polis as a unity of order, with its emphasis on the ultimate human end as a shared normative reason, sharpens and extends Miller's plausible teleological reading of the claim that the polis is prior to the individual. Although the ultimate normative significance of a flourishing polis is found in its

68 Kempshall (1999: 100).

69 Kempshall (1999: 100).

70 See Keyt (1991: 136).

71 Aristotle also countenances the possibility that a polis can be in a state of wellbeing when only most, or even some, of its members are flourishing (*Pol.* II.5, 1264b18).

capacity to promote individual wellbeing, from a teleological perspective the polis is prior (see *Pol.* I.2, 1252b28, 1253a31–3) because a well-ordered and self-sufficient community (1252b26–1253a18) is integral to the full realisation of human nature.[72]

The merits of this reading, which connects the normative force of the common advantage to its status as a form of political justice constituted by acts of virtue directed to a shared goal, can be seen by reference to the difficult case of the law's claim upon a citizen's obedience. In the *Rhetoric*, Aristotle considers military service laws as a privileged example of legal norms directing human conduct for the sake of the community and notes their importance of to the political justice which governs relations between citizens (*Rh.* I.13, 1373b19–24).[73] This passage suggests that political justice is the most compelling normative reason for the weighty demand that individuals subordinate their own flourishing to the wellbeing of the community. If a political association provides for the realisation of possibilities of human flourishing impossible outside of that association, and is a constituent part of each member's wellbeing, then this may require in some circumstances that citizens sacrifice their immediate interests, and even individual flourishing, in order to maintain the association. Without acknowledgement of this aspect of the common advantage it is difficult to see how there could be any decisive reason for a member of a political association to defend their community against external threats or to submit to a law that promotes the good of the community, but is at odds with an aspect of individual flourishing. It is doubtful, moreover, whether the normative import of the demand for sacrifice can be explicated solely by reference to instrumental and aggregative conceptions. This is because the intelligibility of personal sacrifice for the common advantage presupposes that there is a good of community beyond the individual benefit that it provides.[74] The wellbeing of the polis as a unity of order – identifiable with political justice – thus serves as an end of action which provides good reasons to abide by the law, even when legal directives may not serve a citizen's perceived self-interest.

The motivational and normative aspects of the common advantage thus perform different yet complementary explanatory roles in Aristotle's account of the polis.[75] If Aristotle were *merely* claiming that the common advantage is a set of instrumental conditions and aggregated interests and *also* claiming that it is the good condition of the community as a whole, then his position would potentially be inconsistent. The common advantage, however, works along different dimensions. Aristotle's

[72] See Miller (1995: 56): '[T]he priority claim rests on the principle of community that individuals can realise their potential only if they are subject to the authority of the *polis* . . . [t]he *polis* is a whole in the sense of a community: its natural end is a common good in which the individual members directly participate.'

[73] This passage should be read in conjunction with Aristotle's claim that it is the person with virtue who acts most courageously and nobly in dangerous situations because they have more to lose (*NE* III.8, 1117b10–15).

[74] See Pakaluk (2001: 88–94).

[75] Cf. Kahn's analysis (1990: 382) in terms of the concepts of expediency and justice.

explanation of the motivational genesis of the polis appeals to the advantages that accrue to each citizen. These advantages remain on foot once a polis has been established. Yet the common advantage is irreducible to the benefits that accrue to each individual because the polis is a unity of order which is in a good condition when it achieves a state of political justice dependent upon the exercise of virtues promoted by law. The lawful ordering of the polis towards a common goal of flourishing is, in this sense, a truly shared good.

Acknowledgement of Aristotle's appeal to motivational and normative aspects of the common advantage thus allows the interpreter to avoid the simplistic dichotomies mentioned in Section 1. On the extreme holist position, the political community is akin to an organism in the sense that it has an end that is not only distinct from, but supersedes, the ends of its parts.[76] On an extreme individualistic interpretation, by contrast, the promotion of the common advantage is understood solely in terms of the promotion of the interests of individuals.[77] While the extreme holist position understates the instrumental and aggregative aspects of the common advantage, according to which it serves as a motivating reason for individuals to enter the polis, an extreme individualist position contradicts Aristotle's appeal to the common advantage as a shared good identifiable with political justice. The better view is that Aristotle is a 'compositional' individualist and 'teleological' holist.[78] The polis arises because individuals are motivated to form larger communities from smaller associations in order to attain goods that are inaccessible outside the self-sufficiency of a 'complete' political community. Yet law-makers and citizens also seek the political good of justice, understood as a normative reason and distinctive *telos* of community.

It turns out, then, that Aristotle is both a 'moderate individualist' and a 'moderate holist'. Aristotle's conception of the polis is moderately individualistic in the sense that humans participate in the polis for mutual benefit and the common advantage is best construed, from this perspective, as both instrumental and aggregative. Aristotle's conception is also moderately holist, however, because the end of the polis is irreducible to actions of the parts. Although members of an association are able to act independently, there are actions and goals that each individual can only achieve through their activity as part of a whole. Insofar as members of a polis are brought together and guided by a common goal, therefore, they constitute a structured unity. The wellbeing of the polis as a unity of order is, moreover, dependent upon the establishment of a condition of political justice inseparable from the enactment of just laws.

In closing, one important consequence of the claim that the polis is a unity of order for Aristotle's account of *nomos* becomes clear from the following passage in *Nicomachean Ethics* X.9:

76 Miller (1995: 194).
77 Miller (1995: 194). An individualist interpretation along these lines is Nussbaum (1988: 148–214).
78 Miller (1995: 199–251).

> Only in the city of the Lacedaimonians (or it together with a few others) is the legislator (*ho nomothetēs*) held to have taken care for the rearing and the regular practices of the citizens. But in most cities, what concerns such things has been utterly neglected, and each lives as he wishes (*hekastos hōs bouletai*), 'laying down the sacred law (*themisteuōn*) for children and wife' in the manner of the Cyclops. The most excellent thing, then, is for the common care (*koinēn epimeleian*) to be correct (1180a24–30).

Aristotle's approval of the scope of Spartan legislation and emphasis upon the need for laws governing the upbringing and conduct of citizens is a corollary of the view that the aim of *nomos* is the common advantage in a distinctive sense. The association of the common advantage with political justice and the flourishing of a community, considered as a unity of order, imparts a comprehensive authority to legislative activity that precludes a conception of the law as merely as a means of limiting the capacity of individuals to encroach upon the freedom and material interests of each other. While the attribution of totalitarianism to Aristotle's account of the polis is anachronistic, the wide coverage of law in the practical works does reflect a view of the flourishing of the whole political community as a genuine good that is worthy of promotion.[79]

79 For the totalitarianism attribution, see Barnes (1990).

5

Stability and Obedience

If a just and well-ordered political community is integral to the good for an individual, then it would seem incumbent on the architectonic legislator and prudent statesperson to aim at the optimal condition of the polis and hence to reform defective regimes and laws. The normative structure of Aristotle's constitutional theory – with its conception of the best regime as an ideal and appeal to the common advantage as a central criterion for distinguishing correct and defective constitutions – likewise suggests a progressive stance towards correction of political injustice. The overall attitude towards the reform of constitutions and laws which emerges from the *Nicomachean Ethics* and *Politics* is nonetheless cautious and conservative. In the current chapter I consider the motivations for this circumspection and argue that it reflects both the importance of habituation to the effective functioning of law and a recognition of the limits of law's capacity to promote virtue and human flourishing. Section 1 engages in a close reading of Aristotle's treatment of the advantages and disadvantages of legal reform in the *Politics* Book II.8 discussion of Hippodamus' legislative proposal to honour innovation. In Section 2, I examine Aristotle's account of constitutional change and stability in light of his theory of ethical virtue. Finally, in Section 3, I turn to political obedience and argue for its dual justification within Aristotle's practical thought.

SECTION 1 HIPPODAMUS AND LEGISLATIVE REFORM

Aristotle's eudaemonistic practical thought would seem to motivate a progressive stance towards constitutional and legal reform. Both political naturalism (*Pol.* I.2, 1253a1–30) – with its claim that humans are by nature political – and the identification of the flourishing of the political community with the human end (*NE* I.1, 1094b7–11) entail that individual wellbeing depends on the good condition of the polis. Insofar as the good condition of the polis in turn depends upon the justice of its prevailing constitutional form (*Pol.* III.6, 1279a18 and III.12, 1282b17–18; *EE* VII.9, 1241b13–15), and the laws enacted relative to that form, then it would seem incumbent on the legislator to do everything possible to establish good regimes and laws. Conversely, defective regimes and laws would appear incompatible with the flourishing of either the individual or the polis. It thus seems a normative requirement, on the assumptions of Aristotelian practical philosophy, for the legislator to endeavour to improve the constitutional and legal conditions of unjust political communities.

The stance towards constitutional and legal reform which emerges from the *Nicomachean Ethics* and *Politics* is nonetheless more cautious than these points would suggest. Aristotle's circumspection reflects, as Chapter 1 has demonstrated, the importance of habituation to the effective functioning of the law and the law's limited capacity to instil virtue in the majority of citizens. The first section of the current chapter develops this point, which is inseparable from the predominance of the defective regimes, by reference to Aristotle's most sustained discussion of legal reform: the *Politics* II.8 examination of Hippodamus' proposal that a law should be enacted which honours those who have discovered something that is useful for the polis (*Pol.* 1268a6–8).[1]

Hippodamus' legislative proposal is that cities should honour those advancing something beneficial for the political community (1268a7–8). One obvious concern with such a proposal is the difficulty, in the political domain, of deciding whether any proposal is in fact beneficial. Aristotle's treatment of Hippodamus' proposed law, however, sets this concern to one side and works on the assumption that the advantageousness of new laws has already been determined. The question Aristotle considers is therefore whether it is harmful or advantageous for political communities to change the traditional laws (*tous patrious nomous*), if and when better laws are available (1268b18–29).[2] Aristotle, that is to say, assumes for the sake of argument that the proposed new laws are not only good, but superior to the ancestral or traditional laws which they are designed to replace.

The assumption that change in the laws is for the better strengthens the argument for legal reform which already seems built into Aristotle's eudaemonistic account of practical affairs. Every craft, inquiry, action and choice is held to aim at some good (*NE* I.1, 1094a1–2) and every community, including the most authoritative political community, is constituted for the sake of some good (*Pol.* I.1, 1252a1–5). The proximate good of the political community is the common advantage, which is identified with political justice (*Pol.* III.6, 1279a18 and III.12, 1282b17–18; *EE* VII.9, 1241b13–15), and this is inseparable from the enactment of just laws (*NE* VI, 1129b11–14 and *Pol.* VII.2, 1324b23–9). If good laws are necessary for both individual and communal flourishing, then a change to better laws, especially when it is clear that those proposed do in fact constitute an improvement, appears to be a demand of

1 Aristotle initially presents the arguments for and against legal reform in an aporetic or dialectical manner (see, for example, the use of the optative of *phēmi* at 1268b38). From 1269a12, however, Aristotle seems to transition from an aporetic mode of speech to an assertoric (*ek men oun toutōn phaneron hoti*).

2 As Susemihl and Hicks point out (1894: 276), ancestral laws include unwritten norms and conventions.

practical rationality. Aristotle suggests as much when he states that where better legal arrangements have been discovered, then it would seem to be for the common good (*koinon agathon*) to dissolve the regime or laws (*Pol.* II.8, 1268b32). It is in this sense that the replacement of worse laws with better seems a normative requirement for Aristotle's political science.

There are further considerations in favour of beneficial legal reform beyond the eudaemonistic assumptions of Aristotelian practical philosophy. Several of these considerations are discussed by Aristotle in his articulation of the position of an advocate of legal reform for the good. These include an analogy with other applied modes of rationality and a general appeal to progress.

The advocate of legal reform's first argument appeals to the benefits of progress in the scientific and technical realms. This comparison is not as implausible as might first be thought. While political science (*politikē*) and law-making expertise (*nomothetikē*) are modes of *phronēsis* (*NE* VI.8, 1141b23), and hence cannot be scientific in the strict sense of *Nicomachean Ethics* VI.3 and *Posterior Analytics* I.2, the enactment of constitutions and laws applies universal principles derived from experience to variable phenomena (*NE* X.9, 1180b20–8), and employs rationality (1180a21–b29) to augment the natural tendency humans possess to form ordered political communities. As argued in Chapter 2, law-making expertise thus falls under the broader *Metaphysics* VI.1 sense of *epistēmē* as a mode of intellectual inquiry concerned with a particular domain. It also shares with a *technē* like house-building the bringing-into-being of something that would not occur purely as a natural process (*Pol.* I.2, 1253a33). With applied sciences and crafts it is uncontentious that the 'state-of-the-art' progresses and implementation of discoveries is often beneficial. With medicine, for example, a more effective cure should be adopted, given that the promotion of health is an agreed good. Both medicine and gymnastic have in fact changed, Aristotle notes, from their traditional ways (II.8, 1268b35) in cases where improvements have been recognised. The categorisation of law-making with other domains of applied rationality also appears to be supported by the 'historical' consideration that there are seemingly self-evident (*autōn tōn ergon*) advances in law-making similar to those which are found in medicine and gymnastic (1268b37).

Aristotle also offers a general appeal to progress in support of beneficial legal reform. It seems implausible to deny that legal advancement is possible, given that many older laws were simplistic and barbaric (*tous gar archaious nomous lian haplous einai kai barbarikous*) or naïve (*euēthē*). Examples offered by Aristotle include a law governing the purchase of wives between Greeks (1268b37) and homicide laws allowing plaintiffs to provide witnesses from their own family (1269a3). Earlier humans were likely simple-minded, so it would be strange to persist with their opinions. Just as medicine can advance due to increasing technical sophistication and serve the clear good of health, so too might the enhanced experience of humans in the governance of their political communities bring about beneficial legal reforms directed towards the more authoritative end of overall human flourishing. As a general principle (and it is a principle that is surely foundational to philosophy as such), Aristotle notes succinctly, people seek what is good rather than what is traditional (*zetousi d' holōs ou to patrion alla tagathon pantes*) (1269a4) and they are right in so doing.

A final consideration offered by the advocate of beneficial legal reform appeals to the same limitations on fixed and written law presented in *Politics* III.15–16. In the case of political arrangements – which concern actions and particulars – it is impossible for everything to be captured precisely once and for all by universal written pronouncements (*Pol.* 1269a9–11). It would thus seem obtuse to think that laws enacted in a particular context should be immune to improvements formulated on the basis of subsequent changes in circumstance and improved knowledge. Although Aristotle does not make the point explicitly, the position of the advocate of beneficial legal reform cannot therefore be dismissed because it assumes an overly idealistic or sanguine view of the benefits of written law. One can rather see the arguments in favour of legal reform as based on an acknowledgement of law's limitations as a rational guide to conduct.

The considerations in favour of beneficial legal reform thus appear multiple and compelling. What is more, by assuming that the relevant legal reforms are in fact beneficial, Aristotle circumvents the objection that it is difficult to determine whether legal changes are indeed for the good. At this point, the internal normative logic of Aristotle's practical philosophy seems to necessitate the reform of irrational, ineffective and unjust constitutions and laws when doings so would promote the ultimate human end of *eudaimonia* at the level of both the individual and political community.

In the face of all these considerations, *Politics* II.8 nonetheless endorses a circumspect approach to legal reform. The strongest conclusion Aristotle is prepared to draw from the reasons above is that some laws must be changed some of the time (*phaneron hoti kinēteoi kai tines kai pote tōn nomōn estin*) (*Pol.* 1269a12–13). The principal consideration in an assessment of legal reform, Aristotle assumes, is what is advantageous and harmful to the polis (1269a17). From this perspective, the small benefits of minor changes to the law in the direction of the good are frequently outweighed by the harm that is caused by habituating citizens not to respect the law and to disobey the rulers (1269a18–19). It is a bad thing, Aristotle asserts, to habituate people to the reckless dissolution of the law (1269a15–16). Even on the assumption that a legal reform is advantageous because the content of the new law is more rational or just than its predecessor, the good condition of a polis depends upon effective habituation in the ways of the regime and its legal conventions.

Aristotle's position on the importance of habituation for the effective functioning of the law, as noted in Chapter 1, is clearly stated in the *Nicomachean Ethics* X.9 transition to the *Politics*. For most people, it is impossible to have the correct upbringing necessary to develop the ethical character virtues independently of good education laws. Habituation and law are mutually supporting in the development of ethical virtue. A moderate and controlled life is painful to the many, especially the young, but will be less so once they are accustomed or habituated (*sunēthē*) to act in the correct way (1179b33–5). Even in adulthood, citizens must be habituated to virtue. The primary function of *nomos* from this perspective is to habituate citizens so they can develop the ethical virtue necessary to participate in a just political community (1180a1–3). Yet Aristotle's analysis of the ethical virtues in Books II to IV of the *Nicomachean Ethics* suggests that the character (*ēthē*) of a person is manifested primarily in the character dispositions (*ēthikai hexeis*) contained in the desiring part of their soul.[3] Souls must be prepared by means of habits (*tois ethesi*) so as to rejoice and feel hatred in a noble way, just as earth which is to nourish a seed (1179b25–6). This entails that law does not operate solely or even primarily through engagement with the rational faculties, but rather employs compulsion on the desiring parts of the soul, particularly in the case of the many (1180a1–18). The effective operation of the law thus depends upon its capacity to work at the sub-rational level upon the desires of citizens. A minor reform in the law's content to make it more rational and just risks undermining its central function to restrain passions through habit.

It is the dependence of the effective functioning of the law upon habituation which explains why the argument from analogy with change in crafts (*technai*) is misleading. Change in craft is not like change in the law (*ou gar homoion to kinein technēn kai nomon*), because law has no strength with respect to obedience apart from habit, and this must be established over a lengthy period of time (*nomos ischun oudemian echei pros to peithesthai para to ethos, touto d' ou ginetai ei mē dia chronou plēthos*). The easy alteration of existing laws in favour of new laws therefore tends to weaken the power of the law itself (*asthenē poien esti tēn tou nomou dunamin*) (*Pol.* II.8, 1269a19–24).

A key difference between law and crafts like medicine and gymnastic, this passage implies, is that the effective functioning of the former depends upon obedience.[4] Habituation does play a role in the attainment of the end of medicine and gymnastic – health – because a regimen can improve outcomes or make exercise easier and more pleasurable. The key to understanding why Aristotle rejects the model from the other arts, based on the importance of habituation, must therefore be found in the element of compulsion, constraint and force (*NE* X.9, 1180a11–18) that is necessary to secure obedience. While constraint and compulsion play some role in the habitual practices of other crafts, these crafts are not as dependent on force for their successful functioning as law.

There is another key difference between law and the crafts suggested by Aristotle's discussion. Medicine and gymnastic both operate upon the material of the human

[3] Further to this point see Bobzien (2014: 88).

[4] As Lockwood (2015: 74) notes.

body. In a sense, so does the law, insofar as it regulates the conduct of citizens and threatens them with punishments in the case of transgression. Whereas medicine and gymnastic concern specific domains of bodily health, however, the law regulates the entire sphere of human conduct. Legislative activity thus has an extremely wide scope – the human good – and must deal with the entire ethical realm as such.

As discussed in Chapter 1, Aristotle nonetheless has a realistic view of the capacity for law to promote virtue. Ethical virtue in the genuine sense presupposes practical wisdom. Few possess this and few and are capable of possessing it (*NE* VI.8, 114b1–30).[5] Practical wisdom strictly speaking is, moreover, truly exercised only by legislators and rulers. True opinion (*doxa alēthes*), not practical wisdom (*phronēsis*), is the virtue of one ruled (*archomenou*) (*Pol.* III.4, 1277b25–7). The best that can be expected from the law in most cases, Aristotle suggests, is to promote a kind of secondary virtue according to which citizens may not necessarily do the right thing for the right reason, but at least do the right thing. Doing the right thing without a rational justification for why it is the right thing is a form of obedience and it requires habituation of long duration. An innovative approach to medicine or gymnastic might undermine an existing way of performing a treatment or exercise. In the case of law, however, an innovative approach to any particular law undermines the very habit of obedience which legislative expertise presupposes for its effective functioning.

Aristotle's final verdict on the merits of legal change is thus negative overall, even with reforms that in themselves can readily be acknowledged as improvements. While in some cases, legal reform will be desirable (Aristotle approves, for example, of the auditing of legislators introduced by Solon (*Pol.* III.2, 1281b30–5)), the success of any reform is contingent upon the particular character of the relevant political community and proposals for legal innovation should always keep in view both the limits of law and the limited potential for true virtue.[6]

In closing this section, it is worth noting one implication of the fact that legislative activity, unlike medicine and gymnastic, concerns the human good and hence the entire practical domain. Legislative expertise deals with humans motivated by passions and is hence resistant to a strict theoretical treatment. Aristotle's excursus on the desirability of legal reform occurs within his critique of Hippodamus, who is presented – in a passage unusual for its focus upon detailed personal characteristics – as a political innovator who adopted an extraordinary (*perittoteros*) appearance and lifestyle due to his love of honour and who also sought to understand nature as

5 Broadie (1991: 258). See also Rosler (2005: 185) and George (1993: 25).

6 Kraut (2002: 61). A further possible reason for Aristotle's cautious approach to legal reform is commitment to the views that human existence is eternal (*Mete.* II.14, 352b16–17; GA. II.1, 731b24–732a3, II.6, 742b17–743a1; DA. III.4, 515a25–b7) and that human civilisation is cyclical. In *Politics* II.5 Aristotle thus states, in his criticism of Socrates' proposals regarding property, that nearly everything has been discovered, though some things have not been synthesised, and others known but not practised (*Pol.* 1264a2–5). See Lockwood (2015: 75).

a whole (*Pol.* II.8, 1267b22–8).[7] In addition to the law concerning the award of honours to those who discover something beneficial to the polis, Hippodamus' other legislative proposals overestimate the practical applications of theory. Due to a fixation with the number three, for example, Hippodamus categorised the subject matter of law into three kinds: hubristic conduct, injury to persons and property and killing. This proposal, which neglects the educational and habitual aspects of law, delimits 'justice to violations of the harm principle'.[8] An overly positive view of the potential good achieved by radical reform or innovation, Aristotle implies, is commonly associated with the theoretical idealism of those lacking experience in practical affairs. Perhaps the most serious errors that one could make from such a naïve theoretical perspective are the assumptions that a legislator can presuppose that most humans are good by nature and that *nomos* is capable of instilling genuine virtue in those who either have bad natures or upbringings or both.

Even if one accepts that Aristotle's belief in the limits on the capacity for the law to promote genuine virtue largely explains his circumspection with respect to constitutional and legal reform, the desirable features of stability and order in the case of imperfect and unjust regimes still need to be explained. It is to this question that I now turn in the second section of the chapter.

SECTION 2 IMPROVING IMPERFECT REGIMES

Aristotle's advocacy of a cautious approach to legal reform in *Politics* II.8 is consistent with the centrality of the theme of constitutional preservation (*sōtēria*) to *Politics* V and VI. Laws are relative to particular constitutional forms (*Pol.* III.11, 1282b8–13, IV.1, 1289a14–22) and the detrimental impact of revolution or reform of entire regimes with respect to habituation in the law would far exceed that following from minor legal changes. Democracy, oligarchy and tyranny are, however, radically defective regimes. As a consequence, it is difficult to see how Aristotle can simultaneously uphold a conception of politics as directed towards human flourishing and the common advantage while also defending the preservation of regimes which do little to further those ends. It is thus tempting to conclude that Aristotle's discussion in *Politics* II.8 assumes that the hypothetical new and better laws are to be enacted in a correct regime. Yet a close examination of the *Politics* V discussion of regime preservation reveals that Aristotle's circumspection regarding legal reform extends to defective regimes. In order to reconcile this conservatism with Aristotle's eudaemonist political commitments, I argue in this section, it is necessary to examine the implications for Aristotle's constitutional method of the predominance of the defective democratic and oligarchic regimes.

7 See Pangle (2013: 83–5). Further to Hippodamus, see also Susemihl and Hicks (1894: 331–4).

8 Lockwood (2015: 74).

Book V of the *Politics* begins by introducing into Aristotelian political science the sources of preservation (*sōtēria*) of regimes and the manner by which they might best be maintained (*Pol.* V.1, 1301a23–5). In *Politics* VI.5, Aristotle reiterates that the preservation of constitutions, and not merely their establishment, should be a central concern of the law-giver (*nomothetou*). The student of politics should consider the causes of preservation and destruction of constitutions (*sōtēriai kai phthorai tōn politeiōn*) with a view to their safety (*asphaleian*). This involves enacting unwritten and written laws (*nomous, kai tous agraphous kai tous gegrammenous*) that will most of all promote the security and preservation of the constitutions discussed in Books IV–VI (VI.5, 1319b33–1320a2). Troublingly, however, these constitutions include the defective forms of democracy, oligarchy and tyranny. Indeed, the middle books not only dedicate particular attention to the most prevalent constitutional forms of democracy and oligarchy, and the manner by which they are preserved, but contain recommendations for the maintenance of tyranny. It thus seems that the normative criteria for good constitutions – the common advantage and political justice – have dropped out of the picture in favour of pragmatic advice oriented to stability.

Aristotle's advice to law-makers regarding regimes also pertains to the preservation of laws. One reason legislators should enact laws relative to the constitution (*Pol.* III.11, 1282b8–13, IV.1, 1289a14–22), is that even minor legal reforms can lead to constitutional overthrow. In Thurii, a group of ambitious youths sought to repeal a law in which the office of general could only be held at four-year intervals. The law's repeal led to the dissolution of the entire regime and the establishment of a dynasty (V.7, 1307b1–19). Although the original constitution at Thurii was aristocratic, Aristotle asserts that law-makers in all regimes must avoid small changes to the laws (1307b26–32). This advice echoes the cautious approach to legal reform in *Politics* II.8, while widening its scope.

An interpretation according to which Aristotle expresses caution regarding the reform of the traditional laws in correct regime-forms but advocates for radical constitutional and legal change in the case of defective regimes thus appears difficult to maintain. It is true that Aristotle concludes his discussion of legal reform in *Politics* II.8 with an at least implicit suggestion that the desirability of legal reform depends upon the specific kind of regime in question (*Pol.* 1269a25–7). The methodological approach of Books IV–VI nonetheless consistently assumes a perspective according to which the political scientist and legislative expert should be aware of how to preserve and stabilise all regime-types inclusive of the defective forms of democracy, oligarchy and tyranny.

Aristotle's inclusion of regime and law-preservation for defective constitutions within the subject matter of political science has frequently troubled interpreters.[9] It is not so much that eudaemonism would seem to entail that the legislative expert

[9] See the discussions in Kahn (1990), Rowe (1991), Polansky (1991), Garver (2011) and Destrée (2015).

should seek to reform constitutions in the direction of the theoretical best regime according to prayer. Aristotle's emphasis upon regime preservation, even for defective regimes, also appears in tension with the normative presuppositions of the more 'realistic' categorisation of constitutional forms according to whether they aim at the common advantage. Immediately after the passage cited above regarding the enactment of laws that will preserve the regime, Aristotle refers specifically to the need for the good legislator to ensure not that laws are democratic or oligarchic to the greatest degree, but rather that they are enacted in such a way as to cause the regime to continue under its current governance for the longest amount of time (*ho pleiston chronon*) (*Pol.* VI.5, 1320a1–5). Aristotle's inclusive approach to regime-preservation thus appears to combine a Machiavellian pragmatism regarding maintenance of political rule with a privileging of stability and order as political ends.[10]

The major concern in this vicinity is articulated in an instructively strident way by Garver. According to Garver, Aristotle's discussion of *stasis* or faction in Book V of the *Politics* upholds 'stability [as] ... a value apart from all regard for the justice of the regime defended'.[11] In pursuing stability, Garver suggests, Aristotle neglects justice and adopts a relativistic or even arbitrary perspective which may be considered not only 'ethically neutral' but also 'ethically dubious'.[12] If Garver's interpretation is correct, then Aristotle's focus upon the preservation of regimes simply eclipses the eudaemonist normative dimensions of his practical thought, with its appeal to the common advantage and justice as preconditions for development of individual and communal flourishing.

One option in the face of this dilemma is to offer an historical explanation for Aristotle's methodological emphasis upon stability and preservation of regimes in the middle books of the *Politics*. In his study of ancient and modern constitutionalism, for example, McIlwain strongly emphasises the far-reaching and violent nature of revolution and factional conflict in the Greek world.[13] Stability assumes the status of a genuine 'value' or good in relation to the 'dread' of the alternative. This historical reading of Aristotle's methodology in the middle books of the *Politics* is certainly consistent with the emphasis upon avoidance of *stasis* or faction which dominates the Book V account of constitutional change. Aristotle's wide-ranging analysis of *stasis* – with its coverage of psychological factors such as resentment and sociological factors such as the distribution of honour and material goods – plausibly reflects a real concern to avoid the sources of conflict which undermine political order and threaten dissolution into violence and civil war.[14]

10 Nichols (1992: 100). See Coby (1988: 906) for a contrasting view.

11 Garver (2011: 135).

12 Garver (2011: 136).

13 McIlwain (1947: 38–9).

14 Skultety (2009) provides plausible arguments that Aristotle intends to restrict *stasis* to open sedition and civil war. On political change more generally see Polansky (1991), Keyt (1999) and Hatzistavrou (2013).

More recently, Saxonhouse explains Aristotle's emphasis upon stability by reference to the need for clear 'political attribution' in external relations.[15] As discussed in Chapter 3, Aristotle locates the identity conditions for political communities in the *politeia* considered as the form of the polis (*Pol.* III.3, 1276b7–10). On Aristotelian assumptions, constitutional instability renders problematic the question of political responsibility i.e. whether past unjust acts committed by the rulers of one polis against another in war can be attributed to the former polis in cases of regime change.[16] Saxonhouse thus also ascribes Aristotle's privileging of stability to prevalence of violent conflict.

While these interpretations are not without historical plausibility, they fail to provide a fully satisfactory reconciliation of the eudaemonist and conservative tendencies in Aristotle's constitutional theory. An interpretation which can point to the genuine merits of constitutional and legal stability has better prospects, insofar as it allows for an explanation according to which political science must be cognisant of competing normative demands which are at least partially reconcilable through different levels of analysis. In order to be persuasive, however, such an interpretation must also explain how Aristotle's emphasis upon stability and preservation does not entail a complete eclipse of the normative considerations of the common advantage, justice and, pre-eminently, human flourishing, which play such a fundamental role in his practical thought.

An uncontroversial starting point is to acknowledge that regime preservation and stability have normative value for Aristotle because a basic level of political order and freedom from violent faction is a necessary condition for human flourishing. This is to suggest that Aristotle's political thought is animated by a 'double teleology' according to which the polis was established for the sake of human survival or life in a more basic sense, but its ultimate goal is the realisation of the good life (*to eu zēn*) (*Pol.* I.2, 1252b28–30).[17] The stability of regimes consequently derives normative weight from the fact that an ordered polis is a structural requirement for both individual and communal wellbeing. This 'double teleology' can even make intelligible Aristotle's notorious recommendations for the preservation of a tyranny in *Politics* V.11. Aristotle's first set of recommendations – which entail that tyrants should make their subjects think small thoughts and be distrustful of each other – serves the minimal goal of preservation. Yet Aristotle also counsels the tyrant to modify the regime in the direction of a kingship. Although this advice could enhance the security and duration of the regime, it should be understood as primarily designed to guide the ruler of a clearly defective regime in the general direction of virtue and the common advantage.[18]

15 Saxonhouse (2015: 196–7).
16 Saxonhouse (2015: 196–7).
17 Kahn (1990: 369).
18 Kahn (1990: 383).

The identification of a double teleology in Aristotle's political thought still does not totally satisfy as an explanation of the normative value of stability. If one accepts Garver's reading, Aristotle's approach to political change and innovation privileges stability at the *expense* of the common advantage and justice, and does not merely stipulate it as a necessary condition for the good life. It is noteworthy that Aristotle, moreover, consistently characterises innovators and innovation negatively (*Pol.* V.7, 1307b19, V.8, 1308b20, VII.10, 1330a28, VII.14, 1332b29).[19] In his Book II discussion of Phaleas' proposal for levelling of property, for example, Aristotle relates indulgence of political innovation to faction by noting that novel proposals for land redistribution encouraged people to become *neōteropoioi*, i.e. advocates of radical innovation (II.7, 1266b14).

In order to develop a more satisfactory account of Aristotle's normative commitment to stability, it is necessary to appreciate the implications of the predominance of the defective regimes. The most obvious reason for this predominance is that political communities generally divide into factions of the people and the wealthy, thus preventing the development of a 'middling' constitution which looks to the common advantage rather than partisan interests (IV.11. 1296a22–b1).[20] Different regimes reflect diverse conceptions of justice and the democratic and oligarchic conceptions of justice are both mistaken: the former identifies equality with respect to freedom as equality simply, whereas the latter identifies inequality with respect to wealth as inequality simply (V.1, 1301a34–40). Democratic and oligarchic laws mirror these mistaken political commitments. Actual political communities thus tend to be riven by sectional tensions informed by mistaken views of justice. It is those with virtue who have the best claim to engage in factional disputes on the grounds that they are treated unjustly, if they are in fact unequal and yet treated as equal, but they are least likely to do so (1301a40–b1). This is presumably not only because virtue discourages divisive political action, but also because of the paucity of their numbers.

The Aristotelian legislator and statesperson thus confronts a situation in which those with virtue are almost invariably outnumbered by citizens with mistaken views of justice. Good birth and virtue are as rare as wealth and free status are common (1301b39–1302a1) and hence the political scientist must acknowledge the probability that democracies and oligarchies will prevail rather than the 'correct' counterpart regimes. Viewed from this perspective, indeed, the other constitutions can all be viewed as mixtures or blends of democracy and oligarchy (V.7, 1307a5–16, V.10, 1310b2–7), because wealth and free status are by far the most prevalent criteria for the distribution of political offices and honours. Once such assumptions are in place, then the most viable form of political innovation will be, as *Politics* IV.11 suggests, of an incremental kind towards the 'mean' of polity i.e. towards a regime which at least

19 Lockwood (2015: 73).

20 On partisan identities, and their determination by incorrect views of *eudaimonia*, see Skultety (2008).

attempts to balance and mediate the competing (and ultimately mistaken) principles of 'distributive' justice advocated by democrats and oligarchs. Polity thus emerges as the 'realistic ideal' for the Aristotelian legislator and politician (*Pol.* IV.12, 1296b35).

This relative privileging of polity as a 'middling' regime that is actually attainable under the right conditions by political communities – especially democracies and oligarchies – reflects limits on the capacity for human virtue which are rarely overcome. Aristotle notes in this context that while it is difficult for one or a few to be outstandingly good in all virtues, it is possible for a larger number to be so with respect to the military virtue (III.7, 1279a39–b2) that is required by the hoplite class of a polity. Polities possess more stability than democracies and oligarchies because they mitigate the potential for *stasis* which eventuates when a regime is framed around unjust principles of distribution based on freedom (where equality in free status is applied to other domains) and wealth (where inequality in wealth is applied to other domains) respectively.[21] Polity hence serves as an imperfect approximation of the best polis (or as the best polis relatively speaking) insofar as citizens have ethical virtue, but in an attainable way which is associated with military excellence.

It is Aristotle's commitment to the rarity of virtue and advocacy of polity as an attainable goal for actual political communities that in large part explains the specificity of his recommendations for preservation of the defective regimes in *Politics* IV–VI. The discussion of democratic and oligarchic legislative artifices (*sophismata tēs nomothesias*) (*Pol.* IV.13, 1297a36), for instance, is framed around the assumption that a legislator should seek a just blend (1297a39–40) of constitutional forms towards the direction of the middling regime. A picture therefore emerges in which democracy or oligarchy almost invariably prevail and the best that can be hoped for is the balancing of their unjust elements through limited and cautious constitutional and legal reform.[22] As *Politics* IV.11 makes clear, however, even the middling regime is difficult to realise in practice.

The predominance of democracy and oligarchy also means that it is necessary for the law-giver and true politician to consider the better and worse forms of those regimes (*Pol.* IV.4, 1291b31–1292a39, 1292a39–b10) in relative terms. Analysis of the different forms of democracy and oligarchy, in *Politics* IV.4 and 5, reveals that the versions of these regimes 'governed' by *nomos* are superior to those in which human rulers are able to make arbitrary decrees (see, in particular, 1292a1–40). With respect to property assessments determining eligibility for office in an oligarchy, for example, a regime where citizens follow the laws and there are moderate assessments remains oligarchic, but tends towards the middling regime (IV.14, 1298a35–40). By contrast, the 'most oligarchic' form of oligarchy is where officials have authority over the laws (1298b1–5). Adherence to the 'rule of law' thus emerges as a way of

[21] Destrée (2015: 214–15).
[22] See Ober (1998: 290–347).

differentiating best and worst versions of the defective regimes. This relativisation of the defectiveness of democracy and oligarchy to whether they adhere to the rule of law reflects that where laws do not rule, there is in a sense no regime at all (IV.4, 1292a33–4).

Aristotle's account of the best version of democracy instructively identifies it with the oldest sort (*archaiotatē*) in which farmers predominate under law (*Pol.* VI.4, 1318b6–1319a20). Such a regime will be well-governed (*politeuesthai kalōs*) because the majority of citizens are more concerned with their farm work than politics. This promotes a political arrangement in which all citizens elect the magistrates and call them to account, but the more important offices are elected from citizens who meet the higher property qualifications (1318b27–34). The higher classes will also be satisfied with such arrangements, Aristotle suggests, because they will not be governed by those inferior to them (1318b37–8). Most importantly of all, this arrangement – with its laws governing the auditing of officials – ensures that the upper classes do not act in a grasping way. Aristotle makes the general point in this context that it is not advantageous for people to be able to do what they wish, because such a power (*exousia*) cannot guard against that which is bad in all humans (*prattein ho ti an ethelē tis ou dunatai phulattein to en heskastō[i] tōn anthropōn phaulon*) (1318b40–1319a2). Older laws that are well-established in custom mitigate this tendency (1319a10). The examples Aristotle provides of such laws – legislation by Oxylus and the Aphytaeans – served to promote the necessary conditions for an agricultural version of democracy (with its particular range of limited virtues) and restrain the capacity for the upper classes to become too wealthy (1319a6–19).

There are hence at least three levels of normative ideal for the Aristotelian legislative expert and statesperson to keep in view: the regime according to prayer, the middling regime and the predominant regimes under the rule of law. In the case of the third and most attainable level – democracies and oligarchies where partisanship and arbitrary decision is tempered to some extent by adherence to the rule of law – the legislator must also consider what will promote *continued* adherence to the rule of law. This requires habituation in obedience to the laws, particularly those that impede change towards those forms of the defective regimes which barely deserve the name. The most effective and important means of preserving regimes and their laws is accordingly education relative to the constitutional form (*Pol.* V.9, 1310a13–15). Consistent with the principle of the constitutional relativity of law, Aristotle states that there is little point in having the most beneficial laws when those sharing in the regime have not been habituated in the appropriate modes of life consistent with the ends of that regime (1310a17–19). While the focal case of habituation in the law pertains to legal norms enacted under a 'correct' regime, Aristotle's analysis acknowledges the rarity of virtue and correct conceptions of justice. And reflection on the relatively good or preferable forms of predominant defective regimes reveals that these are particularly dependent upon adherence to the rule of law and the habituation this presupposes. These considerations all militate against an innovative stance to constitutional and legal reform.

Aristotle's circumspect assessment of the desirability of constitutional and legal change can thus be found largely to rest on assumptions regarding the prevalence of democratic and oligarchic regimes, which reflects in turn the scarcity of genuine virtue and correct conceptions of justice. The limited capacity for the majority of citizens in most constitutional orders – particularly democracy and oligarchy – to develop full-blooded virtue finds its clearest expression, as is appropriate, in the *Politics* VII discussion of the constitution 'according to prayer'. Here Aristotle states not only that happiness is the best thing (*estin eudaimonia to ariston*), and that this is the actualisation of virtue and a certain complete practice of it (*aretēs energeia kai chrēsis tis teleios*), but also that only some persons are able to partake of it (*metechein autēs*) while others are able to do so only to a small degree or not at all. This, Aristotle concludes, is the ultimate cause of there being several kinds and varieties of polis and several sorts of regime (*Pol.* VII.9, 1328a36–b2).

Aristotle's methodological commitment to different levels of constitutional analysis flows to a significant extent from a prudent recognition of the predominance of democracy and oligarchy and the resultant need for legislators to promote the establishment of the least defective versions of these regimes. As noted in Chapter 3, Aristotle's constitutional methodology distinguishes between (1) the best constitution, (2) the constitution appropriate for particular political communities, (3) the constitution relative to a particular 'hypothesis' or underlying assumptions and (4) the constitution that is most fitting for actual political communities (*Pol.* IV.1, 1288b22–35). The focus of Aristotle's constitutional analysis in the middle books of the *Politics* is (3) and (4) and consequently the imperfect regimes of democracy and oligarchy dominate the discussion. In relation to (3), of particular concern are the assumptions underlying the predominant defective constitutions. In the case of (4) the principal concern is how these imperfect constitutions can be improved.[23] In adopting the perspective of (4), a prudent law-maker might, moreover, reasonably adopt the cautious approach to legal reform advocated by Aristotle in *Politics* II.8. The perspectives of (3) and (4) thus reflect the scarcity of genuine virtue and concomitant prevalence of defective regimes.

In sum, Aristotle's attribution of normative significance to stability reflects that the main function of *nomos* is to provide rational guides to conduct which promote, through habituation, a limited virtue within the better versions of defective regimes for citizens lacking the requisite natures or fortune required for the development of true virtue. With this conclusion in place, it is clear enough why regime change and even legal reform would undermine the power of the law to provide its far from

[23] Destrée (2015: 212–13).

perfect guidance. Ultimately, Aristotle's views on the limited capacity for virtue explains why he assumes the prevalence of defective regimes and is resistant to constitutional and legal innovation. This is not to suggest that regimes and laws which promote the common advantage and political justice are less desirable than their defective counterparts. Nor is it to deny the important role played by the common advantage and political justice in providing normative criteria for the assessment of regimes. It is to suggest that the 'double teleology' in Aristotle's constitutional theory is not simply a matter of stability providing the necessary conditions for human flourishing. The double teleology also reflects real constraints on political eudaemonism.

On Aristotle's conception of practical philosophy, it belongs to the law-giver and true politician to assume a broad perspective which comprehends not merely the best regime, but also the predominant regimes which reflect constraints on the human capacity for virtue. In adopting such a perspective – which is most prevalent in the middle books of the *Politics* – considerations of stability are pronounced because of the need to take into account the ethical limitations of citizens who make up actual political communities. This explains why constitutional and legal stability often takes precedence over political innovations directed to the human good in a more expansive sense.

SECTION 3 OBEDIENCE AND OBLIGATION

A plausible corollary of Aristotle's commitment to the importance of constitutional and legal stability would seem to be that the laws of a polis ought to be regarded as authoritative and binding by citizens, at the very least when correctly enacted and just (*Pol.* III.11, 1282b2–3, III.15, 1286a21–4). Some scholars, indeed, have argued that Aristotle takes the necessity of obedience to the law as a simple given and has little to offer by way of justification for political authority and obligation in the sense familiar from modern political philosophy.[24] Although it is true that Aristotle does not provide an explicit justification for political authority and obligation, it is possible to extract from the practical works an implicit normative argument for obedience to the law. In the final section of this chapter, I first consider Aristotle's statements relevant to the theme of a generic and presumptive obligation to obey the law.[25] I then contend that it is mistaken to ground an Aristotelian account of legal obligation solely in the practical reasoning capacities of individuals.

24 See, for example, Mulgan (1977: 57), Robinson (1995: 14) and Kraut (2002: 271).

25 An obligation to obey the law is *generic* if it is considered in relation to each law taken simply as an instance of law and *presumptive* if in some cases it may be outweighed by countervailing moral considerations. See Finnis (1984) and Duke (2013).

The claim that the concept of political authority – and corresponding notion of obligation – exists at all in Greek thought is controversial.[26] Some concerns in this vicinity include the complex path of derivation from the Latin *auctoritas* to the modern conception of authority and the status of the former as a specifically Roman concept.[27] Perhaps the most well-known recent source of scepticism regarding authority in classical Greek thought is found in Arendt's argument that the concept is Roman in origin and that 'neither the Greek language nor the varied political experiences of Greek history shows any knowledge of authority and the kind of rule it implies'.[28] The interpretative difficulties on this topic are only exacerbated by the fact that the concept of legitimate political authority is strongly contested in contemporary political theory.[29] For present purposes, legitimate political authority can be defined as a right to rule or justified power to change the normative situation of persons. Corresponding to such a right or power are duties or obligations on the part of subjects of authority. Given this definition, it would be misguided to conclude that the Greeks lacked experience of authority simply because they did not have a single concept capturing all aspects of that experience.[30] As Rosler has demonstrated in some detail, the terms *kurios*, *archē* and *krisis* are frequently employed in the *Politics* to express meanings similar to the contemporary understanding of the concept of authority as entailing a right to rule.[31]

In light of this demonstration, and as noted in Chapter 1, Rosler reconstructs Aristotle's account of authority relations by reference to Raz's 'service' conception of the role of authority.[32] Rosler finds something closely akin to Raz's concept of an exclusionary reason for action at work in Aristotle's putative claim that the flourishing of individuals within a political community depends on reciprocal relations of ruling and being ruled.[33] Such relations do not necessarily presuppose a renunciation of practical rationality on the part of those who are ruled, insofar as the order of political communities, and the laws enacted under their rule, provide citizens with reasons to obey legal directives, on the proviso that those directives ultimately promote their best interests. This is to suggest that political authority and

26 Rosler (2005: 88).

27 See Heinze (1925) and Rosler (2005: 88). Evidence for this scepticism about the applicability of the concept of authority to Greek political thought can be found in Cassius Dio's (c. 150–235) inability (in his *Roman History*) to find a Greek term for the word *auctoritas* (L V 3.5) and the fact that the Greek translator of the *Res gestae vivi Augusti* had to employ the term *axiōma* as an equivalent for *auctoritas*; a term that captures the notion of dignity or standing of a person contained in the Roman concept of *auctoritas*, but not the influence that such a person exerts by virtue of their personal qualities and standing.

28 Arendt (1977: 91–141).

29 For a recent attempt to define legitimate political authority see Perry (2013: 1–74).

30 Lütcke (1968: 47).

31 Rosler (2005: 112–15).

32 Rosler (2005: 112–15) and Raz (1986: 23–37).

33 Rosler (2005: 101–12).

obligation can be justified on Aristotelian assumptions insofar as they serve the interests of individual citizens who are seeking to achieve virtue and *eudaimonia*.

Aristotle's implicit justification for political authority depends, in this reading, on perfectionist premises regarding the necessity of polis membership for individual flourishing. If one assumes that excellence and human flourishing require participation in a polis with a constitution (*NE* VI.8, 1142a9–10), and that the order provided by a constitution requires in turn that the laws enacted under it are considered authoritative (*Pol.* III.4, 1276b28–9, III.11, 1282b2, VI.5, 1320a15–16), then this seems to entail a generic and presumptive obedience to law.[34] The 'order and control which are provided by the government of the polis', and the underlying assumption that it is rational to act in conformity with the laws (*prattein kata tous nomous*) (*Pol.* VI.8, 1322a4), are, on this interpretation, necessary conditions for the ethical perfection that is the ultimate aim of practical philosophy.[35] It appears reasonable, given acceptance of all these assumptions, to attribute to Aristotle both a 'service' conception of authority and obligation (according to which the authority of law is justified by the benefits it provides to those living under its directives) and an instrumental account of the role of practical authority and law in the promotion of individual flourishing.[36]

While such a reconstructive interpretation of Aristotle's stance towards political authority and obligation is cogent enough, however, it is one-sided in its emphasis upon the normative force of individual flourishing as the foundation for obedience. Even within a more perfectionist framework, Aristotle's account of obedience is not grounded solely in individual wellbeing, because, as considered in the previous chapter, the common advantage cannot be reduced to its instrumental and aggregative aspects. Undoubtedly the good order of a political community promotes the interests of a citizen through the conditions of stability and predictability necessary for pursuit of individual aims. Yet a well-ordered polis is irreducible to the set of conditions for individual flourishing and has its own good as the flourishing of the community as a whole (*Pol.* VII.1, 1323b30–6, VII.1, 1337a27–30). If this is true, then one must consider whether obedience to the law is also valuable because it is conducive to the wellbeing and order of the community.

Aristotle's *Politics* IV.8 discussion of good governance (*eunomia*) speaks against construing legal obligation solely in individualistic and instrumental terms. Good governance (*eunomia*) does not exist where the laws have been well enacted (*eu keisthai*) yet are not obeyed (*mē peithesthai*). It is one sort of good governance when the laws upheld are finely enacted (even badly enacted laws can be obeyed) and another sort when laws are obeyed as enacted. The inhabitants of a polis may either obey the laws that are the best possible for them, or those that are the best simply

34 Rosler (2005: 181). Rosler cites Miller (1995: 232) for similar views on the relationship between perfectionism and political obligation. See also Zingano (2013: 203).

35 Mulgan (1977: 25).

36 See Rosler (2005: 178–9).

(1294a1–9). In addition, it is not only the case that *eunomia* is impossible when a polis is ruled viciously, rather than by the best citizens (*aristokratoumenēn*), but a city without good governance cannot be ruled in an aristocratic manner. Aristotle in this passage does not simply assert that *eunomia* is a necessary condition for a flourishing polis where citizens seek ethical virtue, but that just laws, or laws reasonably conducive to the development of virtue or quasi-virtue, are necessary for the community to be well-ordered. The good order of the political community has its own rationale beyond instrumental benefits it provides. This rationale is encapsulated in Aristotle's attribution to the polis of the potential for flourishing in the same way as an individual (VII.1–2, 1323b30–1324a13).

The political condition of *eunomia* does of course imply that a regime possesses good laws.[37] In the case of a truly aristocratic regime, such laws seek to promote human excellence. Viewed from a different perspective, however, the laws of a regime cannot be taken in isolation from the order of the whole regime. Without political stability and predictability, laws may be ever so good and just and conducive to virtue, but the conditions necessary for citizens rationally to obey such laws, in particular the expectation that other citizens will also be obedient, would be lacking. In order for the law to operate effectively it must be regarded as a seamless web such that the subjects of the law cannot pick and choose which laws to obey based on their sectional or private interests.[38]

Aristotle's distinction between two dimensions of *eunomia* points to a justification for obedience to the law that is not grounded merely in individualist perfectionism. Obedience to laws which are 'finely enacted' promotes a good condition of the political community conducive to human flourishing. Although 'finely enacted' laws can be understood both in terms of the best possible laws and the best possible laws under certain circumstances and constraints, even in the latter case it may be acknowledged that obedience to the law would be more conducive to *eudaimonia* than a state of anarchy. There is nonetheless a sense of *eunomia* according to which the fact that laws are obeyed as enacted (*to peithesthai tois keimenois nomois*) is normatively significant. Obedience to the law promotes order and justice in the community and hence the wellbeing of the polis as a whole. The normative significance of obedience to the laws is thus not simply to be understood on the presumption that the laws in question are good and just because they promote attainment of individual goods. This presumption implies that the fact of obedience is significant solely because it promotes the good condition of the polis which is a necessary condition for individual flourishing. Aristotle's identification of different dimensions of *eunomia* suggests a more subtle view according to which obedience to law, and the resultant stability, has a distinctive value.

[37] On *eunomia* as a good condition of a polis see Ostwald (1969: 62–95).
[38] Finnis (1984: 120).

In order to understand this qualified good of political obedience it is necessary to return once again to Aristotle's discussion of the function and limits of law. As noted often above, *Nicomachean Ethics* X.9 describes the purpose of law as habituation towards virtue and ascribes the need for law to the fact that the many do not find living in a moderate and controlled way pleasant (*sōphronōs kai karterikōs zēn ouk hēdu tois pollois*) and obey the governance of necessity more than reason (*anankē[i] mallon ē logo[i] peitharchousi*) (1179b33–1180a5). The role of the legislative expert and true statesperson is accordingly to frame laws with a 'view' to virtue (*pros aretēn*) and to encourage citizens in the 'direction' of virtue (*parakalein epi tēn aretēn*). This circumspection regarding the capacity of law to promote virtue reflects, as noted earlier, that genuine *aretē* presupposes a practical wisdom (*NE* VI.8, 114b1–32) which is hard for most citizens to attain.

If Aristotle is sceptical of the capacity for most citizens to develop genuine virtue in most actual regimes, then the justification for political obedience appears in a different light. In the majority of cases, obedience to the law will not promote true excellence and perfection. Often the most one could say is that obedience to the law will promote a secondary form of virtue allowing a citizen to act consistently with what genuine virtue would require.[39] As Aristotle puts it in *Nicomachean Ethics* X.9, a person reared and habituated (by the laws) in a noble manner, will subsequently lead his life in such a way and do nothing base, whether voluntary or involuntary (1180a15–17). The claim is not that laws allow a citizen to develop virtue in the full-blooded sense of human excellence, which presupposes *phronēsis*, but that their external conduct will be the same as a person with virtue.

It is the limited capacity of *nomos* to promote true human virtue which explains both the need for the legislator to focus on the moderation and stability of defective regimes and to extoll the merits of obedience to the law. From this perspective, a significant reason to promote obedience to the law is its capacity to forestall a state-of-affairs in which disorder and vice prevail. Of course, the establishment of political order facilitates, and in most cases is a precondition for, the development of the practical reasoning capacities of individual citizens. Yet Aristotle is realistic about the potential for most citizens in most regimes to develop such capacities to the full extent. The necessity of obedience to law for Aristotle should therefore not be understood as exclusively motivated by its instrumental function in relation to individual practical reasoning. The merit of obedience to law is also identified, at least in the case of most actual regimes, with the legislator's reasonable promotion of the minimally ethical conduct necessary for constitutional order and good governance.

There is hence a risk of anachronism in ascribing to Aristotle a defence of the value of obedience to the law that is grounded primarily in terms of its capacity to

[39] As discussed in Chapter 1, this secondary or 'ground-level' form of virtue is exemplified by the civic courage which, while motivated by honours rather than the noble or *kalon*, is nonetheless directed to the common advantage of the political community and is preferable to a disposition to act that is motivated purely by external goods or fear alone. For further discussion see Hitz (2012: 263–306).

establish the conditions for the ethical perfection of autonomous rational agents. Although it is possible to read back into the regime according to prayer in the later books of the *Politics* a conception according to which citizens are free and equal members of a rational political community, Aristotle's presentation of the principal function of law and the importance of obedience remains grounded throughout in a sober view of the practical reasoning capacities of most citizens and an awareness of the limits of politics.

In closing, it is worth noting that these considerations explain why it is also necessary to be cautious about the attribution to Aristotle of something akin to a 'right of revolution' against tyrannical regimes.[40] Aristotle's statement that no free person willingly endures tyrannical rule (*Pol.* IV.10, 1295a20–3) is not a recommendation that in all such cases a tyrant should be overthrown and a better constitution installed.[41] The broader context of the discussion of tyranny, and constitutional and legal change more generally, suggests that rather than defending a general account of the conditions under which the overthrow of a sub-optimal regime would be justified, Aristotle rather points to the need to consider the consequences of forcibly removing governing authorities. The detrimental impact of any sort of 'revolutionary' political conduct from an Aristotelian perspective would, moreover, need to be taken into account even apart from proper consideration of the disconnect between ethical perfectionism and the circumstances of politics. As Aristotle notes, it is those who are most outstanding in virtue who are most justified in engaging in factional conflict, but they are also the least likely to do so (*Pol.* VI.1, 1301a39–40). While it is reasonable and even just for those with virtue to be unequal in an unqualified sense (1301b1–2), realism demands a prudent recognition of the limited benefits of most forms of political change.

40 Kraut (2002: 373–4) and Rosler (2005: 239).
41 Destrée (2015: 218).

6

Natural Justice and Natural Law

The question of Aristotle's natural law credentials has often divided interpreters.[1] In the current chapter, I argue that much of this disagreement stems from insufficient attentiveness to both the details of Aristotle's account of the just by nature in *Nicomachean Ethics* V.7 and the ambiguity of the term 'natural law'. The chapter thus proceeds from the assumption that a precondition for any adequate assessment of Aristotle's status as a natural law theorist is a close analysis of the V.7 discussion of natural justice.[2] Such an investigation, the main concern of Section 1, reveals that Aristotle's characterisation of the politically just as partly natural and partly conventional does indeed entail that nature serves as a normative ground for law. With this conclusion in place, Section 2 then turns more directly to Aristotle's relation to the natural law tradition. Despite important differences between Aristotle's account of the normative foundations of law and those found in the paradigmatic natural law teachings of the Stoics and Aquinas, I argue, there are nonetheless features of later natural law thought on the purpose and evaluation of law which are genuinely Aristotelian in orientation.

SECTION 1 NATURAL JUSTICE

At no point in the practical works does Aristotle use a compound term directly equivalent to 'natural law'. The closest approximation is found neither in the *Nicomachean Ethics* nor in the *Politics*, but rather in the *Rhetoric*, which distinguishes between particular and common law (*nomon ton men idion ton de koinon*)

[1] Miller (1991) and Burns (1998 and 2011) both offer arguments in support of significant natural law tenets in Aristotle's practical works. See also Siegfried (1942: 57–62), Barker (1946: 366), Trude (1955: 177) and von Leyden (1967). Representative criticisms of the claim that Aristotle is a natural law theorist are found in Jaffa (1952), Mulgan (1977: 141), Yack (1993: 140–1), Lisi (2000: 47), Schroder (2003: 37–51) and Corbett (2009: 229–50).

[2] I use 'natural justice', 'natural right' and 'the just by nature' interchangeably as translations of *phusikon dikaion*. It needs to be remembered, however, that Aristotle's primary focus in *NE* V.7 is with 'the just' (external facts of 'right': *to dikaion*) See Chapter 4, note 48.

by stipulating that the latter consists of things agreed upon by all persons and hence in accord with nature (*kata phusin*, *phusei*) (*Rh.* I.13, 1373b9–13, I.15, 1375a31–b2). Even if one regards the *Rhetoric* as a reliable source of Aristotle's considered views, however, its account of law is internally inconsistent and provides insufficient textual grounds for a natural law doctrine.[3] Aristotle's better-known discussion of natural right in *Nicomachean Ethics* V.7 has recommended to some interpreters an explicit or implicit natural law view. This is despite the fact that Aristotle's description of the politically just as partly natural and partly legal seems to contrapose, rather than conjoin, nature and convention (*tou de politikou dikaiou to men phusikon esti to de nomikon*) (*NE* V.7, 1134b18–19 cf. *MM.* I.33, 1194b30–1). Aristotle's partition, taken at face value, suggests that the just by nature and the just by convention are distinct parts of a political community's principles of justice, not that positive law derives its normative justification from a transcendent source that is external to politics.

It would nevertheless be overly hasty to conclude that the attribution to Aristotle of natural law commitments is simply anachronistic. While natural justice cannot be regarded straightforwardly as a transcendent or even ante-political source of positive law's validity, it does provide a ground for the evaluation of positive law as just or unjust. In order to work through this complexity, it is best to begin with an examination of the discussion of the natural part of political justice in *Nicomachean Ethics* V.7. The difficult question of Aristotle's natural law credentials, that is to say, is best approached through a prior consideration of his difficult statements on the topic of natural right or the just by nature.

Political justice, as seen in Chapter 4, refers to the rightful ordering of relations (inclusive of offices, honours and material goods) between the citizens of a polis who are governed by law. In *Nicomachean Ethics* V.7, Aristotle divides this political justice (*politikon dikaion*) into natural and conventional parts:

> Of the just in the political sense, one part is natural, the other, conventional [or legal] (*tou de politikou dikaiou to men phusikon esti to de nomikon*). The natural (*phusikon*) is that which has the same capacity (*dunamin*) everywhere (*pantachou*) and is not dependent on being held to exist or not, whereas the conventional (*nomikon*) part is that which at the beginning (*ex archēs*) makes no difference (*ouden diapherei*) whether it is thus or otherwise, but once people have set it down (*hotan de thōntai*), it does make a difference (1134b18–22).

The contrast, within political justice, between the natural (*phusikon*), as what has the same power everywhere, and the conventional or legal (*nomikon*), as what is posited by particular communities, seems at first to be a fairly standard application of

[3] In Book I.10 (*Rh.* 1368b7–8) Aristotle says that particular law is written, whereas in Book I.13 (1373b56) he says that particular law is either written or unwritten. This inconsistency is discussed further below. The reliability of the *Rhetoric* as a source of Aristotle's considered views is also discussed in more detail in Section 2.

the *phusis* and *nomos* distinction familiar from mid to late fifth century BCE Greek thought and associated most readily with the sophistic movement.[4] This initial impression is corroborated by Aristotle's subsequent reference to the commonplace example of the burning of fire as a natural phenomenon because it occurs in the same way in Greece and Persia (1134b27). From the perspective of this dichotomy between the invariance of the natural (*phusikon*) and contingency of the conventional or legal (*nomikon*), the idea of a natural law which serves as a transcendent or ante-political normative ground for the evaluation of positive law is paradoxical.[5]

Aristotle's partition of the natural and conventional parts of political justice does not, however, map neatly onto the *phusis* and *nomos* distinction. In the first instance, Aristotle's conception of nature is conceptually richer than that associated with the sophistic movement. In *Metaphysics* V.4, Aristotle distinguishes several senses of nature. These include primary matter, the form or substance which is the *telos* of the process of becoming, substances as such, and the origin or principle of primary movement which inheres in each natural entity intrinsically and non-accidentally. This latter sense of nature – the source or internal principle of change – is privileged for theoretical enquiry.[6] In the practical domain, however, Aristotle's emphasis is on the systematic relationship between the nature (*phusis*) of a thing, its function (*ergon*) and its end (*telos*).[7] From this viewpoint, the end or *telos* of a natural entity is to realise or actualise its nature in the performance of its function (*NE* IX.7, 1168a6–9).

In the second instance, conventional justice (*nomikon dikaion*) appears to have a narrower scope than *nomos* (inclusive of positive law and custom). Aristotle's examples of the conventionally just exemplify 'original indifference': the specific sum of money for a ransom, the choice to sacrifice a goat rather than two sheep, specific legislative (*nomothetousin*) provisions such as the details of the sacrifice to Brasidas and decrees (*psēphismatōdē*). All of these examples describe particular determinations which are ethically indifferent prior to enactment (they could be otherwise and not involve injustice), but ethically (or at least practically) significant subsequent to enactment, because they function as guides to conduct which co-ordinate the activities of the citizens of a polis. The conventionally just, therefore,

4 On the sophistic contrast between *phusis* and *nomos* see Guthrie (1971: 55–134) and Kerferd (1981: 111–30). As Guthrie notes at 53, Aristotle's standpoint is closer to the sophists than Plato on some issues. Aristotle employs or discusses the opposition between *phusis* and *nomos* in a number of places including *NE* I.3, 1094b15–16, V.5, 1133a30, V.7, 1134b18; *Pol.* I.3, 1253b21, I.4, 1254a13–15, I.5, 1254b19–21, 1255a1, I.6, 1255b13–16, III.6, 1278b33; *MM.* I.33, 1194b32; *SE.* 12, 173a7–30. The passage from *Sophistical Refutations* is particularly revealing insofar as it considers the use of the *phusis-nomos* dichotomy in Plato's *Gorgias* and the sophistic view that convention represents the majority opinion, whereas the wise speak according to the standard of truth and nature.

5 As Dodds (1959: 268) notes, when Callicles employs the expression *kata nomon ge ton tēs phuseōs* at *Gorgias* (483e) he is 'coining a new and paradoxical phrase', albeit one anticipated by Thucydides 5. 105. 2.

6 Miller (2000: 322).

7 Reeve (2009: 512).

does not seem to include all legislative enactments and customs, but legal provisions and decrees in relation to particulars (*epi tōn kath' hekasta*) (NE V.7, 1134b23). This leaves open that legislation could include both natural and conventional elements, in the sense that, for example, it might be 'in the nature of things' for all communities to legislate on religion, yet for the precise determination of such laws to remain a matter of positive stipulation allowing law-makers to select from a delimited range of 'originally indifferent' choices without injustice. This construal of conventional or legal justice points forward to the Thomistic natural law doctrine of *determinatio*, according to which legislators can choose from a range of eligible options for the common good of their political communities.[8]

Aristotle's assertion of the 'changeability' of the just by nature also speaks against reading the partition of political justice in terms of a simplistic construal of the *phusis* and *nomos* distinction. If one assumes, as 'some people' (*eniois*) do, that what is by nature is unchangeable and has the same capacity everywhere (*akinēton kai pantachou tēn autēn dunamin*) (1134b24–5), then it is difficult to see how anything politically just could fail also to be conventional and hence changeable. As a consequence, the whole domain of justice would exclude the natural. Yet this is true, Aristotle insists, only in a sense. While it certainly might be unintelligible in the case of the Gods, in the human realm it is possible for there to be something that is by nature and yet also changeable. By nature the right hand is stronger (*kreittōn*) and yet people can become ambidextrous, so that in one sense what is by nature is fixed and in another sense it is subject to variations and habituation. The just by convention is a function of agreement and the pursuit of advantage (*ta de kata sunthēkēn kai to sumpheron*) and hence is not the same everywhere (just as measures for amounts of corn and wine are not the same everywhere). What is just at the human level, but not by nature is also not the same everywhere (*ta mē phusika all' anthrōpina dikaia ou pantachou*), as may be seen by reference to the different constitutions that are established. Nonetheless, Aristotle concludes, there is only one constitution that is everywhere by nature the best (*mia monon pantachou kata phusin hē aristē*) (1134b25–1135a5).

The obscurity and difficulty of V.7 is undeniable. In what follows, I attempt to argue that Aristotle's examples of the stronger right hand and the best constitution justify an interpretation according to which nature serves as a normative foundation for the enactment and evaluation of positive law. Before I turn to these examples, it is helpful to consider some broader interpretative issues at stake.

Aristotle's inclusion of natural justice within political justice seems in tension, it was suggested above, with an appeal to a higher source of justification for law beyond a practically reasonable legislator's conception of the common advantage. As

8 Aquinas recognises that many norms which are part of the *ius civile* (civil law) can only be rational guides to action if they are *posited* and that such norms are selected (determined) by relevant authorities from a *range* of reasonable schemes for serving the common good. ST I-II q95 a2. See also Finnis (2011: 183 and 280–9).

discussed in Chapter 4, political justice obtains between citizens who are free and equal and governed by law (V.6, 1134a25–32) and presupposes an association of 'universal justice' with the 'lawful' (V.1, 1129b1–2) i.e. a legislative interpretation of complete virtue in relation to others. There is accordingly little suggestion in the practical works that nature serves as an 'external' normative standard for legislation. It might be thought a short step from this to the conclusion that the just by nature plays a limited role in Aristotle's account of law. If the content of ethical virtue for each community is predominately determined by positive law, then appeals to nature as a normative criterion appear to be of both limited relevance and application in the political domain.[9]

Such a conclusion underestimates the normative significance of Aristotle's derivation of law from the practical rationality of a legislative expert and the capacity for political science to track ethical truths. The above points do nevertheless rule out a 'vertical' interpretation of the relationship between the just by nature and the just by law of the kind associated with the Stoics, Roman jurists and Thomistic natural law traditions.[10] The categorisation of the just by nature as a part of political justice is rather suggestive of a 'horizontal' relationship, in which the naturally just and the conventionally just are either mutually exclusive parts of political justice or interwoven within the positive laws of a polis.[11]

On a 'mutual exclusion' interpretation, natural justice and conventional justice concern different objects and something politically just could either be naturally just or conventionally just but never both.[12] If the 'mutual exclusion' view is true and conventional justice is identifiable with positive law, then this would seem to rule out the possibility that nature could serve as a normative foundation for legislative enactments.[13] Yet the mutual exclusion view seems erroneously to assume an exact correspondence between conventional justice and positive law. As noted above, Aristotle limits the sphere of the conventionally just to 'originally indifferent' detailed specifications within legislative enactments and decrees, rather than identifying it with positive law *simpliciter*. Aristotle's discussion also appears to allow for evaluation of positive laws by reference to natural justice.[14] One could imagine, for instance, a detailed specification of the religious norms of a political community which was so violent or barbaric as to counteract, rather than promote, the goods which can be instantiated through the regulation of the human inclination towards religious respect and worship. In addition, Aristotle's wording in V.7 does not necessarily entail that natural justice has no existence at all independent of political justice. The characterisation of political justice as partly natural and partly

9 An interpretation along these lines is proposed by Kelsen (1957).
10 Burns (1998: 148) and Yack (1993: 233).
11 Burns (1998: 148).
12 Weirnick (1998: 102). Weirnick translates *nomikon* exclusively as 'legal'. This risks a misleading strict identification of conventional justice with positive and customary law (*nomos*).
13 Weirnick (1998: 102).
14 Weirnick (1998: 112).

conventional leaves open the possibility that the naturally just is in some sense 'prior' to, or independent of, the politically just, but is subsequently embedded within positive legal enactments. On this reading, the establishment of political justice through legislative enactments will be informed by the just by nature, albeit different communities will determine the precise specification of their laws in diverse ways.[15] Nature could accordingly serve as a normative foundation for the evaluation of law, because (at least some) legal enactments would contain both natural and conventional elements.

The most plausible interpretation of the relationship between natural and conventional justice is hence either in terms of 'double aspect' or 'partial overlap'.[16] According to 'double aspect', a law that is politically just would contain elements of both the naturally and conventionally just. According to 'partial overlap', some politically just laws would be both naturally and conventionally just, while others just in one sense only.[17] Once mutual exclusion is eliminated, however, then the difference between these readings is less significant than might first appear. If one assumes that conventional justice refers to the legal specification of particular matters that are 'originally indifferent', and that natural justice refers to normative content embedded within the laws of all (just) political communities, then laws in the focal sense possess a double aspect. While the content of some legislative norms may seem originally indifferent, the mere fact that the flourishing of the political community – which is understood in terms of the development of natural capacities – requires the order introduced by law, entails that the content of those norms will contain an element of the just by nature. From an alternative perspective, it is possible to imagine legal norms that are accepted as valid and binding by the members of a political community, but so completely antithetical to the human good that they contain no content that is just by nature. One could equally say, however, that in such circumstances the subject matter is no longer positive laws that fall under the scope of the politically just, given the restriction of that notion to correct constitutional forms and the relations which obtain between free and equal citizens ordering their communal life through just law (*NE* V.6, 1134a25–32).

In any case, on either reading, politically just positive legal norms may contain both natural and conventional elements. There are a range of human relationships and transactions within any political community which require the co-ordination of law. While it pertains to the very nature of political communities to legislate in areas such as the duration of offices, economic exchanges or arrangements for religious worship, the precise content of legal norms is a matter of determination for those in positions of legislative authority within particular political communities at a certain time and place. That a community would need to enact laws for the regulation of private property, for instance, could be taken to reflect certain facts about human

15 Cf. Miller (1995: 122), Kraut (1996: 758) and Burns (1998).
16 Weirnick (1998: 102).
17 Weirnick (1998: 102).

nature and the practically reasonable regulation of the sphere of property relations.[18] Yet the specific content of particular laws enacted to achieve that natural purpose (including, say, the penalties associated with theft), can, within a reasonable range, differ from one community to another. A law prohibiting murder may also be understood as containing both natural and conventional aspects. All political communities require legal norms which proscribe unprovoked acts of violence. The detailed content of such laws – including provisions for trial and punishment – nonetheless has a conventional aspect which admits of alternative determinations.

With this general picture of the relationship between natural and conventional justice in place, it is now possible to turn to Aristotle's two examples of things which are by nature, but which nonetheless undergo change. Both examples – ambidexterity and constitutional regimes – indeed point to nature as an underlying normative foundation for just legislative enactments. While nature serves as a normative criterion for the enactment and the evaluation of constitutions and laws, however, Aristotle does not lose sight of either the political contingencies of law-making or its positive (human) source.

Aristotle's analogy between natural justice and right-handedness assumes as a premise that the right hand is by nature stronger or superior (*kreittōn*) to the left.[19] In *Progression of Animals* Aristotle argues that the right side is better (*beltion*) than the left by nature for all animals, but particularly in the case of humans, insofar as humans are also 'more' according to nature (*kata phusin*) than the other animals (*PA* 4, 706a18–20). It is the nature of the right hand to initiate movement (705b33–706a1) and it is better because of its function in achieving a beneficial and necessary end.[20] The justification is hence teleological: what is better (*beltion*) is also what is more according to nature (*kata phusin*) (*PA* 2, 704b12–18).[21] While naturally better, however, the superiority of the right hand applies in most cases, not all. Even apart from those who favour the left side from their youth, it is possible for the naturally right handed to become ambidextrous through habituation (*NE* V.7, 1134b33 and *MM.* I.33, 1194b33).

In applying the analogy back to the just by nature, the obvious starting point is Aristotle's political naturalism. As argued in Chapter 2, the three tenets of political naturalism – that the polis exists by nature, that humans are by nature political animals, and that the polis is by nature prior to the individual (*Pol.* I.2, 1253a2–26) – all lead to the

[18] Cf. Miller's argument (1995: 91) that Aristotle, while not subscribing to a modern view of subjective rights possessed in a pre-political state of nature, 'denies that individuals possess rights merely by convention' and hence can be ascribed a theory of 'natural' rights that is based on natural justice and determinative for political rights. For critique see Kraut (1996). As Kraut's analysis suggests (1996: 755), it is more convincing to argue that Aristotle has an incipient concept of rights than that 'rights have a central place' in the practical works.

[19] This analogy reoccurs at I.33 of *Magna Moralia*. On the difference between the two accounts, see Miller (1991: 286). The *Magna Moralia* expressly identifies the natural with what happens for the most part (*hōs epi to polu*).

[20] Miller (1991: 292).

[21] Miller (1991: 290).

conclusion that political life is necessary for the fulfilment of distinctive rational human nature. Given the threat that unchecked political authorities will rule in their own interest, or tyrannically, a corollary of this conclusion is that the governance of the polis through just law is conducive to virtue and human flourishing (*NE* V.6). If one then assumes, consistent with the 'double aspect' interpretation sketched above, that the content of legislative enactments interweaves elements of the just by nature and convention, then constitutions and laws will be just by nature insofar as they promote the natural human end of rational thought in conformity with virtue.

Reference to political naturalism and the natural human end does not in itself, however, explain why it is that the just by nature – particularly as embedded in legal norms – is associated with what is naturally stronger or superior. Aristotle's *Politics* I.6 discussion of the debate between those who regard slavery as always conventional and those who assert that it can also be natural provides perhaps the clearest example of a normative connection between what is superior and natural justice.

The initial defence of natural slavery in *Politics* I.4–5 famously asserts that men who are as inferior with respect to rationality and deliberation as the body is from the soul, or as beasts are from humans, would be slaves by nature (1254b18–20).[22] In *Politics* I.6, Aristotle considers the claims of those who argue, with reference to captives in war, that slavery is by convention rather than natural. Although Aristotle notes that slavery and the slave are spoken of in a double sense – and thus considers the possibility that some captives could be slaves by convention rather than nature (1255a4–5) – he also acknowledges that this matter is disputed even among the wise (*tōn sophōn*). Aristotle then proceeds to attempt to bring greater clarity to the debate by stating its underlying cause (*aition*):

> Virtue (*aretē*), once it obtains the necessary resources, is in a certain manner particularly able to apply force (*biazesthai*), and what is dominant (*kratoun*) is always preeminent in some good (*agathou tinos*), so it is held that there is no force without virtue (*dokein mē aneu aretēs*), and that the dispute concerns only the plea of justice (*dikaiou*); for on this account the ones hold that good will (*eunoian*) is the measure of what is just, while the other hold that this very thing, the rule of the superior, is just (*auto touto dikaion, to ton kreittona archein*). At any rate, if these arguments are set on one side, the other arguments – which assume that what is better in virtue ought not to rule or be master – have neither strength (*ischuron*) nor persuasiveness (1255a13–23).

Although Aristotle's presentation of this debate is dialectical, certain claims are seemingly accepted or endorsed. In particular, Aristotle notes the distinction between just and unjust wars and states that no-one would assert that a person (i.e. a Greek who was previously free) undeserving of enslavement ought to be slave (1255a25–7). This claim appears to assume that there are in fact slaves by nature (as

[22] An insightful discussion of the issues at stake in Aristotle's defence of slavery is found in Kraut (2002: 277–305).

suggested by *Politics* I.4–5) – namely non-Greeks or barbarians – and that the primary criteria for natural mastery and slavery are virtue and vice respectively (1255a39). While those who seek to assert that slavery is purely conventional speak with some reason, they extrapolate from one type of circumstance in which nature has been subverted by convention to the incorrect conclusion that it is impossible to uphold the principle of the natural superiority of virtue. It is this natural superiority which supports the claim that slavery is advantageous for both the master and the slave when it is in accordance with nature i.e. when the slave lacks the capacity for rationality and human excellence.

For Aristotle it is naturally just for those with virtue to rule over those lacking in virtue. It would seem to follow from this that laws will be just by nature insofar as their content reflects the natural superiority of virtue. Yet even the laws of a genuine aristocracy, based on virtue as the correct interpretation of merit, would imperfectly reflect this superiority. Human development is informed not only by nature, but also by reason (*logos*) and habit (*ethos*) (*Pol.* VII.14, 1332b4–5).[23] This necessarily complicates legislative attempts to enact laws in conformity with true virtue in a way that is helpfully explicated by returning to the analogy with right-handedness and ambidextrousness. While the right hand is naturally stronger, and ambidextrousness remains a possibility unrealised for the most part, the role of reason and habituation in human development entails that the naturally superior is frequently unable to rule. In the first instance, true virtue is not strictly speaking a natural capacity (*NE* II.1, 1103a19, II.5, 1106a9). Unlike natural virtue (*phusikē aretē*), true virtue requires choice (*prohairesis*) and an appreciation of the noble or fine (*kalon*) (III.8, 1116b23–33, 1117a4–9, VII.13, 1153b28–30) and this only develops through habituation. The development of virtue through habituation is also subject to contingency, as evidenced by the fact that although nature 'desires' that the children of those with virtue will be similarly excellent, it is not always able to achieve this end (*Pol.* I.6, 1255b2–3). In the second instance, the polis is not straightforwardly a naturally arising entity, but rather requires the supplementary rational direction of a practically reasonable law-maker. While the legislative expert should intend to enact a constitution and laws in conformity with nature, this will often be impossible owing to limitations of the law-maker, the citizens of the community, or even the climate and natural surroundings.[24] In addition, and partly as a consequence, most actual regimes are determined by a conception of the good life which differs from what is truly according to nature. The less excellent has become the dominant principle in actuality, just as if left-handedness were to become the norm.

Aristotle's second example of the just by nature – the best constitution – likewise reflects the priority of virtue. As discussed in Chapter 3, Aristotle's best constitution is one in which participation in political office is granted on the basis of virtue or merit

23 Aristotle notes at *Pol.* VII.14, 1332b4 that animals can also be habituated to some extent.

24 In *Politics* VII Aristotle considers in this context the size of the best city (VII.4), its territory (VII.5) and its access to sea and naval power (VII.6). For discussion see Kontos (forthcoming: 5).

(*Pol.* III.13, 1283b23–40). Orientation by virtue, then, is what defines the best regime, regarded as a genus of which absolute kingship, aristocracy and the aristocratic polity of *Politics* VII and VII are species.[25] The just things that are not natural, but human (*ta mē phusika all' anthrōpina dikaia*), are not everywhere the same (*ou tauta pantachou*), and this is reflected in the different regimes. On the one hand, there is only one regime that is in accord with nature, the best regime (*alla mia monon pantachou kata phusin hē aristē*) (NE VII.16, 1135a3–5). On the other hand, Aristotle's acknowledgement of different species of the best regime suggests that the just by nature is not completely unchangeable in the political domain. In the case of absolute kingship, there is one individual who so surpasses other individuals in virtue that they should rule. In the case of a genuine aristocracy or an aristocratic polity, there are a few citizens or a group of citizens who exceed others in their excellence. The contingency of political affairs, such that it is difficult to predict how many individuals will in each situation acquire the requisite level of virtue, thus points to the variability of what pertains to political justice, albeit the ultimate natural standard remains the same in all cases.

The predominant actual regimes, of course, tend to judge merit on the basis of the status of being a free citizen or wealth rather than virtue. This does not entail, however, that the just by nature is completely absent from the legislative enactments of defective democracies and oligarchies. Aristotle's constitutional methodology, as discussed in Chapter 5, allows for recognition of better and worse forms of defective regimes (*Pol.* IV.4–5, 1291b31–1292b10). The versions of defective regimes governed by law are superior to those in which rule is by arbitrary decree (IV.4, 1292a1–40). Insofar as democracies and oligarchies enact laws regarding, for example, property relations and procedures for the judgements of disputes, then the content of such laws will retain, in however distant or diluted a manner, some orientation by human virtue and, as a consequence, also reflect the just by nature.

The just by nature is hence best interpreted by reference to human excellence and virtue (*aretē*). All political communities distribute offices, honours and other goods on the basis of an interpretation of the correct human end. A regime which judges merit on the basis of true human excellence is most in accord with what is just by nature, but even the laws of such a regime will contain particular determinations that are 'originally indifferent'. Conversely, the laws of defective regimes ordered by a conception other than true flourishing will also contain at least some content which may be considered just by nature insofar as these legal norms seek to promote, however imperfectly, the human good.

There is accordingly a sense in which nature serves as a normative foundation for the evaluation of positive law on Aristotelian assumptions. The best regime is a natural standard for the practically wise legislator seeking to enact laws that promote the human good. A polis is in a natural, and just condition, if it has

[25] Keyt (1991: 257) and Miller (1995: 191–3).

a correct constitution, and in an unnatural, or unjust condition, if it has a deviant constitution (*Pol.* IV.1, 1289a14–17). If political justice is inseparable from the good ordering of a polis (I.2, 1253a31–9), then the most just constitution is that which best serves the common advantage and promotes the fulfilment of distinctly human nature.[26] While this allows for variability in the way political communities legislate to promote the practical good, Aristotle assumes that just laws – by establishing the conditions for human excellence and promoting the common advantage – play an important role in allowing humans to fulfil their natures. Laws which contain content that is reflective of the just by nature – understood in terms of virtue – are those which will best promote the human end of flourishing. In this sense at least, nature does indeed serve as a standard for human law-making.

SECTION 2 NATURAL LAW

Disputes over Aristotle's natural law credentials reflect not only the obscurity of his account of natural justice, but also the ambiguity of the compound term 'natural law'. This second section assumes that it is futile to examine whether Aristotle is a natural law theorist without reference to some of the specific commitments associated with the distinct, yet related, strands of the natural law tradition. Consideration of these claims leads to the unsurprising result that Aristotle holds to some, if not all, central commitments associated with natural law positions. Although this cautious conclusion may seem of limited interest, close examination of Aristotle's relationship with central strands of the natural law tradition elucidates the normative foundations of positive law in his practical thought.

As noted in Section 1, the closest approximation to a reference to 'natural law' in the Aristotelian corpus is the distinction between common (*koinos*) and particular (*idios*) laws in the *Rhetoric*. Common law is unchanging because it is according to nature (*kata phusin, phusei*) (*Rh.* I.13, 1373b9–13, I.15, 1375a31–b2) and made up of things agreed upon by all persons (I.10, 1368b7–9, I.13, 1373b6–9). Particular law is defined differently by political communities and is a covenant by which they govern themselves (I.10, 1368b7–8, I.13, 1373b4–5). In drawing this distinction, Aristotle notes that an act may be consistent with particular law while contravening common law, citing the case of Sophocles' Antigone and her burial of Polyneices against the order of the tyrant of Thebes (I.13, 1373b9–13, I.15, 1375a31–b2). The *Rhetoric* thus appears to offer an account – albeit in outline – of a form of non-positive 'common' law which could potentially serve as a normative foundation for the evaluation of legislative norms.

While suggestive, there is insufficient material in the discussion of common and particular *nomos* in *Rhetoric* I. 10, 13 and 15 to build a systematic natural law interpretation. In the first place, the focus of the *Rhetoric* is alternative rhetorical

26 Kahn (1990: 382–3).

and argumentative forms and it must therefore be employed with caution as a source of Aristotle's considered views on law.[27] While the definitions of practical concepts in the *Rhetoric* often resemble the more precise accounts in the *Nicomachean Ethics* and *Politics*, they are also usually presented in a more provisional fashion (i.e. as indicated through the use of hypothetical imperatives such as *estō*) consistent with the primary emphasis of the work upon effectiveness in persuasion. This lack of precision is evident in the treatment of *nomos* within Book I. In I.10 common law is unwritten and particular law written, whereas in I.13 particular law is either unwritten or written. While such inconsistency may reflect the contextual variability of unwritten law (*agraphos nomos*), it does compromise attempts to use the *Rhetoric* to illuminate the account of natural justice in the *Nicomachean Ethics* V.7 or to offer a natural law interpretation more generally.[28]

Although natural law interpretations of Aristotle are relatively common it is, moreover, an overstatement to say that 'when discussing law and justice philosophers and historians almost invariably claim that Aristotle is the father of natural law'.[29] This is the case even if Aristotle's status as a natural law theorist is framed quite broadly in terms of the question whether he is an advocate of the view that there is an absolute standard of justice which transcends conventional opinion and positive law. Recent scholarship has correspondingly tended either to uphold Aristotle's status as a natural law theorist with reservations or point to the incompatibility of his political conception of justice and law with the central commitments distinctive of the mainstream natural law tradition.[30]

One obvious concern with the attribution to Aristotle of natural law commitments is a form of anachronism which reads into the *Nicomachean Ethics*, *Politics* and *Rhetoric* natural law doctrines which, although nourished by Aristotelian influences, rest upon quite remote Christian presuppositions.[31] Another source of anachronism arises from assuming that Aristotle's views on law can be understood by reference to contemporary debates between natural lawyers and legal positivists. Such debates focus on a notion of validity within a legal system that has limited applicability to the concept of *nomos*. As discussed in the introduction, although *nomos* refers to an order that is (or ought to be) held valid by those who live under it, this sense of validity includes conventions and customs and is broader than the intra-systemic positive validity of contemporary legal systems.[32]

These kinds of anachronisms are not hard to find in defences of Aristotle as a natural law theorist. Burns, for example, rightly acknowledges that it is difficult to extract from *Nicomachean Ethics* V.7 a commitment to many of the doctrines

[27] See Shellens (1959: 79–81).
[28] See Ostwald (1973) on the contextual variability of *agraphos nomos*.
[29] Shellens (1959: 72). Shellens does not offer citations for this claim.
[30] See note 1 above.
[31] See Jaffa (1952).
[32] Ostwald (1969: 20) and Heinemann (1965: 59–89).

generally associated with Thomistic natural law theory, but then appears to proceed on the assumption that the terms 'natural justice' and 'natural law' can be used interchangeably.[33] Von Leyden frames his advocacy of Aristotelian natural law by reference to Hart's definition of legal positivism as the view that there is no necessary connection between law and morality.[34] Such a framing presupposition is dubious on several levels, including that it operates with an account of legal positivism developed in the context of modern legal systems, postulates a clear cut distinction between moral and legal norms of doubtful applicability to classical Greek thought, and assumes a definition of legal positivism that is now considered incorrect by many contemporary proponents.[35] The examples von Leyden offers in support of the contention that Aristotle 'on the whole' rejects Hart's positivism demonstrate the inadequacy of the approach.[36] These include the *Politics* III claim that there can be no law contrary to a prudent ruler and the observation that 'Aristotle's preference is for laws which are generally and absolutely the best.'[37] Given that *Politics* III.15–16 presents a debate on the merits of the rule of law and the rule of the best man, it hardly offers persuasive material for a natural law interpretation. And a preference for better rather than worse laws is a position so widely held as to be of limited use in determining natural law commitments.

My main intention here is not to undermine specific interpretations of Aristotle's natural law credentials. The relevance of these anachronisms and interpretative infelicities is that discussions are often led astray by lack of clarity on what constitutes the natural law position in the first place. This reflects that the concept of natural law has been understood in different ways by diverse thinkers. The best method is thus to respect the equivocality of the term 'natural law' while employing a general definition which captures core features shared by theories of law brought together under its banner.

For current purposes, natural law theories – considered as theories of law – can be characterised in general terms as accounts of positive law's dependence upon extra-positive normative foundations. More precisely, it is distinctive of natural law positions to hold that the existence and content of positive law depends in some way on normative facts.[38] The most obvious, and historically prevalent, normative

33 Burns (1998: 142). According to Burns, Aristotle is a proponent of a 'formal' conception of natural law according to which it is 'a logical impossibility for positive law to conflict with the requirements of natural law'.

34 Von Leyden (1967: 12).

35 See Gardner (2001: 199–227).

36 Von Leyden (1967: 12).

37 Von Leyden (1967: 13).

38 Murphy (2017: 354). The claim here, it should be noted, is not that the existence and content of positive law depends *exclusively* on normative facts: no-one could sensibly deny that the existence and content of positive law depends on some non-normative (i.e. so-called 'social') facts such as particular acts of legislating. Murphy's definition plausibly captures other commitments that are often associated with natural law positions. It is also distinctive of natural law positions, for example, to assert that there are certain actions which are wrong or unjust in and of themselves (*mala in se*) rather than

foundations for positive law are the divine, nature and reason. In what follows, I therefore consider Aristotle's practical thought in relation to each of these potential normative foundations.

In relation to divine foundations, it should be uncontentious that many of the core presuppositions of Aristotle's practical thought diverge significantly from those of medieval Christian natural law theory. One need not even subscribe to the claim that for Aristotle there is 'no moral horizon beyond the political horizon', to accept that medieval natural law theory, as developed in particular by Aquinas in the *Summa Theologiae*, rests on some assumptions that are decidedly foreign to Aristotle's philosophy of human affairs.[39] This does not entirely settle, however, Aristotle's stance on the divine normative foundations of law. Insofar as Aquinas is the 'paradigmatic' natural law theorist, it is helpful to examine this question by comparing the fourfold division of types of law in Question 91 of the *Prima Secundae* with both Aristotle's account of natural justice as developed in *Nicomachean Ethics* V.7 and the concept of the common law according to nature (*kata phusei*) that is set out in Book I of the *Rhetoric*.[40]

Eternal law (*lex aeterna*) is defined by Aquinas as the order of divine providence that is promulgated from eternity by God according to which all creatures – both the rational and the non-rational – are ordered towards the good of the universe.[41] *Natural law* (*lex naturalis*) is the participation in this eternal law by intelligent creatures employing their practical reason insofar as they are ranked under divine providence; the capacity of natural reason to discern what is good and evil, moreover, is due to the imprint of the divine light that is within us.[42] *Human law* (*lex humana*) arises from the human need to enact specific arrangements in accord with practical reason (*ratio practica*) for the common good (*bonum commune*) of the political community.[43] Finally, *divine law* (*lex divina*) is the revealed law which gives us certitude in relation to what is to be done and what is to be avoided, leading us towards our supernatural end (*supernaturalem finem*) by governing both our interior and exterior acts.[44]

On the Thomistic conception, then, the natural law is our rational participation in an eternal law which manifests the order of divine providence. With respect to the

mala prohibita. This commitment would seem to depend, however, on the existence of an extra-positive normative foundation, insofar as such a foundation is understood to function as a higher standard allowing for an assessment of the justice or otherwise of the positive law(s) of any particular community and also for the identification of some of its laws as 'merely' conventional.

39 Jaffa (1952: 30).

40 For the claim that Aquinas is the paradigmatic natural law theorist see Murphy (2003: 241). Strictly speaking Aquinas outlines five types of law: the 'law of the *fomes*' refers to sensual inclinations natural to animals but also present in humans after the Fall. ST I-II q91 a5. A full comparison of Aristotle and Aquinas on the theme of natural and positive law would require attentiveness to Aquinas's account of natural and positive, and special and legal, forms of right and justice in ST II-II q 57–8 and the Commentary on Aristotle's *Nicomachean Ethics* V.7. My intention here is merely to point to some pertinent differences with respect to divine normative foundations.

41 ST I-II q91 a1.

42 ST I-II q91 a2.

43 ST I-II q91 a3.

44 ST I-II q91 a4.

created world, divine wisdom is encapsulated in the notions of *creation* (according to which God is an artificer whose wisdom serves as an exemplar for the creation of the world as God's artefact) and *governance* (according to which God is the ruler and director of the movement of all things).[45] Eternal law has primacy over other forms of law – natural, divine and human – and is known to God absolutely and to created creatures to some extent through its effects.[46] The eternal law is accessible to human reason through a natural habitual cognition (*synderesis*), which is equivalent in the practical order to an understanding of first principles (*intellectus*) in the speculative order.[47] The first principle of the natural law founded in the eternal law is that good is to be done and evil is to be avoided.[48] Precepts of natural law derived on this basis all pertain to what is apprehended by practical reason as human goods, such as the preservation of individual life, the preservation of the species and the good of reason (which includes knowledge of God and what promotes the *summum bonum* of the political community).[49] Practical reason, Aquinas assumes, proceeds from more general principles to particular considerations.[50] While natural law pertains to activities which humans have a natural inclination to engage in, and the general principles of natural law and right and truth are in this broad sense known by everyone, with respect to particular situations it is not the case that the same thing is practically right or true.[51] The Thomistic natural law, that is to say, is not an algorithm allowing for precise practical deductions from a set of precepts.

In comparison with the Thomistic account of natural law, Aristotle's V.7 account of natural justice considered in the previous section contains no reference to either eternal or divine law and is in fact distinctly sublunary. Whereas Aquinas considers natural law to arise from the participation of practical reason with an eternal law and divine order, for Aristotle by contrast the naturally just is a part of political justice and conceptualised within the frame of the philosophy of human affairs.

While Aristotle's account of the just by nature does not postulate a divine normative foundation for positive human law, the *Rhetoric* discussion of common law according to nature might seem to provide more fertile ground.[52] As noted above, in explicating the common law according to nature, made up of things agreed upon by all, Aristotle refers to Antigone's appeal to non-positive law (I.13, 1273b1–18, I.15, 1375a33–b2).[53] The discussion of Antigone nonetheless emphasises the status of common law as unwritten, and hence invariable, rather than its divine origin.[54] In

45 ST I-II q93 a1.
46 ST I-II q93 a2–3.
47 ST I-II q94 a1.
48 ST I-II q94 a2.
49 ST I-II q94 a3.
50 ST I-II q94 a4.
51 ST I-II q94 a4.
52 Miller (2007: 94).
53 For the view that unwritten justice is part of the common law according to nature see Grimaldi (1993: 297–8). For a convincing critique of this view, see Weirnick (1998: 157–8).
54 Miller (2007: 94).

the *Politics*, moreover, Aristotle suggests that unwritten laws are based on customs (*Pol.* III.16, 1287b6) and are reflections of the way of life of particular communities, not universally valid norms.[55] Following the interpretative principle that the *Rhetoric* is to be employed cautiously as a source of Aristotle's views – and that where the *Rhetoric* conflicts with the *Nicomachean Ethics* and the *Politics* there is a presumption in favour of the latter – then *Rhetoric* I.15 offers inadequate evidence to construct a divine natural law theory.

For the sake of completeness, it is also worth noting that Aristotle's surviving work demonstrates little commitment to the ambiguous variant of political theology found in Plato's *Laws*. In the preamble to the law against atheism in Book X of the *Laws*, the Athenian Stranger admonishes those who set up a strict demarcation between nature (*phusis*) and convention (*nomos*) and seek to derive all ethical standards from the latter (*Laws*, 888e–890b). In opposition to this view, the Athenian Stranger insists that the cosmos is directed by a divine soul that is concerned with human matters (893c–899b; 901d–903c).[56] Although Aristotle echoes Plato's (890d) association of law and reason, he at no point directly appeals to a divine creator that troubles itself with human affairs.[57] The divinities of Aristotle are the eternal substances thinking true thoughts on which all change in the cosmos depends (*Met.* XII.7, 1072b13–1073a13; *NE* X.8, 1178b8–25). These divinities 'do not guarantee that justice will be done'.[58]

On the basis of the foregoing, it is clear that Aristotle's practical thought does not contain an appeal to divine sources of the kind found in the Thomistic account of natural law. The case with respect to the natural and rational normative foundations of law is, as I will now demonstrate, more complex.

The sense in which Aristotle's account of natural justice establishes nature as a normative foundation for the evaluation of positive law has been discussed in detail in the previous section. It is nonetheless helpful, in thinking about the relationship of these commitments to the more mainstream natural law tradition, briefly to compare Aristotle's practical thought with Stoic teachings on nature and law. In his discussion of the subject of nature in Stoic philosophy in *De Finibus*, Cicero writes as follows:

> The same honour is also bestowed with good reason upon Natural Philosophy, because he who is to live in accordance with nature must base his principles upon the system and government of the entire world. Nor again can anyone judge truly of things good and evil, save by a knowledge of the whole plan of nature (*nisi omni cognita ratione naturae*) and also of the life of the gods, and of the answer to the question whether the nature of man (*natura hominis*) is or is not in harmony with the nature of the universe (*De Finibus*, III, 73).

55 Weirnick (1998: 157).

56 On the implications of Plato's appeal to the divine in Book X of the *Laws* see Stalley (2007: 71).

57 The closest approximation is perhaps *Physics* II.4, 196a25ff. On *theologikē* in Aristotle see Menn (2012: 422–64).

58 Kraut (2002: 203).

In *De Finibus*, Cicero distinguishes between several senses of *natura*, including the *prima naturae* or primary inclinations (e.g. life, knowledge) (*De Finibus*, III, 16–18) and the features of *natura* that are discoverable by human reason in natural philosophical investigation (*De Finibus*, III, 73, IV, 12).[59]

What is salient here about Cicero's presentation is the Stoic construal of the idea that the human good is to live in accordance with reason and nature.[60] On the Stoic view, the good is sought through inference (*collatio rationis*) from what is in accordance with nature (*secundum naturae*), rather than directly accessible as the practical end of human intentionality (*De Finibus*, III, 33). This contrasts with the Aristotelian perspective, according to which ethical enquiry always remains practical in its orientation (*NE* II.2, 1103b25–30) in the sense that the good is the internal end at which all activity aims.

At this point it is instructive to recall that Aristotle's account of natural justice as outlined in Section 1 is situated within a discussion of political justice and remains practical in orientation throughout. In *Nicomachean Ethics* V.6, as seen in Chapter 4, Aristotle states that the just in the political sense exists among those for whom there is law (*esti gar dikaion ois kai nomos pros autous*) (1134a30–1). Justice is a judgement about what is just and unjust and the law is required in particular where there is the possibility of injustice. Law serves a natural need by bringing order to political communities in light of the limits on the human capacity to act with complete virtue in relation to others. This explains the desirability of the rule of law as a restraint on the natural tendency to distribute honours and other goods to suit one's own interest in a tyrannical way (1134b35–7). Political justice in the central sense exists where citizens share a life in common and are free and equal, either in accord with geometrical proportion or arithmetically (1134a26–8). Judgements about the just and unjust are in one sense *naturally* expressed in law (*kata nomon gar ēn, kai en ois epephukei einai nomos*) (1134b14–16). Yet positive laws remain an articulation of practical judgements on the good by human – albeit in the ideal case prudent and insightful – legislators (I.9, 1099b29–32, I.13, 1102a7–25, X.9, 1180a34, 1180b25–30). Law is therefore natural on Aristotelian assumptions principally in the sense that it arises from practically reasonable reflection on the human good, not in the sense that it can be derived from nature understood as a transcendent or even extra-political source of external ethical standards.

Another passage that elucidates the role of nature as a normative foundation for human law-making is Aristotle's discussion of *logos* as distinctively human. The sense in which humans are more truly political animals by nature than other gregarious animals like bees (*Pol.* I.2, 1253a1–25) reflects the active role of practical reason in the development of law. Humans are distinguished from other animals

59 While a non-standard Stoic, I assume here that Cicero remains close to Stoicism on moral questions. For a more detailed exposition of the different senses of *natura* in Cicero's *De Finibus* see Finnis (2011: 375–6).

60 Finnis (2011: 375–6) citing *De Legibus I*, 55.

because they have a natural capacity for rational speech (*logos*), which allows them to express opinions on the expedient and inexpedient and the just and the unjust, in contrast to other animals, which are only capable of expressing pleasure or pain (1253a8–14). Once again, it is through this natural capacity for rational speech and practical choice and action that humans develop a sense of the just and the unjust, the good and the bad, which culminates in the distinctly political association and law.[61]

In sum, Aristotle's conception of the role of law within political communities is informed by the view that laws play an indispensable role in allowing humans to fulfil their natures. The fulfilment of human nature involves rational activity in accordance with virtue, but it also requires the formation of political communities governed by law. In this sense, and keeping in mind the discussion of Section 1, it is true to say that nature serves as a normative foundation and evaluative standard for human law-making.

In the context of debates surrounding Aristotle's natural law credentials, it is worth noting that the claim that laws are best when they are enacted in conformity with a true conception of human flourishing need not culminate in an illicit derivation of normative claims from factual premises regarding nature. This is because the sense of nature most pertinent to understanding Aristotle's account of law is not that found in a descriptive investigation of 'bare nature', but rather that articulated in practically reasonable reflection on the fulfilment of human capacities. In order to understand human nature, Aristotelian practical philosophy implicitly assumes, it is necessary to understand human capacities, in order to understand those capacities, it is necessary to understand their acts, and in order to understand those acts, it is necessary to understand their objects.[62] Ultimately the objects of practical reflection are human goods accessible to practical reflection as directive propositions about what it would be best to do. It is thus not the fact that humans are political by nature which justifies certain sorts of constitutions and laws but rather the capacity of practically reasonable agents to apprehend participation in a complete and just political community as conducive to human flourishing. If this conception of human nature and practical rationality is characteristic of natural law theory, then in this respect Aristotle may indeed be classified as a natural law theorist.

It remains to consider the sense in which rationality serves as a normative foundation for law on an Aristotelian conception. As discussed at length in Chapter 1, the claim that law is 'intellect (*nous*) without desire' (*Pol.* III.16, 1287a33), the seemingly intellectualist characterisation of *nomos* in X.9 of the *Nicomachean Ethics* as rational speech (*logos*) derived from practical wisdom (*phronēsis*) and intellect (*nous*) (1180a22–3), the identification of *nomos* with order (*taxis*) (*Pol.* VII.4, 1326a30 cf. II.5, 1263a23, III.16, 1287a18), and the attribution of a significant role to

61 Cheery and Goerner (2006: 563–85).

62 Finnis (1998: 29 and 90). Finnis cites *De Anima* II.4, 415a16–22 and ST I-II q87 a3.

the practical reason of the law-giver in the establishment of constitutions and law, all undoubtedly reflect an appreciation of the rational content of law. Laws are also evaluated in the *Politics* as better or worse depending on both the capacities of the law-giver and the particular end that they intend to promote (*Pol.* IV.9, 1293b42–1294a7). In the best regime, legal norms have a trans-historical rational content because they are oriented by the natural human end. In less than ideal regimes, laws may still promote a limited form of virtue and mitigate sectional rivalries. The relativisation of the defectiveness of democracy and oligarchy to whether they adhere to positive law reflects Aristotle's view that where laws do not rule, there is in a sense no regime at all (*Pol.* IV.4, 1292a33–4). Aristotle thus also subscribes to 'the rule of law' in the sense that adherence to the law differentiates the best and worst versions of the defective regimes. Positive law can accordingly serve as a rational standard that the good citizen should follow.[63]

From this perspective, there are obvious affinities with the Thomistic account of law developed under Aristotelian influence. Aquinas defines law (*lex*) in the *Summa* as 'nothing other than an ordinance of reason for the common good, made by the person who has care of the community, and promulgated' (*legis, quae nihil est aliud quam quaedam rationis ordinatio ad bonum commune, ab eo qui curam communitatis habet, promulgate*).[64] This definition does not expressly appeal to divine sources in its insistence that law, properly speaking, is the outcome of human practical rationality in its directedness towards the common good. Aquinas' definition also incorporates reference to a law-giver: the law is understood as an achievement of practical reason and it is the political common good that serves as the normative criterion for assessing the justice of particular legal enactments. All these points suggest that it is indeed legitimate to talk of a common Aristotelian-Thomistic tradition of legal thought.

In light of this affinity, it is instructive to consider Aristotle's relationship to the natural law dictum that an unjust law is not a law (*lex iniusta non est lex*).[65] Contemporary natural law theorists such as Finnis and Murphy have sought to avoid the counter-intuitive implications of interpreting this dictum to mean that unjust laws are necessarily legally invalid, while continuing to uphold a connection between central or non-defective cases of law and practical reasonableness.[66] For Finnis, an unjust law is not a law in the focal sense.[67] A person's history with another person might make him count as friend, even though disloyalty prevents him from being a friend in the focal sense. Likewise, a law might meet a particular legal system's requirements for validity, even though its injustice makes it a non-focal instance of law. Murphy approaches *lex iniusta non est lex* in a more metaphysical

63 Lisi (2000: 42).

64 ST I-II q90 a4.

65 The dictum is not *directly* attributable to either Augustine or Aquinas. See Kretzmann (1988: 100–1).

66 Finnis (2011: 23–55) and Murphy (2005a: 15–28).

67 Finnis (2011: 364).

key by reference to law's 'non-defectiveness conditions'. On Murphy's view, natural law theories characteristically assert theses of the form that '[l]aw exhibits N, where N is some normative feature' (like being a legitimate practical authority or being just).[68] On a strong reading, this core natural law thesis entails a necessary universal generalisation: that 'necessarily, if x is a law, then x is legitimately authoritative, or just'. On Murphy's favoured, weaker reading, it asserts that it is necessarily the case that non-defective law 'is backed by decisive reasons for compliance'.[69] Falling short of this rational standard makes a law defective as such. Both approaches thus reconcile the tradition's view that true laws are rational guides to action with an acknowledgement that defective laws may still be intra-systemically valid.

Aristotle can intelligibly be regarded as at least incipiently subscribing to both Finnis' theory of law in the focal sense and Murphy's weak natural law thesis. As noted in Chapter 4, when Aristotle asserts that all the lawful (*nomima*) things are somehow (*pōs*) just (*NE* V.1, 1129b13), the indefinite correlative adverb *pōs* suggests that this passage should be interpreted by reference to law in the focal sense. Aristotle also states in this passage that the laws pronounce on all things in their aiming at the common advantage (either of all persons, or the best, or those with authority, either in accord with virtue, or in some way) and that those things apt to produce or preserve wellbeing for a political community are just (1129b15–19). The reference to the common advantage and *eudaimonia* indicates that the lawful is just in the sense that it conforms to the normative point of law. Aristotle is accordingly not claiming that any legislative enactment or unwritten custom is necessarily just, but rather pointing to the assumed purpose of law to promote political justice and hence also the overall human good. The association of law with the common advantage of a political community and human flourishing thus situates Aristotle within a natural law tradition that has sought to differentiate between practically reasonable and just laws and laws that fall short of those rational standards. This is true even if, as is plausible, Aristotle would not seek to deny the status of defective laws as laws in a qualified sense, a view that is in any case advocated by most prominent adherents of contemporary natural law theory.

In conclusion, Aristotle does appeal, in a non-trivial way, to nature and reason as normative grounds for the enactment and evaluation of positive law. While it is necessary to avoid strict identifications of Aristotle's concerns with those of medieval Christian natural theory, or with contemporary critiques of legal positivism, his practical works are committed to law's non-positive normative foundations.

68 Murphy (2013: 5).
69 Murphy (2013: 5).

7

Equity and the *Spoudaios*

Aristotle's discussion of equity (*epieikeia*) is perhaps his most influential contribution to jurisprudence.[1] Like the English doctrine of equity it informed, Aristotelian *epieikeia* is intended to rectify deficiencies arising from the strict application of the letter of the law to all circumstances.[2] The extension of the concept of the 'decent' or equitable into the legal domain might nonetheless seem to undermine some of the most desirable features of the rule of law, including impartiality and predictability. In this final chapter, I argue that Aristotle addresses this concern regarding potential arbitrariness by deriving equitable decisions from the rational content of the legislative expert's judgements. More generally, while the exemplary ethical agent is a measure of practical reasonableness, it is the content of their judgements which ultimately serves as 'normative bedrock'. Section 1 examines Aristotle's use of equity to balance the universality of the law's pronouncements with the need for adjudicators to assess particular circumstances. Section 2 then turns to Aristotle's appeal to the judgements of the exemplary practically reasonable agent as a normative criterion and contends that this need not culminate in arbitrariness or decisionism.

SECTION 1 EQUITY

In *Nicomachean Ethics* V.10 and *Rhetoric* I.13 and 15 Aristotle employs the concept of *epieikeia* to identify and explain the circumstances when it is justified to correct the law. Laws, in contrast to decrees, are stated in the form of universal propositions and cannot cover all practical contingencies. By conceptualising equity as the correction of law when a strict or literal interpretation would lead to an unjust outcome, Aristotle thus intends to achieve a balance between law's universality and the limited scope for precision in practical affairs. This is nevertheless a difficult balancing act. Universality is precisely what often makes the authority of law

[1] Shiner (1987: 174). See also Hamburger (1951: 89–90) for the originality of Aristotelian *epieikeia*.

[2] For the influence of the Aristotelian concept of *epieikeia* (mediated through Giles of Rome's *De Regimine Principium*) on the fifteenth century development of English equity see Cromartie (2008: 8 and 18).

preferable to the more partisan authority of human rulers. Correction of law's 'blind' universality thus threatens to culminate in the reintroduction of the arbitrariness of human rule and its tendency to follow passions and promote selfish or sectional interests. Aristotle's appeal to the intentions of the legislator as the criterion for correct equitable judgement, moreover, might be thought only to exacerbate this concern, given that actual law-makers are undoubtedly subject to the same psychological and affective weaknesses as any human authorities. My primary concern in this first section of the chapter is to argue that Aristotle's derivation of both positive law and equitable outcomes from the content of sound practical judgements prevents a reduction of legal adjudication to arbitrary decision. Before I prosecute this argument, it is first necessary to consider both the motivations and context for Aristotle's application of equity to the legal domain.

Aristotle's main discussion of equity (*epieikeia*) is located within his broader investigation of some difficulties regarding the ethical virtue of justice in Book V.10 of the *Nicomachean Ethics*. The relationship between justice and equity is puzzling, because they appear to be neither the same, nor to be of a different genus (1137a32–5). People tend to praise the equitable and the equitable person as good (*tou agathou*), but also to regard the equitable as better (*beltion*) than the just, which is a strange outcome, given the status of justice as complete or perfect (*teleia*) virtue (1137b2–13). The solution to this quandary is found in the proposition that although the equitable is indeed just, it is not what is just according to law (*to epieikes dikaion men estin, ou to kata nomon*):

> The equitable is instead a correction of the legally just (*epanorthōma nomimou dikaiou*). The cause of this is that all law is universal (*nomos kathalou pas*), but concerning some matters it is not possible to speak correctly in a universal way (*ouk oion te orthōs eipein kathalou*). In those cases, then, in which it is necessary to speak universally, but it is not possible to do so correctly, the law takes what is for the most part the case (*to hōs epi to pleon lambanei ho nomos*), but without being ignorant of the error involved in so doing. And the law is no less correct for all that: the error resides not in the law or in the law-giver but in the nature of the matter at hand (*ouk en tō[i] nomō[i] oud' en tō[i] nomothetē[i] all' en tē[i] phusei tou pragmatos*) (1137b11–19).

Equity hence arises as a response to the tension between the inflexible universality of law and the variability of practical affairs. When the law 'speaks' universally, without sufficient specificity to cover all cases, or in a manner which allows for exceptions, then it is not incorrect, but rather incomplete. The role of equity, in a legal context, is to rectify this incompleteness by reference to the intention of the legislator. An equitable judge thus corrects a deficiency in the law (*epanorthoun to elleiphthen*), by saying what the law-giver would have said, had they been there, and what they would have put into the law, were they aware of the specific circumstances of the case (*ho kan ho nomothetēs autos an eipein ekei parōn, kai ei ēdei, enomothetēsen*) (1137b20–4). Aristotle concludes that equity is both just and better than the just i.e. the equitable is not better than what is just in an unqualified way, but better than (i.e. it corrects) the error which arises whenever what is just is stated, in legal contexts, in an unqualified or indeterminate way (1137b24).

Aristotle's legal employment of the concept of equity should be read against the background of both the traditional meaning of *epieikeia* and the broader notion of the equitable person or *epieikēs*. In its widest sense the term *epieikēs*, Aristotle suggests, is used to commend the decent person with ethical virtue (more or less equivalent, as will be seen in Section 2, to the *spoudaios*). The designation of someone as *epieikēs* also connotes that they are fair and capable of forgiveness or sympathy (*sungnōmē*) (1138a1–3, VI.11, 1143a19–24 and *Rh.* I.13, 1374b4–19).[3] This traditional sense of the term is retained in Aristotle's legal concept of *epiekeia* insofar as the equitable person is characterised as someone who intentionally takes less for themselves, even with the law on their side (*kaiper echōn ton nomon boēthon*) (*NE* V.10, 1138a1–2). The equitable person is a just person, but one who is not exacting to a fault about the just in the strict legal sense (1137b34–1138a1).

A narrower and more obviously proto-legal sense of equity, which is presupposed and refined by Aristotle's discussion of *epieikeia*, places it both in close proximity and opposition to justice (1137b37–8). As Brunschwig notes, an equitable decision in this sense is one that only arises as an alternative to what would be considered a just decision according to conventional standards.[4] An equitable judgement of this kind is exemplified by Achilles' decision to obtain a new chariot race prize for Eumelos, while allowing Antilochus to retain his prize. Here a just judgement is required, yet a distribution or correction which followed standards of conventional justice is inadequate from the perspective of affected parties. Aristotle's adjudicative employment of the concept of equity – which characterises it as both just itself and better than the legally just – can be understood as at least in part an attempted clarification of this ambiguity.

It has nonetheless been argued that Aristotelian equity imports a new ambiguity in its synthesis of (1) the traditional view of *epieikeia* as a virtue manifested in a concessive attitude and (2) a philosophical–jurisprudential conception of the equitable as the correction of the legal.[5] If the equitable in the second sense is understood as the correction of 'gaps' in the law, then there appears to be a lack of correspondence between the two conceptions, because the rectification of the law's 'incompleteness' need not entail any concessive attitude on the part of a judge. This concern, however, rests on the mistaken view that Aristotle's account of *epieikeia* is primarily intended to address 'gaps' in the law. Aristotelian *epieikeia* is enlivened principally in circumstances where there is a relevant law, but its rigid application

[3] See Weirnick (1998: 90) and Nussbaum (1993).

[4] Brunschwig (1996: 120). See *Illiad* 23.537. Cf. Herodotus 3.53.4 and Euripides, frag. 645N.

[5] Georgiadis (1987: 165). Georgiadis distinguishes in the context between 'virtue equity' and 'value equity'.

would result in an unjust verdict.[6] Equity is hence less a response to 'gaps' in the law than the inherent deficiencies resulting from its universality. Recognition of this point allows for a partial harmonisation of equity as the virtue of a person who takes less than they are entitled to (the opposite of someone who is animated by *pleonexia*) and the disposition to do what justice requires, even where this diverges from the literal directives of positive law.[7] An equitable judgement is 'concessive' in the sense that the adjudicator recognises that a truly just outcome is not always that dictated by a strict and inflexible reading of legal norms.[8] Although this does not mean that a judge 'takes less' (except metaphorically), the traditional meaning of *epieikeia* informs the more technical legal sense of V.10 insofar as extenuating or mitigating circumstances are taken into account by the reasonable adjudicator.[9]

Aristotle's concrete illustration of the application of equity in adjudication corroborates this interpretation. His main example – wounding with an iron ring in *Rhetoric* I.13 – sets out from the assumption, familiar from Book III.15–16 of the *Politics*, that the universality of the law, while in many respects beneficial, can also be a form of deficiency (*elleipei*) (*NE* V.10, 1137b26). This deficiency may be viewed under multiple aspects.[10] A law-giver, in framing laws, may not have considered possible exceptional circumstances, yet often it may simply be infeasible, or even undesirable, to specify all the possible permutations.[11] A further source of the deficiency of law arising from its universality is that legal terms may, by necessity or design, be vague or imprecise.[12]

> For that which is equitable seems to be just (*epieikes dokei dikaion esti*), and equity is justice that goes beyond the written law (*epieikes to para ton gegrammenon nomon dikaion*) . . . omissions are sometimes involuntary, sometimes voluntary, on the part of legislators (*tōn nomothetōn*); involuntary when it may have escaped their notice, voluntary when, being unable to define for all cases, they are obliged to make a universal statement (*katholou eipein*), which is not applicable to all, but only to most cases; and whenever it is difficult to give a definition (*diorisai*) owing to the infinite (*apeirian*) number of cases (*Rh.* I.13, 1374a25–33).

In the case of a law prohibiting wounding with an iron instrument, it would be impractical to list all possible scenarios. Since legislation is stated in universal terms,

6 Shiner (1987) and Brunschwig (1996: 137).

7 Horn (2006: 165).

8 Guest (2017: 16). Guest cites *NE* I.13, 1102b10, V.8, 1128a18, V.9, 1128b21–3, VIII.8, 1159a22, IX.6, 1167b1, X.1, 1172b11 and X.5, 1175b24.

9 Weirnick (1998: 90).

10 Aristotle has also been accused of conflating the distinction between the universal and the general e.g. by Barnes (1994: 83). A more charitable reading, as suggested by Weirnick's interpretation, is that law requires the supplementation of equity both because it is universal (i.e. it addresses instances of a type of conduct) and because it is general (i.e. it applies widely to a set of circumstances, although its range can be more or less specific). See Weirnick (1998: 84–6).

11 Weirnick (1998: 82).

12 Weirnick (1998: 83).

such a law might deal inadequately, for instance, with a man who strikes when wearing an iron ring. Equity is necessary, Aristotle concludes, because while according to the written law such a man would be guilty of the specific wrongdoing, in reality this would not be a just finding (1374b1–2). An equitable judge will hence apply a penalty that is more concessive or less strict than a literal reading of the law mandates.

The deficiency of the written law is thus not always a fault of the law-maker, but also reflects the universal propositions with which the law deals. Equity, indeed, is necessary even in circumstances where a practically wise legislator has enacted just and decent laws. The discussion regarding the complexity of Solon's laws in 9.2 of the Aristotelian *Athenian Constitution* provides support for this claim. Although some unnamed critics argued that Solon made his laws deliberately obscure in order to give the people greater decision-making power, the author of the *Athenian Constitution* avers that this is unlikely. A more plausible explanation is that the obscurity of some Solonian laws arises from the impossibility of including the best solution for every instance in a universal provision (*to mē dunasthai kathalou peribalein to beltion*). It is accordingly inherent to the law, which is expressed in universal terms, but grounded in practical judgements about what happens 'for the most part' (*epi to pleon*), that there will be difficulties of application. This is why Aristotle states that the law (i.e. the practically wise law-maker responsible for enacting the law) is not unaware of the errors of the law. When laws are framed badly, this obviously exacerbates its deficiencies, yet even in the central case of laws enacted by the true legislative expert there remains an unavoidable distance between law's universality and its concrete application to cases.

One instructive way to approach this distance is to consider the fact that laws are stated in the form of propositions which pick out types of conduct and circumstances, rather than specific events. In the example above, the law on wounding with an iron ring necessarily takes the form of a prohibition of a kind of action, without specifying the full range of contextual factors which could inform the action. The law is thus stated in universal form but its application involves reference to practical, and hence contingent, particular 'material' (*hē tōn praktōn hulē estin*) (*NE* V.10, 1137b19).

Aristotle also acknowledges that there are some matters which cannot, on account of their specificity or variability, be adequately dealt with by universal laws at all. Such matters should instead be governed by decrees pertaining to particulars (*to psēphisma pros to pragmata*). Whereas laws have wide scope and are intended to have validity across a long duration, decrees direct temporally specific circumstances. This specificity of decrees means that, taken as a category of legal norm, they are indeterminate and adaptable to the concrete situation. When the matter with which the law deals is indeterminate or limitless, then the measure must also be indeterminate or limitless (*tou gar aoristou aoristos kai ho kanōn estin*) in a manner akin to a Lesbian rule (1137b28–33). Yet to set down specific decrees for every aspect of human conduct requiring rational guidance would obviously not only be practically impossible, it would also have undesirable normative consequences insofar as it would allow for inconsistency and arbitrary decision.

The potential arbitrariness of decrees, in fact, points to the main difficulty with Aristotelian equity. As the previous chapters have demonstrated, law, while limited in its capacity to inculcate genuine full-blooded virtue, is nevertheless necessary to promote the flourishing of individuals and political communities. Yet the desirable features of law, such as universality, impartiality and predictability, are precisely what the concept of equity seems to undermine. By appealing to the concept of equity, Aristotle hence appears to risk compromising the beneficial features of law and reintroducing a lack of consistency that is conducive to the promotion of partisan interests.

The reproach that Aristotelian equity promotes arbitrariness in legal adjudication can be made from perspectives internal and external to the practical works. From an internal perspective, in *Rhetoric* 1.1 (1354a31–b22) Aristotle offers a seemingly unequivocal endorsement of legislative determinacy. Laws which are enacted correctly (*tous orthous keimenous nomous*) should define everything to the greatest extent possible and leave little discretion to those responsible for adjudication (*tois krinois*). The reasons for this are several. In the first instance, it is difficult to find people who are sufficiently practically reasonable to frame good legislation or to adjudicate well (*eu phronountas kai dunamenous nomothetein kai dikazein*). When a good legislator enacts laws, these norms prevail over a long duration and can compensate for the weaknesses of subsequent adjudicators. Secondly, legislators may examine matters carefully when drafting laws, in contrast to judges forced to make immediate decisions. Thirdly, and most significantly of all, a judgement by a law-giver is not partial but prospective and universal (*hē men tou nomothetou krisis ou kata meros, alla peri mellontōn te kai kathalou estin*). Members of an assembly or a jury, by contrast, must decide on particular cases brought before them. As a consequence of this particularity, participants in an assembly or jury are easily influenced by feelings of hatred and self-interest and their judgements can by obscured or corrupted by feelings of pleasure and pain (*hēdu ē lupēron*). All these considerations confirm the priority of well-framed legislation within Aristotle's account of *nomos*, but do not appear to be in harmony with the prominent role given to equity in adjudication.

From an external perspective, Aristotle's privileging of *epieikeia* within a legal context may be revealingly contrasted with Plato. In the *Laws*, Plato associates equity with forgiveness or indulgence and states that it represents a departure from 'the complete and rigorous' in a manner that undermines what is just and correct (*to gar epieikes kai sungnōmon tou telou kai akribous para dikēn tēn orthēn esti paratethraumenon, hotan gignētai*) (757d–e cf. 736d–e). Far from being a virtue conducive to just adjudication, then, Plato views equity in this context as a corruption of law. While the assessment of circumstances must be left to the judgement of the judge (875e), Plato's advocacy of law as a necessary second-best to the rarely instantiated kingly science (875a–d) seeks to strictly delimit the circumstances where an adjudicator can 'rectify' legislative enactments.[13]

Aristotelian equity therefore seems to pose a danger to the rule of law and its alleviation of partisanship.[14] By presenting equity as not merely a correction of the law, but as in some sense superior to the legally just, Aristotle might be thought to open up a space for arbitrary legal decision which conflicts with rule of law desiderata such as impartiality, transparency and predictability. The potential indeterminacy resulting from adjudicative correction of the deficiencies of law does not initially appear, moreover, to be assuaged by appeal to what the legislator would have said if present, or would have legislated, if aware of the circumstances. For even if one assumes that Aristotle does not refer to legislative intention in an historical or psychological sense, the problem remains of determining what a legislator would have enacted or said. This concern is especially significant in light of the fact, as noted in earlier chapters, that the rule of law mitigates incorrect interpretations of merit found in predominant defective regimes.

Aristotle's appeal to the law-maker's intention in *Nicomachean Ethics* V.10 is grounded, however, in his privileging of practical legislative expertise. The relevant passage is worth considering in detail:

> Whenever the law speaks universally (*legē[i] men ho nomos katholou*), then, but what happens in a given case constitutes an exception to the general rule, then it is correct (*sumbē[i] d'epi toutou para to kathalou, tote orthōs echei*), where the law-giver omits something (*paraleipei ho nomothetēs*) and erred by speaking unqualifiedly (*ēmarten haplōs eipōn*), to rectify that deficiency (*epanorthoun to elleiphthen*) with what the law-giver himself would have said if he had been present and, if he had known of this case, he would have legislated (*ho kan ho nomothetēs autos an eipein ekei parōn, kai ei hēdei, enomothetēsen*) (1137b20–4).

The first striking feature of this passage is that it seems to prescribe a rectification of the deficiency of legislative enactments through recourse to the very source of the deficiency. Yet Aristotle's broader statements on equity make clear that the deficiency in question is inherent to law and not something that could be overcome by

[13] On the relationship between these passages in Plato's *Laws* and Aristotelian equity see Brunschwig (1996: 126–35). A negative or cautious estimation of the merits of the operation of *epieikeia* in the political or the legal domain is not exclusive to Plato. See, for example, the speech of Cleon in Thucydides 3.37–40 and the other texts cited in Hamburger (1951: 90–1). This Platonic delimitation of judicial discretion and even judgement should be read in light of the workings of the Athenian court system, which neither required jurors to provide reasons for their decisions nor bound future jurors to follow prior decisions in a manner analogous to common law precedent. Athenian jurors were, however, bound by official oaths. See Todd (1993: 54–62).

[14] Weirnick (1998: 96).

even the most practically reasonable or wise legislator. The universality of the law entails that there will potentially always be some exceptional circumstance that defies the capacity of a legislator to account for all instances. This seemingly obvious point is significant because it strongly suggests that the role of equity is to supplement the written law, as enacted by the legislator, rather than to warrant arbitrary departures from it.[15] Although it is tempting to associate equity with appeals to higher justice beyond the legislative enactments of particular political communities, which would indeed threaten to open up a space of indeterminacy in the law given the difficulty of establishing such a standard, Aristotle's intention appears rather to bind the decisions of jurors to the content of practical judgements made by true legislators.

The second important feature of this passage is that Aristotle's appeal to legislative intention as a criterion for correct equitable judgement has a twofold aspect.[16] On the one hand, Aristotle refers to what the legislator would have said, if they were present during the process of adjudication. On the other hand, Aristotle refers to what the legislator would have included in the law, if they were appraised of the circumstances of the case. Whereas the first perspective puts the legislator in the position of a judge, the second perspective allows the legislator a hypothetical retrospective opportunity to revise the legislation so that it captures an omission or deficiency.[17] This twofold character of the appeal to legislative intention is crucial because whereas the first perspective points to an 'irreducible' indeterminacy in the law which is an unavoidable feature of any legal code that promulgates universal directives dealing with what is 'for the most part', the second allows for correction of the law through a principled refinement or supplementation of existing content.[18]

Although these points mitigate the threat of arbitrariness arising from equity as the correction of the law, they do not address the concern regarding the determination of what it is that the legislator would have said or included in their enactments. The 'deficiency' of written law is in one respect simply irreducible, and not only because of the contingency and variability of practical affairs. Aristotle's acknowledgement of the impossibility for a written law to consider all possible circumstances that could require adjudication recalls two important aspects of Plato's critique of writing and law in the *Phaedrus* and *Statesman* respectively. In the first instance, Socrates places in question the benefits of the artifice of writing invented by the Egyptian God Theuth by reference to the fact that written words are fixed so that they signify the

15 See Horn (2006: 152): 'Aristotle means an amplification, not a transformation or an abandoning of written laws. The person who is in possession of *epieikeia* is able to continue the work begun by the legislator by precisely representing his intentions.'

16 Brunschwig (1996: 152).

17 Brunschwig (1996: 152) attempts to establish a correspondence between the two perspectives (legislator as judge/retrospective legislation) with the two categories of shortcomings in the law articulated in the *Rhetoric* (I.13, 1374a28–31): (1) those arising from unintentionally overlooked possible circumstances; (2) those arising from the universality of the law of which the legislator is aware.

18 Brunschwig (1996: 153).

same thing forever, regardless of context, circumstances and listeners. Socrates points out that writing cannot come to its own aid, but requires the assistance of its father (275d–e). In the second instance, and as discussed already above, the law must be regarded, according to Socrates in the *Statesman*, as a flawed but necessary second-best option relative to the practical wisdom of the possessor of the kingly expertise (297a–e). Even allowing for differences between Plato and Aristotle with respect to theoretical and practical knowledge, these passages point to the explanatory motivations for the criterion for correct equitable judgements offered in V.10. Written laws are necessary for the good governance of a political community, but they need to be interpreted in light of both their function and their source in the practical rationality of the legislator. A judge or juror seeking to decide a case equitably, when confronted with a deficiency in the law, should not make an arbitrary decision reflecting partisan biases, but reanimate the content of the law as intended by the *nomothetēs*.

Aristotle's concept of legislative intention accordingly should not be construed in subjective or psychological terms. An interpretation of Aristotelian equity in terms of some variants of contemporary 'originalism' also has the potential to be misleading. Aristotle's legislator in the focal sense is a practically reasonable political expert with access to ethical truths about virtue and the human good. The primary concern of a judge or juror in deciding a difficult case is hence not the intentions of the legislator in a psychological or historical sense, but rather the rational content that the law-maker would articulate if they were aware of the relevant deficiencies of the law as applied to particular cases. On Aristotelian assumptions, members of the assembly and jurors must make decisions in accordance with the law, both written and unwritten, and in this sense are 'subordinate' to the architectonic practical wisdom of the legislator (*Pol.* IV.4, 1292a32–4).[19] The practical wisdom of the legislative expert is in turn, as discussed in Chapter 1, to be understood in terms of the content of their judgements, which correctly track human virtue and flourishing.

As a consequence, while it is inevitable that there is indeterminacy when the written law is applied to particular cases, the assumption that equitable decisions are in conformity with the intention of the practically wise legislator precludes an association of equity with arbitrariness. On Aristotelian assumptions, the content of the judgements of the architectonic law-maker reflects a correct grasp of the good life (*NE* X.9, 1180b13–16). Of course, in actuality, the prospect that a juror would be able to recapture the content of the judgements of a true legislative expert to arrive at an equitable legal decision is undermined by ethical shortcomings and partisan interests. A juror who did arrive at a correct equitable decision would nonetheless do so by recourse to the law-giver's rational intentions (*Rh.* I.13, 1374b11), understood in terms of the content of judgements, not arbitrary whim.

19 Weirnick (1998: 70).

It is therefore the content of the law, as a rational standard derived from practical legislative expertise, which serves as normative bedrock for Aristotelian equity. Although the comparison should not be overstated, Aristotle's account of equity has some affinities with Ronald Dworkin's appeal to principles as standards of justice used by judges to determine the application of legal rules.[20] In its broader sense, a Dworkinian principle is a standard which is reflective of the wider political 'morality' of a community governed by law. Aristotle's appeal to the intention of the legislator may be regarded as drawing on principles in the sense that it requires an adjudicator to take recourse to the rational standards which informed the legislative activity of the true politician. Dworkinian principles, however, can be weighed against other principles such that their employment in adjudication is not dispositive for a correct legal decision, but must rather be balanced against other standards. As the next section examines, Aristotle's appeal to the reasons of the legislator rests upon standards derived from his wider conception of political science and practical reasonableness.

An interpretation of Aristotelian legislative intention as ultimately bound to the rational content of the law is supported by his claim that office holders must be educated by the law-maker for all eventualities (*Pol.* III.16, 1287a25–7). As discussed in Chapter 3, laws both are and should be enacted relative to the ends of a particular constitutional form. In the same way as it is possible to assess laws by reference to a constitutional form, one can assess adjudicative outcomes by reference to the content of the laws legislated within that regime. In this sense, the 'competence [of the *epieikēs*] described by Aristotle always achieves its goal according to an accepted standard' such that two judges confronted with the same set of circumstances adjudicating within the same regime would arrive at identical (and hence not agent-relative) determinations of the law.[21]

The Aristotelian approach to equity assumes that what the law is incapable of determining precisely is of such a nature that no human would be able to determine it precisely either. The law necessarily hands over what is not strictly determined by the law to be judged and administered by the 'most just judgement' of the rulers (*Pol.* III.16, 1287a24–b26). The most just judgements will be those which recapture the principled content of the law embedded in a legislative expert's enactments. These judgements will be genuinely just only, of course, on the assumption that the law-giver enacted a just regime in the first instance. In such a case, adjudicators would act equitably not by filling in gaps in the law through arbitrary discretion, but rather by making judgements guided 'by the general principles and goals of the existing law' set down by the practically wise legislator.[22]

Aristotle's appeal to the intentions of the law-giver in the equitable correction of the law is thus less vulnerable to the charge of introducing arbitrariness into

20 Dworkin (1967: 23).
21 Horn (2006: 153).
22 Georgiadis (1987: 164).

adjudication as first appears. One might nonetheless consider dubious its residual appeal to the practically wise legislator as a normative measure. In the second section of this chapter, I therefore consider more closely the justificatory status of the practically reasonable agent by reference to the Aristotelian *spoudaios*.

SECTION 2 THE *SPOUDAIOS* AS ETHICAL EXEMPLAR

The previous section has demonstrated that the rational content of the legislative expert's practical judgements, not intentions in a psychological sense, is the 'normative bedrock' of Aristotle's account of equitable adjudication. Although the equitable adjudicator goes beyond the strict letter of the law, the decision they reach is not groundless, but rather guided by the rational standard of what a prudent legislator would have said, were they the judge, or would have legislated, had they known of the circumstances. Aristotle's appeal to the rational content of the legislator's enactments as a criterion for legal decisions beyond the latter of the law is nonetheless inseparable from a commitment to the status of the exemplary ethical agent as a normative standard. In this second section, I thus consider Aristotle's use of ethical exemplars as normative measures by reference to the figure of the *spoudaios* or mature practically reasonable citizen.

The terms *epieikēs* and *spoudaios* are sometimes employed interchangeably to refer to an exemplary ethical agent in the *Nicomachean Ethics* (e.g. IX.4, 1166a10–23 and X.5, 1175b24–8).[23] In addition to the quality of 'sympathy' discussed above, an *epieikēs* is an agent who acts for the ethical good (IX.8, 1168a33–5), does not engage in activities deserving of shame (IV.7, 1127b3), feels 'self-love' in the appropriate manner as love for their own intellect (IX.8, 1169a16) and is guided by the truth (IV.7, 1127b3). In a political context, the plural *hoi epieikeis* denotes citizens whose excellent characters mean they would not make errors of judgement in the governance of the polis (*Pol.* III.9, 1281a28, VI.4, 1318b35–1319a4). These passages can be instructively compared with the definition of the *spoudaios* in the Aristotelian *Magna Moralia*: a *spoudaios* is a politically capable (*tois politikois dunaton*) person who possesses the virtues (*to de spoudaion einai esti to aretas echein* (I.1, 1181b24–1181b1). As will be explained below, what is distinctive of the *spoudaios* is that they make correct judgements about the noble and base, pleasant and unpleasant (*NE* III.4, 1113a30–4).

It is plausible that the Aristotelian legislative expert possesses greater practical wisdom than is necessary for an *epieikēs* or a *spoudaios* (*Pol.* III.4, 1277b25–7). All three figures are nonetheless agents who serve as exemplars and normative measures because the content of their practical judgements is correct. In what follows, I therefore examine the figure of the *spoudaios* as a test case for the use of ethical exemplars as justificatory standards within Aristotelian political science.

[23] See Horn (2006: 143) and Bobzien (2014: 83).

The primary meaning of the term *spoudaios* until and inclusive of Plato is 'serious' in both the 'subjective' sense of 'earnest' or 'zealous' and the 'objective' sense of 'worthy of serious consideration'.[24] In Plato there are indications that the term has developed an ethical connotation of 'inner' qualities of excellence (*aretē*) and goodness.[25] It is in Aristotle's practical thought, however, that the meaning of 'seriousness', when applied to a human agent, becomes explicitly associated with the excellence manifested in 'mature judgement' concerning practical matters. Related to the *phronimos* (the practically wise person) and *sophos* (the wise person or sage), the term *spoudaios* now 'embodies a specific norm' of ethical achievement.[26] The *spoudaios* is hence regarded within Aristotle's practical work as an exemplar and measure of the ethical virtues.

The importance of the *spoudaios* to Aristotelian practical philosophy has sometimes been understated, in part due to the tendency to translate occurrences of the term with expressions such as 'the good man' or 'the virtuous man'. These translations are not incorrect insofar as the *spoudaios* indeed embodies excellence or virtue (*NE* III.4, 1113a25–34, IX.9, 1170a8–11, X.5, 1176a15–19). As Schottländer argues, the translation 'virtuous man' nonetheless misses some nuance.[27] While Aristotle holds up the *spoudaios* as an embodiment of virtue, this is in the specific sense of someone who has mature judgement on the basis of insight and experience, particularly in relation to practical matters.[28] The Aristotelian use of the term *spoudaios*, moreover, can be distinguished from the use of other terms to designate aristocratic ethical exemplars – such as *esthlos*, *agathos*, *kalos kagathos*, *aristos* – insofar as it remains applicable to everyday as well as exceptional situations, without this entailing that it is intended as democratic in any polemical sense.[29]

The Aristotelian *spoudaios* can be clarified through comparison with both the *phronimos* and *sophos*. The terms *spoudaios* and *phronimos* are close in meaning and yet not quite co-extensive.[30] The *spoudaios* is closely related to the *phronimos*

24 Liddell and Scott (2000: 741).

25 Plato's use of the term and its cognates in the cave analogy of the *Republic* and also in the Platonic *Seventh Letter* can be considered as transitional. In the *Republic* Plato says that the duty of those who have seen the idea of the good to return to the cave exists whether the toils and honours of the cave-dwellers are of lesser or greater worth or seriousness (*eite fauloterai eite spoudaioterai*) (519d8). The *Seventh Letter* (344c) anticipates Aristotle's use of the term *spoudaios*, while remaining more theoretical in its orientation, in a discussion of the *anēr spoudaios* (serious man) who deals with *ta spoudaiotata*; see Schniewind (1998). For the decline of the ethical ideal represented by the *spoudaios* in Stoic and Christian thought see Duke (2013).

26 Schniewind (1998).

27 Schottländer (1980: 385–95). Schottländer speculates that Aristotle is likely to have introduced the quasi-technical use of the term in response to Speusippos and Xenocrates (the leaders of the Academy after the death of Plato) who, in their strong emphasis upon theoretical knowledge, allowed for the possibility of an agent possessing excellence independently of practical application in judgement or action.

28 Schottländer (1980: 385–95).

29 Schottländer (1980: 385).

30 See Voegelin (1990: 67), Tessitore (1996: 17–19) and Mara (1998: 301–29). Tessitore convincingly argues that Aristotle leaves the identity of the *spoudaios* ambiguous between 'two types of morally serious persons': practically reasonable people more generally and philosophers. This ambiguity, for

because both agents exercise the virtues in an exemplary manner. In the *Categories*, Aristotle asserts that the *spoudaios* is so-called because of their virtue (10b8).[31] The meaning of *spoudaios* seems to differ from *phronimos*, however, in its wider extension, as demonstrated by the *Politics* III.4 discussion of whether the good man can be identified with the 'serious' (*spoudaios*) citizen. Whereas the *phronimos* exemplifies the virtues most in ruling (1277b26), a mature and serious citizen qualifies as a *spoudaios*. Aristotle's demarcation of the *spoudaios* from the *sophos* is implicit in his characterisation of wisdom (*sophia*) as intelligence (*nous*) plus scientific knowledge (*epistēmē*) (NE VI.7, 1141a16–b4). Someone with the intellectual virtue of wisdom has demonstrative knowledge of first principles and what follows from them (1141a16–b4), which is constrained in the realm of practical activity. Yet when Aristotle suggests that practical wisdom (*phronēsis*) is not the most serious (*spoudaiotatēn* (1141a22) knowledge, because humans are not the most serious thing in the cosmos (1141b1–2), this does not undermine the exemplary status of the *spoudaios* from the viewpoint of political science.

The most contentious aspect of Aristotle's use of the term *spoudaios* is its reference to a norm of human excellence that can serve as a dispute-resolution procedure regarding what is truly good, noble or pleasurable. A striking example is the following passage from *Nicomachean Ethics*:

> The *spoudaios* judges these things correctly, and what *appears* true to him in each of these is true. For each sort of character/disposition (*hexin*) there is a particular (*idia*) account of what is noble (*kala*), and what is pleasant (*hedē*). What perhaps most distinguishes the *spoudaios* is seeing the truth (*talēthes*) about each of these things. He is, so to speak, the standard (*kanōn*) and the measure (*metron*) of them (III.4, 1113a30–4).

Similarly, in his discussion of pleasure, Aristotle says that what appears to the *spoudaios* to be the case is indeed the case (*einai to phainomenon tō[i] spoudaiō[i]*) (X.5, 1176a26–9). In an earlier passage, Aristotle emphasises that 'virtue (*arête*) and the *spoudaios* are the measure (*metron*) of each thing' (IX.4, 1166a13; cf. I.8, 1099a13). The *spoudaios* accordingly functions in Aristotle's political science as an exemplar, both in the sense of a model of virtue to which all should aspire and as authoritative source of true practical judgements allowing for resolution of ethical disputes.

There is presumably a deliberate echo of Protagoras' 'man is the measure of all things' dictum in these passages and the reference elucidates the authoritative status attributed to the judgements of the *spoudaios*. The *Nicomachean Ethics*, of course, sets out from the assumption that while all desire *eudaimonia* (I.1–4, 1094a1–1095b14),

Tessitore, is deliberate and reflects Aristotle's mediation between the two audiences in the presentation of his ethics.

[31] As Voegelin says, these definitions suggest that 'the possessor of ... virtue is identified with the *spoudaios*, the mature man; as the possessor of *phronēsis*, however, he is called *phronimos*' (1990: 67).

people have different conceptions of what it consists in. This pluralism of ends leaves the true politician and legislator with the task of adjudicating between competing conceptions of the good. Aristotle's use of the *spoudaios* as a norm reflects the view that the disagreement is best approached by an appeal to the activities of an ethical exemplar. While the ultimate cogency of the approach depends on the truth of Aristotle's practical teaching as a whole, this 'personalisation' of ethical norms is distanced from that of Protagoras through an analogy with health. Just as the experiences of the healthy physically well-functioning person are the measure of judgements in relation to sensations such as sweet and sour etc., so should the mature judgements of the *spoudaios* be privileged in the ethical domain (*NE* III.4, 1113a32ff).

Appeal to the normative authority of an exemplary practically reasonable agent remains a feature of contemporary legal reasoning, particularly in the case of common law systems, albeit in a distinctive watered-down form.[32] Aristotle's analysis of voluntary and involuntary action in *Nicomachean Ethics* III.1–5 – which anticipates distinctions familiar from contemporary criminal law codes – assumes a perspective of what would be reasonable in a set of circumstances. In categorising certain actions as 'indirectly voluntary', for example, Aristotle links instances of such conduct by reference to 'a foreseeable causal chain that has its origin in the agent' (*NE* III.5, 1113b30–3).[33] This notion of foreseeability, familiar from modern tort law, depends upon a conception of the reasonable person that in Aristotelian terms is the *spoudaios* or *epieikēs*. What is distinctive of Aristotle's account is that the status of the *spoudaios* and *epieikēs* as an ethical norm closely tracks the authoritative status of the judgements of the *nomothetēs*. The legislative expert remains the measure in the political domain and the *spoudaios* is defined by the exercise of those dispositions of ethical virtue that the laws of the *nomothetēs* are also intended to cultivate and promote.

An obvious objection to the use of the *spoudaios* as a normative exemplar is that it involves a vicious form of circular reasoning. The assertion that one can establish what is practically reasonable by looking at what a *spoudaios* or *epieikēs* would do seems to presuppose a pre-commitment to the very criteria under investigation. If one assumes, moreover, that an equitable judge must take recourse to the intentions of the legislative expert, considered as the paragon of practical reasonableness, then Aristotle's account of legal judgement appears even more circular.

The main issues at stake are evident in Finnis' contemporary use of the Aristotelian *spoudaios*. At a meta-theoretical level, Finnis employs the status of the *spoudaios* as an ethical exemplar to justify the employment of the methodological devices of central cases and focal meaning discussed in the Introduction. Finnis also contends that attentiveness to the judgements of the *spoudaios* can help

32 The association of the reasonable person of English common law with 'the bald-headed man at the back of the Clapham omnibus' is instructive in this regard. See Bagehot (1873: 325–6).

33 Bobzien (2014: 106).

guide the identification and formulation of the requirements of practical reasonableness.[34]

Finnis' use of the *spoudaios*, it has been argued, conflates explanation and justification.[35] According to Westerman, Finnis writes as if the fact that something has been understood by a 'just and reasonable spectator' means that it is justified as well.[36] This criticism is a variant on the circularity objection above. A description of what the *spoudaios* thinks clearly does not in itself justify the claim that their thoughts are practically reasonable, let alone that they have normative force in relation to others. Finnis, it seems, derives normative conclusions from prior evaluative commitments as to what is practically reasonable that have already been smuggled into the premises. Westerman concludes that Finnis' ethical theory rests on a decisionistic 'pre-moral choice'.[37]

In more general terms, an appeal to the normative force of an exemplar, such as the *spoudaios*, seems to rely on prior ethical commitments. If the criterion for judging whether an act is practically reasonable or not is whether it is what the *spoudaios* would do, then this presupposes a prior determination that the judgements in question are actually good.[38] Indeed, in order to live up to the requirements of practical reasonableness, one must have insight into those requirements, which suggests that one is already a *spoudaios* or has at least been able to appreciate the sense in which someone else has attained that status. The concern is hence not only the potential arbitrariness of evaluations that would allow the *spoudaios* to serve as a normative ideal and ethical exemplar, but the claim that one needs to be a *spoudaios* in order adequately to formulate the principles.

Westerman's critique, however, misunderstands both the purpose and scope of Finnis's employment of the *spoudaios* as an ethical exemplar. Finnis states explicitly that the *spoudaios* does not provide, but rather 'lives up to' the 'requirements of practical reasonableness'.[39] The implication that the *spoudaios* is not 'normative bedrock' is confirmed by Finnis' contention that Aquinas recognised more clearly than Aristotle that standards can be identified and articulated which enable us to judge the actions of an ethical exemplar.[40] It is therefore the fact that the *spoudaios* exemplifies the requirements of practical reasonableness which explains why they are 'the measure' in the practical domain, rather than it being the case that certain dispositions should be considered virtues, or judgements considered just, simply because exemplified by the *spoudaios*.

This analysis can be carried across to both Aristotle's architectonic law-maker, considered as the efficient cause of constitutions and legal norms, and the *epieikēs*,

34 Finnis (2011: 101–3).

35 Westerman (1998: 260 ff).

36 Westerman (1998: 262).

37 Westerman (1998: 261, 275–6 and 283). See also Hittinger (1989: 48).

38 Finnis (2011: 102). Cf. Celano (1995: 226).

39 Finnis (2011: 103).

40 Finnis (1998b: 50 and 57).

considered as a source of equitable judicial decisions. When Aristotle states that an equitable judgement conforms to what the legislator 'would have enacted or said', this is not to suggest that a legal determination would be lawful and just simply because it accurately reflects a judgement made by a particular person at a certain place and time. It is rather assumed that the equitable adjudicator recaptures the content of the judgements of a prudent law-maker who has legislated in conformity with right reason. The rational content of the law-maker's judgements and subsequent legal directives is therefore the 'normative bedrock' which explains their status as an authoritative source of norms, rather than the brute fact that they have promulgated binding laws and that these are generally obeyed.

A central case viewpoint does presuppose that some views are more practically reasonable than others.[41] The difficulty remains that of determining which propositions articulate the requirements of practical reasonableness and it is not obvious that an appeal to the *spoudaios* can be of much assistance. It is insufficient simply to claim that what justifies the privileged status of the *spoudaios* is a more complete and well thought-out understanding of practical matters, although this does explain Aristotle's emphasis upon maturity and experience.[42] One must attend here to the 'reflexivity' of the philosophy of human affairs. The fact that the purpose of ethical inquiry is not primarily contemplation or definitions of virtue, but rather how to become good (*NE* II.2, 1103b26–9; cf. I.3, 1095a5–6, X.9, 1179a35–b4) entails that, in the philosophy of human affairs, the distinction between understanding the content of true practical propositions and excellence 'can only be made as a distinction between two different ways of talking about the same thing'.[43] The subject matter of Aristotelian political science is consequently in a strong sense reflexive insofar as what is studied is oneself and one's reasons for action. As Aristotle says, practical wisdom is about the just and noble and good; but it is a good person's part to do these things (VI.12, 1143b22). If one adds to this the claim that practical wisdom and the ethical virtues can only be acquired together (1144a30), then this implies that someone is 'good' at ethics, as a form of enquiry, only insofar as they are a 'good person'.[44] The status of being a *spoudaios* is partly constitutive of ethical understanding on the Aristotelian conception: it is both the 'subject' and 'object' of investigation and hence functions as a norm for resolving disputes that the enquirer is actively engaged in.

The concerns raised by Westerman regarding circularity and justification accordingly derive from a view of ethics that is animated by very different assumptions than Aristotle's. Aristotle's conception of political science, and correspondingly ethical

41 Finnis (2011b: 80).

42 Finnis (2011a: 112).

43 Chappell (2005: 237–38).

44 Finnis (2011b: 31). Finnis writes that 'the mature person of practical reasonableness . . . can understand the concerns and the reasons for action of the merely self-interested, the mere conformist, the mere careerist, but the converse does not hold'. Finnis, in the same passage, correctly ascribes this insight not only to Aristotle and Aquinas, but also to Plato (on the basis of *Republic* 408d–409e and 582a–e).

enquiry, seeks both to explain and influence human action through internal reflection on goods that certain kinds of excellent activity are capable of instantiating.[45] The reason why apprehension of practical truths is assisted by consideration of the actions of persons with whom we credit it (*NE* VI.5, 1140a24–5), is because reflection on ethics is itself an activity, pre-eminently that of well-habituated and experienced people, who are able to judge correctly about the sorts of goods that it is properly reasonable to pursue. While there is indeed a circularity of sorts in appeals to ethical exemplars, it need not be regarded as vicious. Like the 'doctrine' of the mean, appeal to the *spoudaios* is 'unhelpful' in the sense that it does not in itself explain whether a particular action is reasonable or not.[46] It is by looking at ethical exemplars, however, that one can more clearly apprehend the sorts of activities and ends which are most in conformity with practical reason and truly worthy of promotion.

Although Aristotle emphasises the contingent and circumstantial nature of practical judgements, moreover, this does not entail that principles based on critical reflection are incapable of informing and modifying ethical deliberation and action.[47] Aristotle's political science, as discussed in the earlier chapters, presupposes access to 'for the most part' universal truths regarding human activities and their ends. The problem of justification, accordingly, is not one of legitimating an arbitrary appeal to standards beyond critical scrutiny or discussion, but rather of identifying the abiding principles of practical reasonableness which accurately reflect the human good.[48]

The problem of determining the content of practical reasonableness, inclusive of legal enactments and their equitable correction by a just adjudicator, is thus to determine – through both ethical reflection and rational dialogue – the principles that should guide human choices. Arriving at sound conclusions regarding these principles requires good judgement and experience and the reflection of an ethical exemplar has a privileged normative status. Although practical wisdom is concerned with particulars, it is misleading to characterise ethical choices as arbitrary. Decisions between competing instantiations of human good are made on the basis of principles of practical reasonableness developed through a form of ethical reflection that is inherently reflexive.

In sum, Aristotle's appeal to the intentionality of the legislative expert in his account of equity privileges the role of practical reason in the development of legal norms without reducing the content of the law to contingent, let alone arbitrary, decisions. The fact that law in the focal sense, and its equitable correction, is an achievement of practical reason precludes the irrationality of its content: the rule of law turns out to be the rule of the truly practically reasonable agent.

45 Cf. Salveker's (1990: 13–56) discussion of Aristotelian teleology and 'evaluative' explanation.

46 Finnis (2011: 102 and 128).

47 See Gill (2005: 15–40).

48 On the role of dialogue in identification of principles of practical reasonableness see Finnis (2011a: 43).

Conclusion

If humans are political animals by nature, then the ordering of their communal life requires the guidance of a prudent law-giver and practically reasonable laws. The purpose of the political community is both to allow individuals to satisfy basic wants and to realise the potentiality of human flourishing. Neither the political community in its fully developed sense nor its laws, are, however, at least without further assistance, naturally arising. They rather emerge through the direction of a law-maker who employs insight and practical rationality to legislate for the community's good. This ordering of a political community, on the basis of a legislator's practical wisdom, and prevailing authoritative opinions about justice, is nothing other than its law.

From a philosophical perspective, the benefits of law become particularly evident in the transition from reflection on the nature of human excellence to the good of the community which is one of its preconditions. The development of human virtue in the genuine sense is difficult for the best natures, let alone for the less fortunate. An urgent need for law – understood as a communal set of obligatory rational guides to conduct supported by coercion – thus derives from the fact that both the full and partial development of virtue depend on correct habituation and education. Even for individuals only able to partake in a small part of virtue, the law (when it is just and good) provides a guideline for correct behaviour that is at least consistent with the demands of reason.

All human activity is motivated by the end of some apparent or real good. In the domain of politics, which has a rightful claim to be authoritative over other practical domains because its concern is the whole human good rather than particular or discrete goods, legislative expertise has a privileged role. Laws are an articulation of prevailing beliefs as to the activities citizens should engage in and abstain from. A practically wise law-maker responsible for the establishment of a constitution and laws thus has a decisive function in ordering the political community so that it promotes the development of individual virtue and the flourishing of that community as a whole.

The pre-eminent role of the legislator and legislation in the realisation of the good of a political community entails that laws always articulate a particular conception of the ends of human life. This conception is reflected in the choices made for the arrangement of a political community in terms of its distribution of power and offices and other constitutional provisions. It is not only that laws are enacted relative to a particular conception of the human good and consequent political structure, but that they should be so enacted, if the community is to be stable and well-governed. Laws thus both are and should be established in line with a particular form of political ordering.

The relativity of law to a particular political ordering, or regime, need not culminate in the reduction of law and justice to partisan politics or competing power claims. It is possible to distinguish between different political orderings based on their orientation by the common advantage of the political community and also the consistency of its laws with its overarching conception. Attentiveness to the difference between political orderings motivated primarily by a concern with the common advantage, and those motivated by sectional or partisan concerns, provides a foundation for a normative assessment as to better and worse regimes and also the best regime of all. As a corollary, regimes can be more or less just, depending on their overarching conception.

Even if one accepts the status of laws as universal norms deriving from practical reason, it is also necessary to attend to the predominance of defective regimes guided by unjust partisan interpretations of merit. The prevalence of democratic and oligarchic regimes entails that the wise legislator must consider the importance of stability and obedience as preconditions for the effective functioning of law. While the normative point of law is the provision of conditions for the good life in a robust sense, its more realistic goal in most actual political circumstances is to promote those conditions which support a minimum level of justice and communal wellbeing.

Assessments of the justice of regimes do not, moreover, require recourse to a source of right which transcends the political domain. As complete virtue in relation to others, justice in the universal and political senses can be understood without appeal to divine sources or nature understood as an external criterion. While the law certainly contains rational content, this content is largely a function of the insight and practical reasoning capacity of the legislator, and thus neither a product of prophetic revelation nor 'read off' a theoretical investigation of nature. Law is rather an achievement of practical reason applied to the ordering of communal life for the sake of the good.

There are limits to the efficacy of law which follow from its demotic and universal character. It is always necessary to keep in mind the intention of the legislator to mediate communal relations in an equitable manner in circumstances where a rigid application of the law would result in an unjust outcome. More decisively, it is important to recognise the status of the law as a second-best alternative for the ordering of the political community relative to the practically implausible possibility of a truly wise ruler able to apply their rationality to all relevant circumstances. The beneficial aspects of the law, which follow from its capacity to restrain the tendency for the soul to be overcome by passion, are always shadowed by its shortcomings from the perspective of philosophy and the actualisation of excellence. Ultimately, from the practical point of view, it is the end of an activity that has explanatory priority in an elucidation of its other central features. Law's ultimate normative point is to promote the necessary preconditions for human excellence and flourishing. This, however, is consistent with a recognition of the limits of law, and its status as a second-best alternative to the government of a truly wise and practically reasonable ruler. The fact that the normative point of law remains the promotion of virtue and flourishing explains the privileged status of the mature practically reasonable agent in the rightful ordering of the political community.

References

PRIMARY WORKS

Barker, E. 1946. *The Politics of Aristotle*. Oxford: Oxford University Press.

Barnes, J. 1994. *Aristotle: Posterior Analytics*. Oxford: Clarendon Press.

Barnes, J. 1996. *The Complete Works of Aristotle*. Princeton: Princeton University Press.

Bartlett, R. C. and Collins, S. D. 2011. *Nicomachean Ethics*. Chicago: Chicago University Press.

Dirlmeier, F. 1974. *Aristoteles Nikomachische Ethik*. Berlin: Akademie Verlag.

Dodds, E. R. 1959. *Plato. Gorgias*. Oxford: Clarendon Press.

Everson, S. 1996. *The Politics and the Constitution of Athens*. Cambridge: Cambridge University Press.

Grant, A. 1885. *The Ethics of Aristotle*. London: Longmans, Green and Co.

Grimaldi, W. M. A. 1988. *Aristotle Rhetoric 1: A Commentary*. New York: Fordham University Press.

Grimaldi, W. M. A. 1993. *Aristotle Rhetoric II: A Commentary*. New York: Fordham University Press.

Inwood, B. and Woolf, R. 2013. *Eudemian Ethics*. Cambridge: Cambridge University Press.

Irwin, T. 1999. *Aristotle: Nicomachean Ethics*. Indianapolis: Hackett.

Keyt, D. 1999. *Aristotle Politics V–VI*. Oxford: Clarendon Press.

Kraut, R. 1997. *Aristotle Politics VII–VIII*. Oxford: Clarendon Press.

Lord, C. 2013. *Politics*. Chicago: Chicago University Press.

Newman, W. L. 1887–1902. *The Politics of Aristotle*. 4 vols. Oxford: Clarendon Press.

Reeve, C. D. C. 2014. *Nicomachean Ethics*. Indianapolis: Hackett.

Reeve, C. D. C. 2016. *Metaphysics*. Indianapolis: Hackett.

Reeve, C. D. C. 2017. *Politics*. Indianapolis: Hackett.

Rhodes, P. J. 1981. *A Commentary on the Aristotelian* Athenaion Politeia. Oxford: Clarendon Press.

Robinson, R. 1995. *Politics III–IV*. Oxford: Clarendon Press.

Schütrumpf, E. 1991–2005. *Aristoteles Politik*. 4 vols. Berlin: Akadamie Verlag.

Simpson, P. 1998. *A Philosophical Commentary on the Politics of Aristotle*. Chapel Hill: University of North Carolina Press.

Stewart, J. A. 1892. *Notes on the Nicomachean Ethics of Aristotle*. 2 vols. Oxford: Clarendon Press.

Susemihl, F. and Hicks, R. D. 1894. *The Politics of Aristotle: A Revised Text*. Books I–V (I–III, VII–VIII). New York: Macmillan.

SECONDARY WORKS

Allen, T. R. S. 2016. "The Rule of Law." In D. Dyzenhaus (ed.) *Philosophical Foundations of Constitutional Law*. Oxford: Oxford University Press.

Ambler, W. 1985. "Aristotle's Understanding of the Naturalness of the City." *Review of Politics* 47: 163–85.

Anagnostopoulos, G. 1994. *Aristotle on the Goals and Exactness of Ethics*. Berkeley: University of California Press.

Annas, J. 1982. "Inefficient Causes." *Philosophical Quarterly* 32: 311–22.

Annas, J, 1996. "Aristotle on Human Nature and Political Virtue." *Review of Metaphysics* 49: 731–53.

Anscombe, E. 1957. *Intention*. Harvard: Harvard University Press.

Aquinas, T. 1993. *Commentary on Aristotle's Nicomachean Ethics*. Trans. C. J. Litzinger. Topeka: O.P. Dumb Ox Books.

Arendt, H. 1977. "What Is Authority?" in *Between Past and Future*. New York: Penguin. 91–141.

Bagehot, W. 1873. *The English Constitution*. London: Chapham and Hall.

Barker, E. 1959. *The Political Thought of Plato and Aristotle*. New York: Dover.

Barnes, J. 1990. "Aristotle and Political Liberty." In G. Patzig (ed.) *Aristoteles' Politik: Akten des XI. Symposium Aristotelicum*. Göttingen: Vandenhoeck & Ruprecht. 249–63.

Bates, C. 2003. *Aristotle's "Best Regime."* Baton Rouge: Louisiana State University Press.

Bobzien, S. 2014. "Choice and Moral Responsibility in *Nicomachean Ethics* III 1–5." In R. Polansky (ed.) *The Cambridge Companion to the Nicomachean Ethics*. Cambridge: Cambridge University Press.

Bodéüs, R. 1991. "Law and the Regime in Aristotle." In C. Lord and D. K. O'Connor (eds.) *Essays on the Foundations of Aristotelian Political Science*. Berkeley: University of California Press. 234–48.

Bodéüs, R. 1993. *The Political Dimensions of Aristotle's Ethics*. New York: SUNY Press.

Broadie, S. 1991. *Ethics With Aristotle*. Oxford: Oxford University Press.

Brooks, R. and Murphy, J. (eds.) 2003. *Aristotle and Modern Law*. London: Taylor and Francis.

Brunschwig, J. 1996. "The Aristotelian Theory of Equity." In M. Frede and G. Striker (eds.) *Rationality in Greek Thought*, Oxford: Oxford University Press. 115–55.

Burns, T. 1998. "Aristotle and Natural Law." *History of Political Thought* 19: 142–66.

Burns, T. 2011. *Aristotle and Natural Law Theory*. London: Continuum.

Celano, A. J. 1995. "The End of Practical Wisdom: Ethics as Science in the Thirteenth Century." *Journal of the History of Philosophy* 33: 225–43.

Charles, D. 2000. *Aristotle on Meaning and Essence*. Oxford: Oxford University Press.

Chappell, T. 2005. "The Good Man Is the Measure of All Things." In C. Gill (ed.) *Virtue, Norms and Objectivity: Issues in Ancient and Modern Ethics*. Oxford: Oxford University Press. 237–8.

Cheery, K. and Goerner, E. A. 2006. "Does Aristotle's Polis Exist by Nature." *History of Political Thought* 27: 563–85.

Coby, P. 1988. "Aristotle's Three Cities and the Problem of Faction." *Journal of Politics*, 50: 896–919.

Cochran, C. E. 1978. "Yves Simon and 'The Common Good': A Note on the Concept." *Ethics* 88: 229–39.

Code, A. 1997. "The Priority of Final Causes over Efficient Causes in Aristotle's Parts of Animals." In W. Kullmann and S. Föllinger (eds.) *Aristotelische Biologie*. Stuttgart: Steiner. 127–43.

Collins, S. D. 2006. *Aristotle and the Rediscovery of Citizenship*. Cambridge: Cambridge University Press.

Cooper, J. M. 1973. "The Magna Moralia and Aristotle's Moral Philosophy." *American Journal of Philology* 94: 327–49.

Cooper, J. M. 1975. *Reason and Human Good in Aristotle*. Massachusetts: Hackett Publishing.

Cooper, J. M. 1999. "Political Animals and Civic Friendship" in *Reason and Emotion: Essays on Ancient Moral Psychology and Ethical Theory*. Princeton: Princeton University Press. 356–77.

Corbett, R. 2009. "The Question of Natural Law in Aristotle." *History of Political Thought* 30: 229–50.

Cromartie, A. 2008. *The Constitutionalist Revolution: An Essay on the History of England, 1450–1642*. New York: Oxford University Press.

Dancy, J. 2000. *Practical Reality*. Oxford: Oxford University Press.

Depew, D. 1991. "Politics, Music and Contemplation in Aristotle's Ideal State." In D. Keyt and F. D. Miller Jr. (eds.) *A Companion to Aristotle's Politics*. Blackwell: Oxford. 346–80.

Deslauriers, M. and Destrée, P. (eds.) 2013. *The Cambridge Companion to Aristotle's Politics*. Cambridge: Cambridge University Press.

Destrée, P. 2015. "Aristotle on Improving Imperfect Cities." In T. Lockwood and T. Samaras (eds.) *Aristotle's Politics: A Critical Guide*. Cambridge: Cambridge University Press. 204–23.

Duke, G. 2013. "Finnis on the Authority of Law and the Common Good." *Legal Theory* 19: 44–62.

Duke, G. 2013. "The Aristotelian Spoudaios as Ethical Exemplar in Finnis's Natural Law Theory." *American Journal of Jurisprudence* 58: 183–204.

Dunbabin, J. 1982. "The Reception and Interpretation of Aristotle's Politics." In N. Kretzmann, A. Kenny and J. Pinborg (eds.) *Cambridge History of Later Medieval Philosophy*. Cambridge: Cambridge University Press. 723–38.

Dworkin, Ronald. 1967. "The Model of Rules." *University of Chicago Law Review* 14: 14–46.

Finnis, J. 1984. "The Authority of Law in the Predicament of Contemporary Social Theory." *Notre Dame Journal of Law, Ethics & Public Policy* 1: 115–37.

Finnis, J. 1998a. "Public Good: the Specifically Political Common Good in Aquinas." In R. P. George (ed.) *Natural Law and Moral Inquiry*. Georgetown: Georgetown University Press. 174–210.

Finnis, J. 1998b. *Aquinas: Moral, Political and Legal Theory*. Oxford: Oxford University Press.

Finnis, J. 2011. *Natural Law and Natural Rights* second edition. Oxford: Oxford University Press.

Finnis, J. 2011a. *Reason in Action: Collected Essays: Volume I*. Oxford: Oxford University Press.

Finnis, J. 2011b. *Philosophy of Law: Collected Essays: Volume IV*. Oxford: Oxford University Press.

Frede, D. 2013. "The Political Character of Aristotle's Ethics." In M. Deslauriers and P. Destrée (eds.) *The Cambridge Companion to Aristotle's Politics*. Cambridge: Cambridge University Press. 14–37.

Freeland, C. 1991. "Accidental Causes and Real Explanations." In L. Judson (ed.) *Aristotle's Physics: A Collection of Essays*. Oxford: Oxford University Press. 49–72.

Fortenbaugh, W. W. 1991. "Aristotle on Prior and Posterior, Correct and Incorrect Constitutions." In D. Keyt and F. D. Miller, Jr. (eds.) *A Companion to Aristotle's Politics*. Blackwell: Oxford. 226–37.

Gagarin, M. 1986. *Early Greek Law*. Berkeley: University of California Press.

Gagarin, M. 2005. "The Unity of Greek Law." In M. Gagarin and D. Cohen (eds.) *The Cambridge Companion to Ancient Greek Law*. Cambridge: Cambridge University Press. 29–40.

Gagarin, M. and Woodruff, P. 2007. "Early Greek Legal Thought." In D. Miller Jr. and C. Biondi (eds.) *A History of the Philosophy of Law from the Ancient Greeks to the Scholastics*. Dordrecht: Springer. 8–34.

Gardner, J. 2001. "Legal Positivism: 5 1/2 Myths." *American Journal of Jurisprudence* 46: 199–227.

Garver, E. 2011. *Aristotle's Politics: Living Well and Living Together*. Chicago: University of Chicago Press.

George, R. P. 1993. *Making Men Moral*. Oxford: Oxford University Press.

Georgiadis, C. 1987. "Equitable and Equity in Aristotle." In S. Panagiotou (ed.) *Justice, Law and Method in Plato and Aristotle*. Edmonton: Academic Printing & Publishing. 159–72.

Gill, C. 2005. "In What Sense Are Ancient Ethical Norms Universal." In C. Gill (ed.) *Virtue, Norms and Objectivity: Issues in Ancient and Modern Ethics*. Oxford: Oxford University Press. 15–40.

Grimm, D. 2010. "The Achievement of Constitutionalism and Its Prospects in a Changed World." In P. Dobner and M. Loughlin (eds.) *The Twilight of Constitutionalism*. Oxford: Oxford University Press.

Grisez, G. 1983. *The Way of the Lord Jesus: Christian Moral Principles*. Chicago: Franciscan Herald Press.

Guest, J. W. 2017. "Justice as Lawfulness and Equity as a Virtue in Aristotle's *Nicomachean Ethics*." *Review of Politics* 79: 1–22.

Guthrie, W. K. C. 1971. *The Sophists*. Cambridge: Cambridge University Press.

Hamburger, M. 1951. *Morals and Law: The Growth of Aristotle's Legal Theory*. New Haven: Yale University Press.

Hansen, M. H. 2013. *Reflections on Aristotle's Politics*. Copenhagen: Museum Tusculanum Press.

Hardie, W. F. R. 1968. *Aristotle's Ethical Theory*. Oxford: Clarendon Press.

Hardie, W. F. R. 1979. "Aristotle on the Best Life for a Man." *Philosophy* 54: 35–50.

Hart, H. L. A. 1994. *The Concept of Law* (second edition). Oxford: Clarendon Press.

Harte, V. and Lane, M. (eds.) 2013. Politeia *in Greek and Roman Philosophy*. Cambridge: Cambridge University Press.

Hatzistavrou, A. 2013. "Faction." In M. Deslauriers and P. Destrée (eds.) *The Cambridge Companion to Aristotle's Politics*. Cambridge: Cambridge University Press. 301–23.

Heinemann, F. 1965. *Nomos und Physis: Herkunft und Bedeutung einer Antithese im Griechischen Denken des 5. Jahrhunderts*. Basel: Friedrich Reinhardt.

Heinze, R. 1925. "Auctoritas." *Hermes* 60: 348–66.

Henry, D. and Nielsen, K. M. (eds.) 2015. *Bridging the Gap Between Aristotle's Science and Ethics*. Cambridge: Cambridge University Press.

Hittinger, R. 1989. *A Critique of the New Natural Law Theory*. Notre Dame: University of Notre Dame Press.

Hitz, Z. 2012. "Aristotle on Law and Moral Education." *Oxford Studies in Ancient Philosophy* XLII: 263–306.

Hoekstra, K. 2016. "Athenian Democracy and Popular Tyranny." In R. Bourke and Q. Skinner (eds.) *Popular Sovereignty in Historical Perspective*. Cambridge: Cambridge University Press. 15–51.

Horn, C. 2006. "Epieikeia: The Competence of the Perfectly Just Person in Aristotle." In B. Reis (ed.) *The Virtuous Life in Greek Ethics*. Cambridge: Cambridge University Press. 142–66.

Horn, C. 2013. "Law, Governance and Political Obligation." In M. Deslauriers and P. Destrée (eds.) *The Cambridge Companion to Aristotle's Politics*. Cambridge: Cambridge University Press. 223–46.

Inglis, K. 2014. "Philosophical Virtue: In Defense of the Grand End." In R. Polansky (ed.) *The Cambridge Companion to Aristotle's Nicomachean Ethics*. Cambridge: Cambridge University Press. 263–87.

Irwin, T. 1981. "Homonymy in Aristotle." *The Review of Metaphysics* 34: 522–44.

Irwin, T. 1988. *Aristotle's First Principles*. Oxford: Clarendon Press.

Irwin, T. 1990. "The Good of Political Activity." In G. Patzig (ed.) *Aristoteles' Politik: Akten des XI. Symposium Aristotelicum*. Göttingen: Vandenhoeck & Ruprecht. 73–98.

Jaeger. W. 1948. *Aristotle: Fundamentals of the History of His Development*. Trans. R. Robinson, second edition. Oxford: Oxford University Press.

Jaffa, H. V. 1952. *Thomism and Aristotelianism: A Study of the Commentary by Thomas Aquinas on the Nicomachean Ethics*. Chicago: University of Chicago Press.

Johnson, V. 1938. "Aristotle on Nomos." *The Classical Journal* 33: 351–6.

Kahn, C. H. 1990. "The Normative Structure of Aristotle's Politics." In G. Patzig (ed.) *Aristoteles' Politik: Akten des XI. Symposium Aristotelicum*. Göttingen: Vandenhoeck & Ruprecht. 369–84.

Kelsen, H. 1945. *General Theory of Law and State*. Harvard: Harvard University Press.

Kelsen, H. 1957. "Aristotle's Doctrine of Justice." In *What is Justice? Justice Law and Politics in the Mirror of Science*. Berkeley: University of California Press.

Kelsen, H. 1967. *Pure Theory of Law*. Trans. M. Knight. California: University of California Press.

Kempshall, M. S. 1999. *The Common Good in Late Medieval Thought*. Oxford: Oxford University Press.

Kerferd, G. B. 1981. *The Sophistic Movement*. Cambridge: Cambridge University Press.

Keys, M. 2006. *Aquinas, Aristotle, and the Promise of the Common Good*. Cambridge: Cambridge University Press.

Keyt, D. 1991. "Three Basic Theorems in Aristotle's Politics." In D. Keyt and F. D. Miller Jr. (eds.) *A Companion to Aristotle's Politics*. Oxford: Blackwell. 118–41.

Keyt, D. 2017. *Nature and Justice: Studies in the Ethical and Political Philosophy of Plato and Aristotle*. Leuven: Peeters.

Kontos, P. (ed.) 2018. *Evil in Aristotle*. Cambridge: Cambridge University Press.

Kontos, P. Forthcoming. *Aristotle and the Breadth of Practical Reason* (unpublished).

Kraut, R. 1996. "Are There Natural Rights in Aristotle?" *Review of Metaphysics* 49: 755–74.

Kraut, R. 2002. *Aristotle: Political Philosophy*. Oxford: Oxford University Press.

Kraut, R. 2013. "Aristotle and Rawls on the Common Good." In M. Deslauriers and P. Destree (eds.) *The Cambridge Companion to Aristotle's Politics*. Cambridge: Cambridge University Press. 350–74.

Kraut, R. 2018. "The Politikon Kakon." In P. Kontos (ed.) *Evil in Aristotle*. Cambridge: Cambridge University Press. 170–88.

Kretzmann, N. 1988. "Lex Iniusta Non Est Lex: Laws on Trial in Aquinas' Court of Conscience." *American Journal of Jurisprudence* 33: 99–122.

Lane, M. A. 2013. "Founding as Legislating: the Figure of the Lawgiver in Plato's *Republic*." In L. Brisson and N. Notomi (eds.) *Dialogues on Plato's Politeia. Proceedings of the IX Symposium Platonicum*. Sankt Augustin: Akademia Verlag. 104–14.

Lanni, A. and Vermeule, A. 2012. "Constitutional Design in the Ancient World." *Stanford Law Review* 64: 907–49.

Lee, D. 2016. *Popular Sovereignty in Early Modern Constitutional Thought*. Oxford: Oxford University Press.

Lewis, J. D. 2007. *Early Greek Lawgivers*. London: Bloomsbury.

Lewis, V. B. 2006. "Plato's *Minos*: the Political and Philosophical Context of the Problem of Natural Right." *Review of Metaphysics* 60: 17–53.

Liddell, H. G. and Scott, R. 2000. *Greek-English Lexicon*. Seventh edition. Oxford: Oxford University Press.

Lisi, F. 2000. "The Concept of Law in Aristotle's Politics." *Proceedings of the Boston Colloquium on Ancient Philosophy* 16: 29–53.

Lockwood, T. 2015. "Politics II: Political Critique, Political Theorising, Political Innovation." In T. Lockwood and T. Samaras (eds.) *Aristotle's Politics: A Critical Guide*. Cambridge: Cambridge University Press. 64–83.

Lockwood, T. 2017. "Judging Constitutions: Aristotle's Critique of Plato's Republic and Sparta." *Archiv für Geschichte der Philosophie* 99: 353–79.

Lockwood, T. Unpublished manuscript. "Phusis and Nomos in Aristotle's Ethics."

Lockwood, T. and Samaras, T. (eds.) 2015. *Aristotle's Politics: A Critical Guide*. Cambridge: Cambridge University Press.

Lord, C. 1981. "The Character and Composition of Aristotle's Politics." *Political Theory* 9: 459–78.

Lord, C. 1982. *Education and Culture in the Political Thought of Aristotle*. Cornell: Cornell University Press.

Lütcke, K. 1968. *Auctoritas bei Augustin*. Stuttgart: W. Kohlhammer Verlag.

MacDowell, D. M. 1978. *The Law in Classical Athens*. Cornell: Cornell University Press.

MacIntyre, A. 1988. *Whose Justice? Which Rationality?* Notre Dame: University of Notre Dame Press.

Mara, G. M. 1998. "Interrogating the Identities of Excellence: Liberal Education and Democratic Culture in Aristotle's Nicomachean Ethics." *Polity* 31: 301–29.

Martin, C. 1951. "Some Medieval Commentaries on Aristotle's Politics." *History* 36: 29–44.

McIlwain, C. H. 1947. *Constitutionalism: Ancient and Modern*. Indianapolis: Liberty Fund.

Menn, S. 2012. "Aristotle's Theology." In C. Shields (ed.) *The Oxford Handbook of Aristotle*. Oxford: Oxford University Press. 422–64.

Miller, F. D. Jr. 1991. "Aristotle on Natural Law and Justice." In D. Keyt and F. D. Miller Jr. (eds.) *A Companion to Aristotle's Politics*. Oxford: Blackwell. 280–304.

Miller, F. D. Jr. 1995. *Nature, Justice and Rights in Aristotle*. Oxford: Clarendon Press.

Miller, F. D. Jr. 2000. "Aristotle: Naturalism." In C. J. Rowe and M. Schofield (eds.) *The Cambridge History of Greek and Roman Political Thought*. Cambridge: Cambridge University Press. 321–43.

Miller, F. D Jr. 2007. "Aristotle's Philosophy of Law." In F. D. Miller Jr. and C. Biondi (eds.) *A History of the Philosophy of Law from the Ancient Greeks to the Scholastics*. Dordrecht: Springer. 79–110.

Miller, F. D. Jr. 2009. "Aristotle on the Ideal Constitution." In G. Anagnostopoulos (ed.) *A Companion to Aristotle*. London: Wiley-Blackwell. 540–53.

Miller, F. D Jr. 2013. "The Rule of Reason." In M. Deslauriers and P. Destrée (eds.) *The Cambridge Companion to Aristotle's Politics*. Cambridge: Cambridge University Press. 38–66.

Miller, F. D. Jr. 2017. "Aristotle's Political Theory." *Stanford Encyclopedia of Philosophy*. https://plato.stanford.edu/entries/aristotle-politics/.

Moravcsik, J. M. 1974. "Aristotle on Adequate Explanations." *Synthese* 28: 3–17.

Morrison, D. 1999. "Aristotle's Definition of Citizenship: A Problem and Some Solutions." *History of Philosophy Quarterly* 16: 143–65.

Morrison, D. 2013. "The Common Good," in M. Deslauriers and P. Destrée (eds.) *The Cambridge Companion to Aristotle's Politics*. Cambridge: Cambridge University Press. 176–98.

Mulgan, R. 1977. *Aristotle's Political Theory*. Oxford: Oxford University Press.

Mulhern, J. J. 2015. "*Politeia* in Greek Literature, Inscriptions, and in Aristotle's *Politics*: Reflections on Translation and Interpretation." In T. Lockwood and T. Samaras (eds.) *Aristotle's Politics: A Critical Guide*. Cambridge: Cambridge University Press. 84–102.

Murphy, M. C. 2003. "Natural Law Jurisprudence." *Legal Theory* 9: 241–67.

Murphy, M. C. 2005. "The Common Good." *Review of Metaphysics* 59: 133–64.

Murphy, M. C. 2005a. "Natural Law Theory." In M. P. Golding and W. P. Edmundson (eds.) *The Blackwell Guide to Philosophy of Law and Legal Theory*. London: Blackwell.

Murphy, M. C. 2006. *Natural Law in Jurisprudence and Politics*. Cambridge University Press.

Murphy, M. C. 2013. "The Explanatory Role of the Weak Natural Law Thesis." In W. Waluchow and S. Sciaraffa (eds.) *Philosophical Foundations of the Nature of Law*. Oxford: Oxford University Press. 3–21.

Murphy, M. C. 2017. "Two Unhappy Dilemmas for Natural Law Jurisprudence". In G. Duke and R. P. George (eds.) *The Cambridge Companion to Natural Law Jurisprudence*. Cambridge: Cambridge University Press. 342–66.

Nederman, C. J. 1994. "The Puzzle of the Political Animal: Nature and Artifice in Aristotle's Political Theory." *Review of Politics* 56: 284–304.

Neschke-Hentschke, A. 1971. *Politik und Philosophie bei Plato und Aristoteles: die Stellung der "Nomoi" im Platonischen Gesamtwerk und die Politische Theorie des Aristoteles*. Frankfurt am Main: Vittorio Klostermann.

Nichols, M. 1992. *Citizens and Statesmen: A Study of Aristotle's Politics*. Lanham: Rowman and Littlefield.

Nielsen, K. M. 2015. "Aristotle on Principles in Ethics: Political Science as the Science of the Human Good." In D. Henry and K. M. Nielsen (eds.) *Bridging the Gap Between Aristotle's Science and Ethics*. Cambridge: Cambridge University Press. 29–48.

Nussbaum, M. 1988. "Nature, Function and Capability: Aristotle on Political Distribution." In *Oxford Studies in Ancient Philosophy* supp. vol.: 148–214.

Nussbaum, M. 1990. "Aristotelian Social Democracy." In R. B. Douglass, G. M. Mara and H. S. Richardson (eds.) *Liberalism and the Good*. New York: Routledge.

Nussbaum, M. 1993. "Equity and Mercy." *Philosophy and Public Affairs* 22: 83–125.

Ober, J. 1998. *Political Dissent in Democratic Athens: Intellectual Critics of Popular Rule*. Princeton: Princeton University Press.

Ostwald, M. 1969. *Nomos and the Beginnings of the Athenian Democracy*. Oxford: Clarendon Press.

Ostwald, M. 1973. "Was There a Concept of Agraphos Nomos in Classical Greece." *Phronesis* 18: 70–104.

Ostwald, M. 1986. *From Popular Sovereignty to the Sovereignty of Law*. California: University of California Press.

Pakaluk, M. 2001. "Is the Common Good of Political Society Limited and Instrumental?." *Review of Metaphysics* 55: 57–94.

Pakaluk, M. 2005. *Aristotle's Nicomachean Ethics: An Introduction*. Cambridge: Cambridge University Press.

Pangle, T. 2013. *Aristotle's Teaching in the Politics*. Chicago: University of Chicago Press.

Parfit, D. 1997. "Reasons and Motivation." *Proceedings of the Aristotelian Society Supplementary Volume* 71: 99–130.
Parfit, D. 2006. "Normativity." in Russ Shafer-Landau (ed.) *Oxford Studies in Metaethics*, Vol. 1. Oxford: Oxford University Press. 325–80.
Pellegrin, P. 1996. "On the 'Platonic' Part of Aristotle's Politics." In W. Wians (ed.) *Aristotle's Philosophical Development: Problems and Prospects*. Lanham: Rowman and Littlefield. 347–59.
Pellegrin, P. 2012. "Aristotle's Politics." In C. Shields (ed.) *The Oxford Handbook of Aristotle*. Oxford: Oxford University Press. 558–88.
Perry, S. 2013. "Political Authority and Obligation." In L. Green and B. Leiter (eds.) *Oxford Studies in Philosophy of Law: Volume 2* Oxford: Oxford University Press. 1–74.
Polansky, R. 1991. "Aristotle on Political Change." In D. Keyt and F. D. Miller, Jr. (eds.). *A Companion to Aristotle's Politics*. Blackwell: Oxford. 322–45.
Polansky, R. (ed.) 2014. *The Cambridge Companion to Aristotle's Nicomachean Ethics*. Cambridge: Cambridge University Press.
Preus, A. 1977. "Eidos as Norm in Aristotle's Biology." *The Society for Ancient Greek Philosophy Newsletter*. 86.
Raz, J. 1980. *The Concept of a Legal System: An Introduction to the Theory of the Legal System*. Second edition. Oxford: Clarendon Press.
Raz, J. 1986. *The Morality of Freedom*. Oxford: Clarendon Press.
Raz, J. 2002. *Engaging Reason: On the Theory of Value and Action*. Oxford: Oxford University Press.
Raz, J. 2004. "Can There Be A Theory of Law?" In M. Golding and W. Edmundson (eds.) *Blackwell Guide to the Philosophy of Law and Legal Theory*. Malden: Blackwell. 15–28.
Reeve, C. D. C. 1992. *Practices of Reason: Aristotle's Nicomachean Ethics*. Oxford: Oxford University Press.
Reeve, C. D. C. 2000. *Substantial Knowledge: Aristotle's Metaphysics*. Indianapolis: Hackett.
Reeve, C. D. C. 2009. "The Naturalness of the Polis in Aristotle." In G. Anagnostopoulos (ed.) *A Companion to Aristotle*. Oxford: Blackwell. 512–25.
Reeve, C. D. C. 2013. *Aristotle on Practical Wisdom: Nicomachean Ethics VI*. Cambridge: Harvard University Press.
Riesbeck, D. 2016. *Aristotle on Political Community*. Cambridge: Cambridge University Press.
Riesbeck, D. 2016a. "The Unity of Aristotle's Theory of Constitutions." *Apeiron* 49: 93–125.
Ripstein, A. 2009. *Force and Freedom: Kant's Legal and Political Philosophy*. Harvard: Harvard University Press.
Rosler, A. 2005. *Political Authority and Obligation in Aristotle*. Oxford: Oxford University Press.
Rowe, C. J. 1991. "Aims and Methods in Aristotle's Politics." In D. Keyt and F. D. Miller, Jr. (eds.) *A Companion to Aristotle's Politics*. Blackwell: Oxford. 57–74.
Salveker, S. C. 1990. *Finding the Mean: Theory and Practice in Aristotelian Political Philosophy*. Princeton: Princeton University Press.
Saxonhouse, A. W. 2015. "Aristotle on the Corruption of Regimes: Resentment and Justice." In T. Lockwood and T. Samaras (eds.) *Aristotle's Politics: A Critical Guide*. Cambridge: Cambridge University Press. 184–203.
Schniewind, A. 1998. "Remarks on the Spoudaios in Plotinus I 4 [46]," in *Paideia Archive*. Boston: Conference Proceedings of the Twentieth World Congress of Philosophy.
Schofield, M. 2006. *Plato: Political Philosophy*. Oxford: Oxford University Press.

Schottländer, R. 1980. "Der aristotelische 'spoudaios'." *Zeitschrift für philosophische Forschung* 34: 385–95.

Schroeder, D. N. 2003. "Aristotle on Law." In R. O. Brooks and J. B. Murphy (eds.) *Aristotle and Modern Law*. London: Ashgate.

Schütrumpf, E. 1999–2005. *Aristoteles Politik*. 4 vols. Berlin: Akadamie Verlag.

Schütrumpf, E. 2015. "Little to Do With Justice: Aristotle on Distributing Political Power." In T. Lockwood and T. Samaras (eds.) *Aristotle's Politics: A Critical Guide*. Cambridge: Cambridge University Press. 163–83.

Shapiro, S. 2011. *Legality*. Harvard: Harvard University Press.

Shellens, M. S. 1959. "Aristotle on Natural Law." *Natural Law Forum* 40: 79–81.

Shields, C. 2012. "Aristotle's Philosophical Life and Writings." In C. Shields (ed.) *The Oxford Handbook of Aristotle*. Oxford: Oxford University Press. 3–16.

Shields, C. 2015. "The Science of Soul in Aristotle's Ethics." in D. Henry and K. M. Nielsen (eds.) *Bridging the Gap Between Aristotle's Science and Ethics*. Cambridge: Cambridge University Press. 232–53.

Shiner, R. A. 1987. "Aristotle's Theory of Equity." In S. Panagiotou (ed.) *Justice, Law and Method in Plato and Aristotle*. Edmonton: Academic Printing and Publishing. 173–91.

Shute, R. 1888. "On the History of the Process by which the Aristotelian writings arrived at their Present Form. An Essay." Oxford: Clarendon Press.

Siegfried, W. 1942. *Der Rechtsgedanke bei Aristoteles*. Zurich: Schultess.

Simon, Y. R. 1965. *The Tradition of Natural Law: A Philosopher's Reflections*. New York: Fordham University Press.

Skultety, S. C. 2008. "Aristotle's Theory of Partisanship." *Polis* 25: 208–32.

Skultety, S. C. 2009. "Delimiting Aristotle's Conception of Stasis in the *Politics*." *Phronesis* 54: 346–70.

Smith, M. A. 1994. *The Moral Problem*. Oxford: Blackwell Publishers.

Sorabji, R. 1990. "Comments on J. Barnes, State Power: Aristotle and Fourth Century Philosophy." In G. Patzig (ed.) *Aristotle's Politik. Akten des XI Symposium Aristotelicum*. Göttingen: Vandenhoeck & Ruprecht. 264–76.

Sprague, R. K. 1968. "The Four Causes: Aristotle's Exposition and Ours." *Monist* 52: 298–300.

Stalley, R. F. 2007. "Plato's Philosophy of Law." In F. D. Miller Jr. and C. Biondi (eds.) *A History of the Philosophy of Law from the Ancient Greeks to the Scholastics*. Dordrecht: Springer. 57–78.

Stein, N. 2011. "Aristotle's Causal Pluralism." *Archiv für Geschichte der Philosophie* 93: 121–47.

Szegedy-Maszak, A. 1978. "Legends of the Greek Lawgivers." *Greek, Roman and Byzantine Studies* 19: 199–209.

Tessitore, A. 1996. *Reading Aristotle's Ethics*. Albany: State University of New York Press.

Todd, R. B. 1976. "The Four Causes: Aristotle's Exposition and the Ancients." *Journal of the History of Ideas* 37: 319–22.

Todd, S. C. 1993. *The Shape of Athenian Law*. Oxford: Clarendon Press.

Trude, P. 1955. *Der Begriff der Gerechtigkeit in der Aristotelischen Staatsphilosophie*. Berlin: de Gruyter.

Tuck, R. 2016. *The Sleeping Sovereign: The Invention of Modern Democracy*. Cambridge: Cambridge University Press.

Vander Waerdt, P. A. 1985. "Kingship and Philosophy in Aristotle's Best Regime." *Phronesis* 30: 249–73.

Vander Waerdt, P. A. 1991. "The Plan and Intention of Aristotle's Ethical Writings." *Illinois Classical Studies* 16: 231–53.

Van Johnson, L. 1938. "Aristotle on *Nomos*." *The Classical Journal* 33: 351–6.

Voegelin, E. 1990. *Anamnesis*. Trans. G. Niemeyer. Notre Dame: University of Notre Dame Press.
Von Leyden, W. 1967. "Aristotle and the Concept of Law." *Philosophy* 42: 1–19.
Waldron, J. 1995. "The Wisdom of the Multitude." *Political Theory* 23: 563–84.
Weinreb, L. L. 1987. *Natural Law and Justice*. Cambridge: Harvard University Press.
Weirnick, D. 1998. *Law in Aristotle's Ethical-Political Thought*. PhD Dissertation. Rice University.
Westerman, P. 1998. *The Disintegration of Natural Law Theory*. Leiden: Brill
Yack, B. 1993. *The Problems of a Political Animal*. Berkeley: University of California Press.
Zingano, M. 2013. "Natural, Ethical and Political Justice." In M. Deslauriers and P. Destrée (eds.) *The Cambridge Companion to Aristotle's Politics*. Cambridge: Cambridge University Press. 199–222.

Index

Printed by Integrated Books International,
United States of America